Teaching 4- to 8-Year-Olds

National Center for
Early Development & Learning

A Series from the National Center for Early Development & Learning

Series Editor: Donald B. Bailey, Jr., Ph.D.

This book is part of a series edited by Donald B. Bailey, Jr., Ph.D., and developed in conjunction with the National Center for Early Development & Learning (NCEDL). Books in this series are designed to serve as resources for sharing new knowledge to enhance the cognitive, social, and emotional development of children from birth through 8 years of age. For information on other books in this series, please refer to the Brookes web site at www.brookespublishing.com.

Other Books in this Series

The Transition to Kindergarten
Robert C. Pianta and Martha J. Cox

Infants and Toddlers in Out-of-Home Care
Debby Cryer and Thelma Harms

Critical Thinking About Critical Periods
Donald B. Bailey, Jr., John T. Bruer,
Frank J. Symons, and Jeff W. Lichtman

Early Childhood Education and Care in the USA
Debby Cryer and Richard M. Clifford

Teaching 4- to 8-Year-Olds

Literacy, Math, Multiculturalism, and Classroom Community

edited by

Carollee Howes, Ph.D.
University of California–Los Angeles

National Center for
Early Development & Learning

·P A U L·H·
BROOKES
PUBLISHING C?®

Baltimore • London • Sydney

Paul H. Brookes Publishing Co.
Post Office Box 10624
Baltimore, MD 21285-0624

www.brookespublishing.com

Typeset by Type Shoppe II Productions, Ltd., Chestertown, Maryland.
Manufactured in the United States of America by
Victor Graphics, Inc., Baltimore, Maryland.

The National Center for Early Development & Learning is supported under the
Educational Research and Development Centers Program, PR/Award Number
R307A960004, as administered by the Office of Educational Research and Improvement,
U.S. Department of Education. However, no official endorsement by the federal
government should be inferred.

Cases described in this book are composites based on the authors' actual experiences.
Individuals' names have been changed and identifying details have been altered to
protect confidentiality.

Library of Congress Cataloging-in-Publication Data
Teaching 4- to 8- year-olds : literacy, math, multiculturalism, and classroom community /
edited by Carollee Howes
       p.   cm.
       Includes bibliographical references and index.
       ISBN 1-55766-597-4
       1. Early childhood education—United States. 2. Language arts (Early
childhood)—United States. 3. Mathematics—Study and teaching (Early
childhood)—United States. 4. Multicultural education—United States. I. Title: Teaching
four- to eight-year-olds. II. Howes, Carollee.
LB1139.25. T418 2002
372.21—dc21   2002034400

British Library Cataloguing in Publication data are available from the British Library.

10/25/04

Contents

About the Editor vii

About the Contributors ix

Foreword xiii

For the Reader. xv

Introduction. xvii

1 Creating Community-Oriented Classrooms: Nurturing Development
   and Learning
   Jean A. Baker, Laura J. Dilly, and Carol L. Lacey 1

2 Community-Oriented Classroom Practices: Developing Positive
   Teacher–Child Relationships
   Sharon Ritchie 25

3 Early Literacy for Young Children and English-Language Learners
   Linda M. Espinosa and M. Susan Burns. 47

4 Emergent Literacy Practices in Early Childhood Classrooms
   Sharon Ritchie, Jolena James-Szanton, and Carollee Howes 71

5 Fostering Young Children's Mathematical Understanding
   Megan Loef Franke 93

6 Classroom Practices that Support Children's Mathematical Ideas
   Elham Kazemi 113

7 Understanding Multicultural and Anti-bias Education
   Aisha Ray 135

8 Classroom Practices in Multicultural and Anti-bias Education
   Peter Hoffman-Kipp 157

Afterword. 173

Index 177

About the Editor

Carollee Howes, Ph.D., Professor, Division Head, Psychological Studies in Education, Department of Education, University of California–Los Angeles, 3302A Moore Hall, Box 951521, Los Angeles, California 90095

Dr. Howes is an internationally recognized developmental psychologist focusing on children's social and emotional development. She teaches in the applied developmental doctorate program at the University of California–Los Angeles (UCLA). Since 1981, Dr. Howes has been conducting local and national research at UCLA, including being principal investigator on the National Child Care Staffing Study; The Family and Relative Care Study; the Cost, Quality and Outcomes Study; and the Then and Now Study and advisor to the current National Study of Child Care in Low Income Families and the National Head Start Families and Children Experiences and Random Assignment Studies. Her research focuses on children's experiences in child care, their concurrent and long-term outcomes from child care experiences, child care quality, and efforts to improve child care quality.

Dr. Howes has been active in public policy for children and families in California as well as across the United States of America. She recently was appointed to the Los Angeles Round Table and the California School Readiness Master Plan Task Force. She co-chaired the State Task Force on School Readiness in 1987–1988 and served on the more recent Universal Preschool Task Force. She was also part of the 1998–2000 National Research Council Panel on Pedagogy for Early Childhood Education.

About the Contributors

Jean A. Baker, Ph.D., Associate Professor and Co-director, School Psychology Program, Michigan State University, 443A Erickson Hall, East Lansing, Michigan 48824

Dr. Baker is an associate professor of school psychology at Michigan State University. Her research interests are in the area of social-ecological context of schooling and its effects on children's mental health outcomes. She focuses on community and relational aspects of schooling, with an emphasis on student–teacher relationships and classrooms as caring communities. She is interested in school-based prevention and behavior problems, school violence, and academic failure, as well as in social-emotional development of gifted students.

M. Susan Burns, Ph.D., Associate Professor, George Mason University, 4400 University Drive, MS 4B3, Fairfax, Virginia 22030

Dr. Burns is a faculty member in the graduate school of education at George Mason University. She was the study director for the National Research Council's Committee on the Prevention of Reading Difficulties in Young Children and is the author of numerous books and articles related to early childhood literacy development.

Laura J. Dilly, Doctoral Student, Department of Counseling, Educational Psychology, and Special Education, Michigan State University, 401 Erickson Hall, East Lansing, Michigan 48824

Ms. Dilly is a doctoral student in school psychology at Michigan State University. She received her bachelor's degree in psychology from Vanderbilt University. Her research interests include indicators of positive student adjustment and resilience.

Linda M. Espinosa, Ph.D., Co-director, National Institute for Early Education Research, Rutgers University, 120 Albany Street, Suite 500, New Brunswick, New Jersey 08901

Dr. Espinosa has served on numerous boards and advisory committees, including the Boards for Project Construct and the Scholastic Early Childhood

National Advisory Board and is currently a member of the Head Start Technical Work Group on Child Outcomes. She is a consulting editor and book editor for *Early Childhood Research Quarterly,* an editor for *Early Childhood Research and Practice,* and on the editorial board of *The Prevention Researcher.* Dr. Espinosa's research has focused on bilingual preschool education, Hispanic families and children, the effectiveness of family support programs, and early literacy for non-English speakers. She completed her bachelor of arts degree at the University of Washington, her master of education degree at Harvard University, and her doctoral degree in educational psychology at the University of Chicago.

Megan Loef Franke, Ph.D., Associate Professor, Graduate School of Education & Information Studies, University of California–Los Angeles, 2335 Moore Hall, Los Angeles, California 90095

Dr. Franke is an Associate Professor of Education and Director of Center X: Where Research and Practice Intersect for Urban School Professionals at the University of California–Los Angeles. Her work focuses on supporting teachers as they work to create productive mathematical learning environments for all children. She studies the ways teachers and students learn together in the context of mathematical work.

Peter Hoffman-Kipp, Ph.D., Lecturer, California State University–Dominguez Hills, 1000 E. Victoria Street, Carson, California 90747

Dr. Hoffman-Kipp is a lecturer in the Teacher Education Department at California State University–Dominguez Hills. At the University of California–Los Angeles (UCLA), he completed his doctoral degree in education with a focus on teacher learning about cultural diversity and specifically how teachers form their political-pedagogical identities in their preservice programs and professional life. He works with the teacher education programs at California State University–Dominguez Hills and UCLA. Dr. Hoffman-Kipp worked as a K–12 teacher in Los Angeles for 6 years.

Jolena James-Szanton, M.A., Doctoral Student, Urban Education Fellow, Division of Psychological Studies in Education, University of California–Los Angeles, Los Angeles, California 90025

Ms. James-Szanton has been in the education profession, both as a classroom teacher and as a researcher, since receiving her bachelor of arts degree in psychology in 1991. Before her admission to UCLA's Graduate School of Education and Information Studies, she worked as an elementary school teacher in the Watts neighborhood of Los Angeles, then moved to Korea to teach English as a second language strategies to Korean English teachers. She is working with the Los Angeles school district on its Secondary Literacy Plan Evaluation.

Elham Kazemi, Ph.D., Assistant Professor, Mathematics Education, University of Washington, Box 353600, Seattle, Washington 98195

Dr. Kazemi is an assistant professor in mathematics education at the University of Washington. She is interested in how schools nurture the intellectual and social lives of children and adults. She studies how teachers, over the long term, transform their classroom practices through collaborative work focused on understanding children's mathematical ideas.

Carol L. Lacey, Doctoral Student, Michigan State University, 401 Erickson Hall, East Lansing, Michigan 48824

Ms. Lacey is a doctoral student in school psychology at Michigan State University. She received her bachelor of science degree in education and social policy from Northwestern University. Her research interests are focused primarily on teacher–student relationships and their effect on children's school adjustment.

Aisha Ray, Ph.D., Assistant Professor, Erikson Institute, 420 North Wabash Avenue, Chicago, Illinois 60611

Dr. Ray is the director of the Bilingual/English as a Second Language–Multicultural Teacher Training Program at the Erikson Institute for Advanced Study in Child Development. She is a developmental psychologist whose interests are childrearing in African American families, father involvement in childrearing, parenting in high-risk communities, emergent literacy in multicultural early childhood settings, and training early childhood practitioners to respond effectively to diversity in early childhood programs. She focuses on the role of culture in child development and strengthening child, family, and teacher relationships.

Sharon Ritchie, Ed.D., Researcher, Graduate School of Education & Information Services, University of California–Los Angeles, A18 GSEIS, Box 152003, Los Angeles, California 90095

Dr. Ritchie has worked for 25 years as both an educator and researcher. Her primary goal is to support the research and professional development between teachers and children as an integral part of effective education for young children.

Foreword

Over the next decade, we will see a dramatic increase in public funding for programs serving young children, especially 3- and 4-year-olds. The impetus for this funding will come from a variety of sources, but at the heart of much of this effort is an increased national concern about school success. Prekindergarten and early elementary programs will receive more scrutiny in line with a growing awareness that school success is heavily influenced by the skills and attitudes children have when they enter school and the quality of initial school experiences.

Although the emphasis will first be on *program* development and modification, attention will quickly shift to the specific *practices* that occur within those programs, for ultimately it is not the program that affects a child but rather the nature of the child's experiences within that program. These experiences include interactions with the physical environment, toys and materials, peers, and adults. Children's experiences in early childhood programs will vary considerably as a function of the practices and beliefs held by the adults who direct and work in those programs.

This book makes an important contribution to a national discussion of these issues by focusing on elements of prekindergarten and early elementary programs that must be considered in the development and refinement of program models. What will be the overall philosophy of these classrooms? What will be the nature of the relationship that is established between teachers and children? How will parents be involved and supported? What experiences will best prepare children for success in literacy and math? How will early childhood programs meet the needs of children and families in an increasingly diverse society? Researchers with expertise in these areas have written thoughtful chapters about these topics, and conference attendees have summarized and responded to a range of issues that undoubtedly will emerge.

Not everyone will support the message of this book. The authors argue for early childhood programs that emphasize teaching and learning in the context of classrooms that are organized as social communities, with a heavy focus on the social-emotional relationships between children and adults in these classrooms. This perspective suggests that early childhood programs can and should teach children, but that teaching can only occur in an environment that is nurturing, warm, and positive for children. The implication is that programs with an exclusive academic focus that ignore the social-emotional needs of children at this stage of development are not likely to succeed.

Research, politics, and funding will play important roles in the next decade as the debate over appropriate practices plays itself out in the implementation of policy, regulations, and practice. This book articulates a number of the most important issues that will need to be considered in this process and makes concrete suggestions for practices that are likely to promote school success without ignoring the unique nature of early childhood development and learning.

Donald B. Bailey, Jr., Ph.D.
Director
Frank Porter Graham Child Development Institute
University of North Carolina at Chapel Hill

For the Reader

This book was inspired by the National Center for Early Development & Learning's conference *Teaching and Learning in the Classroom: Practices for Four- to Eight-Year-Old Children.* The guest list for the conference included authors of the research-based chapters, all university faculty with illustrious research careers; the researchers of the National Center for Early Development & Learning; faculty from early childhood teacher training programs in the University of California–Los Angeles (UCLA) Department of Education, UCLA Education Extension, and local 4-year and community colleges; and preschool and elementary school teachers. All 200 attendees listened and responded together to the talks given by Dr. Baker, Dr. Espinosa, Dr. Franke, and Dr. Ray. These talks were simultaneously translated in Spanish.

Following the talks, participants divided into groups of 10–15. These groups remained together throughout the entire conference, and one group was conducted entirely in Spanish. Teacher trainers and very experienced teachers who had collaborated with various UCLA projects on teaching and learning facilitated the groups. One person within the group had received the presented paper before the conference and prepared a learning guide intended to help the group focus on discussing the salient issues developed in the paper. Another person within the group took careful notes as the discussion progressed. All small group participants were asked to examine how particular practices, from their experience and/or from the talk, relate to school adjustment and success for children from diverse backgrounds. Dr. Ritchie, Dr. Hoffman-Kipp, and Dr. Kazemi wrote the practice chapters based on their participant observation in these small groups and the notes generated in each small group.

Introduction

As the United States of America begins the 21st century, most 4- and 5-year-old children are enrolled in early childhood programs (Clifford & Early, 1999). The designers of these programs often claim to ready children for school, to give them positive experiences as preschool children, or to provide a safe and nurturing place for them as their parents work. There has been an ongoing debate over what constitutes a high-quality program for these children. Parents, advocates, and researchers have come to agree that high quality means a place where children trust adults to take care of them and to guide their learning and where they encounter interesting activities that stimulate thinking and learning. Longitudinal research has documented that enrollment in a high-quality program for all children is linked to school success (Peisner-Feinberg et al., 2001). For children from low-income families, it may make the difference between school success and failure (Campbell & Ramey, 1994). In most studies, the influences of quality child care on later school achievement is greater for children from low-income families than for children from higher-income families.

Meanwhile, advances in basic cognitive science and developmental psychology illustrate that young children are capable of more complex content learning than previously believed (Bowman et al., 2001). As experienced teachers, program directors, advocates, and researchers with children and families from racially, ethnically, and home-language diverse families, the contributors to this book are aware of differences in the beliefs of adults about how children should be socialized and taught (Coll et al., 1996; Harwood, Schoelmerich, Schulze, & Gonzales, 1999).

These understandings have led us to focus on practices within early childhood classrooms. The construct of practices—that is, the ways in which teachers and children collaborate to teach and learn—is derived from research on teaching and learning in elementary school classrooms rather than on the more familiar early childhood literature that has tended to focus on quality. Early childhood programs that are high quality have very heterogeneous practices (Wishard, Shivers, Howes, & Ritchie, in press).

The range of potential practices in early childhood classrooms is very wide. Again, speaking simply, the range of teaching practices goes from adult-determined drill and practice exercises to adults watching passively as children explore and make sense of a learning environment. Our belief is that the middle of this range, neither adult- nor child-controlled, is the most important and most interesting to examine. In this middle range, teachers and children collaborate to create learning environments requiring both children and teachers to take an active role in the teaching and learning process. In our work at the University of California–Los Angeles (UCLA) with community-based early childhood programs, we have found that the actual practices enacted within this middle range are complex and varied and are influenced by program and community goals (Wishard et al., in press).

Practices are about *what* to teach as well as *how* to teach. Again, the possibilities of what to teach 4- to 8-year old children include a wide range of activities: gardening, reading, sewing, caring for animals, mathematics, and so on. Young children getting ready to enter formal school and in the primary grades need to learn in four areas of practice: literacy, mathematics, multiculturalism, and classroom community. Why these four? Literacy and mathematics are in one sense the basics. Schools, school boards, teachers, and parents generally agree that children need reading, writing, and arithmetic skills. We believe that multiculturalism and classroom community are equally important skills that require teacher practices because, as will be elaborated in the following sections, they make learning the basics possible as they organize children's learning.

LITERACY

Increasingly, teachers report that the children who enter their kindergarten classrooms do not have the literacy skills they need to succeed in school. Unfortunately for many children, the environments in which they spend the majority of their time—home and child care or school—often fail to provide optimal developmental support for emergent literacy skills. In part, this is due to environmental risk factors such as poverty, violence, racial discrimination, poor nutrition, parental illiteracy, and abuse. This is also due to the lack of a system of high-quality early care and education to prepare children for school.

Only 1 in 12 infant-toddler centers and 15%–30% of preschool centers provide developmentally appropriate care (Helburn & the Cost, Quality and Outcomes, Team, 1995). There is an inadequate supply of well-educated and trained teachers and providers who have access to professional development programs that could assist them in developing and implementing emergent literacy curriculum and pedagogy that would better prepare children for elementary school. In addition, little has been written about how to provide in-service training for teachers of young children to become effective teachers of literacy skills. These deficits are compounded by the real needs of second-language learners in classrooms throughout the United States of America, as well as philosophical differences in approaches to teaching young children whose home languages are not English. Some of the theoretical material and practical suggestions found in this book will help teachers to enact positive practices in this critical area.

MATHEMATICS

As much as we are concerned that children enter formal school without the underlying skills and concepts to help them learn to read, we are concerned about children and mathematics. To make the issue even more complex, because most states do not require bachelor's degrees for teachers in early childhood programs, all too often the early childhood teachers have had little or no advanced mathematical training, even in simple algebra. We have observed early childhood teachers avoiding numbers and math altogether. Although many traditional early childhood activities, such as blocks and puzzles, provide opportunities for understanding basic mathematics constructs, it is rare to observe these constructs linked to numbers. By adding numeracy to our list of practices to be included, we intended to enhance our understanding of how to make these links. Again, the goal of this book is to assist teachers in helping children to develop complex mathematical understandings.

MULTICULTURALISM

Children in the 4- to 8-year age range are increasingly children of color and children with home languages different from English. This means first that early childhood classrooms are filled with children different from the white and middle class or affluent children who participated in much of the research that led to accepted practices in early childhood education. Another debate in the early childhood field is whether children from different backgrounds require different practices due to differences in cognitive development or in learning style. To inform this debate, we argue that teachers need to think about culturally competent practices in order to enhance the learning of all children. Furthermore, we suggest that there is sufficient evidence that children from all backgrounds may do best with teaching practices that are tailored to their particular experiences. Moreover, bridges between home and school can best be made when practices within classrooms are culturally sensitive.

The challenge and promise of diverse classrooms is that they are opportunities for children of different backgrounds to experience being within a rich and diverse community that works well together. Children who are learning new material in collaboration with learning partners who are different from themselves learn two sets of skills—the skills inherent in the material (e.g., finding place values, looking up words in a dictionary) and the social skills needed for collaboration when communication is not simple or easy. Children have opportunities to learn not only new vocabularies but also how to communicate clearly when taking into account the partner in the communication.

CLASSROOM COMMUNITY

This brings us to classroom community. Our bias is that children can only learn when they trust teachers to support and guide their learning. Preschool and early elementary teachers are often children's first adult relationships within learning environments. These first teacher–child relationships set the stage for either trusting the teacher and learning ways to collaborate with him or her in learning or for establishing an acrimonious, contentious relationship that interferes with learning. Positive child–teacher relationships are constructed in classrooms where both learning and social relationships are valued. Teacher attention to relationships, child–teacher relationships, and child–child relationships is associated with pro-social and cooperative classroom climates.

CONCLUSION

The conference described in For the Reader and this resulting book were intended to bridge that difficult space between research and practice. By participating in the creation of this book, we increased our understanding of best practices for children in early childhood programs. We hope this book will generate discussion within the early childhood field as well as increase knowledge about the range of practices that enact quality in early childhood programs. We also hope that this book will be useful to the teachers and providers within early childhood as they work to create high-quality environments for children to learn and develop.

REFERENCES

Bowman, B., Donovan, M.S., & Burns, S. (Eds.). (2001). *Eager to learn: Educating our preschoolers*. Washington, DC: National Academy Press.

Campbell, F.A., & Ramey, C.T. (1994). Effects of early intervention on intellectual and academic achievement: A follow-up study of children from low-income families. *Child Development, 65*, 684–698.

Clifford, R.M., & Early, D. (1999). Almost a million children in school before kindergarten: Who is responsible for early childhood services. *Young Children, 54*, 48–51.

Coll, C.G., Lamberty, G., Jenkins, R., McAdoo, H.P., Crnic, K., Wasik, B., & Garcia, H.V. (1996). An integrative model for the study of developmental competencies in minority children. *Child Development, 67*, 1890–1914.

Harwood, R.L., Schoelmerich, A., Schulze, P.A., & Gonzales, Z. (1999). Cultural differences in maternal beliefs and behaviors. A study of middle class Anglos and Puerto Rican mother–infant pairs in four everyday situations. *Child Development, 70*, 1005–1016.

Helburn, S., & the Cost, Quality and Outcomes Team. (1995). *Cost, quality and outcomes: Final report*. Denver: University of Colorado at Denver.

Peisner-Feinberg, E.S., Burchinal, M.R., Clifford, R.M., Culkin, M.L., Howes, C., Kagan, S.L., & Yazejian, N. (2001). The relation of preschool child care quality to children's cognitive and social developmental trajectories through second grade. *Child Development, 72,* 1534–1553.

Wishard, A., Shivers, E., Howes, C., & Ritchie, S. (in press). Child care program and teacher practices: Associations with quality and children's experiences. *Early Childhood Research Quarterly.*

Creating Community-Oriented Classrooms

Nurturing Development and Learning

Jean A. Baker, Laura J. Dilly,
and Carol L. Lacey

Classrooms are important environments in which children ages 4–8 develop the skills they will need for academic success, learn how a classroom is organized, and learn what it means to be part of a community. Classrooms that focus on the development of a sense of community are ideal for school learning.

> Ms. Ling's first-grade class looks like many others—colorful bulletin boards, small tables and chairs, centers with engaging activities—however, it feels different. There is a distinct sense of organization and purpose in the room with students actively engaged in activities. But there is something more. It feels warm and comfortable, and the

The authors gratefully acknowledge the contributions of the School Ecology Study Group at Michigan State University to the ideas expressed in this chapter. This work was supported in part by Grant No. R305T990330 to Randy Kamphaus, Jean A. Baker, and Arthur Horne from the Office of Educational Research and Improvement, Institute for At-Risk Children, United States Department of Education. The views expressed in this chapter are those of the authors and do not necessarily represent those of the United States Department of Education.

1

children look happy to be here. "I've worked very hard to build a community in this class," reports Ms. Ling, "I want the kids to feel secure, to feel supported by me and by the other children, and to really love what we do. We're more like a family than a class."

This chapter defines this community-oriented approach to classroom teaching, provides rationales from psychological and educational perspectives, describes classroom practices that embody community ideals, and illustrates the effectiveness of such models with two examples. By focusing on social-psychological processes that promote learning, it is not our intent to downplay the other factors critical to schooling for young students. Quality education for young children requires content-rich environments, skillful pedagogy, and opportunities to acquire both the knowledge and behaviors necessary for school success; however, the psychosocial structure of the environment is an equally important component of developmentally appropriate instruction for young learners. Intentional community-building practices in the classroom afford teachers powerful vehicles to promote children's competence and adaptation to schooling.

COMMUNITY-ORIENTED APPROACHES TO SCHOOLING

Without a sense of community, people experience loneliness, alienation from others, and disconnection from the society at large. Durkheim (1893/1964) explained that involvement in community is a fundamental human experience that meets emotional needs and helps individuals find a sense of meaning and purpose in their lives. Some contemporary social theorists (e.g., Etzioni, 1993) have applied this idea to the nature of American schools. A community-oriented classroom approach employs these theories of community and emphasizes personal relationships as a vehicle for teaching and learning.

Community is the bond between people with shared values and ideals who are pursuing a meaningful, common goal (Sergiovanni, 1994). Relationships are crucial to the organization of community life. They tie individuals in a community together and provide a sense of belonging to the collective unit. Students have relationships that create a unique bond with each other as well as with the teacher. Members of a community also share common values and ideals. Community activities have a clear focus and purpose. Students and teachers have a shared sense of why they are in the classroom and how the classroom should function. There is a clear sense that school is important or that kindness is valued as a core commitment in the classroom. In addition, a community activity is meaningful; members are committed to and actively engaged in pursuit of a goal. For students ages 4–8, this goal is typically learning the early academic and social skills that permit school success.

The goals within a community are shared. There is a sense of mutuality and support that functions both to cement relationships and to keep the community focused on attaining its goal. There is a sense of "we-ness" in which students help each other and remind each other of the class rules. Finally, there is a collective memory or common "story" to a community; there is an enduring sense of unique history and identity that makes a community distinctive. Stories about common experiences, such as field trips, might be retold or the class might decide on a class name or mascot. Community is essentially a shared social contract that allows individuals to derive a sense of purpose and meaning within a behavior setting. In community-oriented schools, children feel a sense of belonging, commitment, and shared venture in learning.

Community-oriented classrooms are structured around two ideas central to a sense of community (Baker, Terry, Bridger, & Winsor, 1997; Battistich, Watson, Solomon, Schaps, & Solomon, 1991). First, these classrooms intentionally develop rich, warm, interpersonal relationships among students and teachers. Such relationships enhance children's development and help them achieve optimal learning. Second, community-oriented classrooms develop a collective responsibility for achieving goals. Teachers and students in a community-oriented classroom share responsibility for success, so they have a feeling of togetherness. Students and teachers work to develop shared goals (e.g., learning to transition between activities smoothly) and values (e.g., treating each other with kindness or cooperating with each other) that guide the "mission" of the classroom. Practices and instruction in such classrooms support a collective sense of purpose in the context of personally meaningful relationships. Students in community-oriented classrooms feel cared about, care about others, and work in an environment that makes sense to them.

Community-oriented classrooms work differently from traditional American classrooms. In the 19th century, American schools became increasingly structured, formalized, and standardized (Tyack & Cuban, 1995). Schools since then have evolved into institutions with hierarchical administrative structures with formal role expectations (e.g., principal, vice principal, teacher's aide) and a businesslike notions regarding education (e.g., report cards a designated number of times per year, bells to mark the beginning and end of the day). An individual's value is based on his or her ability to "produce" or contribute to the success of the school (Sergiovanni, 1994).

Traditional education reflects this formal organizational model as seen in 1) the enduring interest in the "science" of education as evidenced through the formal study of the discipline and its tenets by scholars; 2) the administrative, structural, and pedagogical emphases in teacher training (e.g., pre-service classes in methods and instructional models); 3) the emphasis on individual achievement and competition among students (e.g., some students are labeled "gifted" whereas others are "challenged"); and 4) the bureaucratic and rule-governed nature of schooling (e.g., the clear differentiation between administrative and teaching positions within schools). Policy initiatives with an emphasis on teacher accountability, standardized testing with high stakes, school choice, and competition illustrate the model of schools as businesses.

Community-oriented classrooms use a different model to organize the purpose, functions, and tasks of schooling. By valuing personal relationships and shared goals and values, community-oriented classrooms seem more like families or neighborhoods than businesses. They teach students by placing them in a supportive, intentionally constructed web of relationships (Schaps & Solomon, 1990). In a learning community, each individual is valued as an important part of the community and is committed to a shared purpose with others in that environment. Children develop a sense of collectiveness that can provide cohesion and motivate them to participate in community activities.

The community-oriented approach addresses the fact that the traditional model of schooling does not work well for all children or for all teachers (Baker, 1998a). The formal structures of school ignore the fact that children enter schools with different developmental capacities and move through the curriculum at different rates. The emphasis on academic study as the primary purpose of schooling ignores the historical mission of schools to socialize children for participation in society. Children need their social, ethical, and civic development nurtured in addition to their academic development. Teachers in traditional schools often are bound by the demand to move children through the curriculum at a prescribed rate and are not able to use their expertise to adapt the classroom so that children's development is adequately supported. These teachers may value similar ideas found in community-oriented classrooms (e.g., the importance of group cohesion, classroom climate, and pro-social norms), but they do not believe these ideas are as important to teach as academic learning. Community-oriented classrooms are distinguished by their intentional focus on the development of community in order to accomplish these goals and their reliance on authentic, meaningful social relationships among members of the classroom community as an important vehicle through which learning occurs.

Because of their roots in sociological ideas such as community, these schools recognize the environments in which learning occurs and pay attention to shaping them in order to influence learning and development of children in the classroom. They typically use intensive staff training as the means to change the school's climate and thereby influence children's academic performances. For example, a community-oriented school might hold an in-service training session on using positive and inclusive language to build cooperation and caring among students. Community-oriented schools pay significant attention to interactions between individuals as opportunities for learning. For example, if two children are fighting, the teacher will use this opportunity to teach students conflict resolution.

A community-oriented classroom environment may be especially important for young children at risk for poor school outcomes. Children who come to school without the social and psychological preparation for learning perform worse on indicators of early school adjustment (e.g., grades, retention, social competence) than peers without such disadvantages (Birch & Ladd, 1997). Some children may not know certain cultural assumptions regarding schooling (e.g., raise hand and wait to be called on) and need additional support from teachers and the social organization of the classroom to learn the school behavior and how to participate in school (e.g., Mrs. Rosa hands John a picture of a student raising his hand when John calls out in class; Ogbu, 1992). Classroom community may act as a bridge between home and school cultures. In a caring classroom community, children are accepted as individuals and encouraged to share their experiences with the class. Home routines and traditions can be incorporated into school activities by teachers who know children well and value their cultural traditions. Because of the intentional focus on social-emotional development in these classrooms, community-oriented teachers can also help children understand and affiliate with the school environment by providing more instruction or practice with school routines they might not be familiar with (e.g., raising hands, doing homework; Wang, Haertel, & Walberg, 1994). Thus, community-oriented experiences at school may provide a compensatory function for children at risk for school failure, helping them feel comfortable with the school's culture and to develop the competencies to support school success.

PSYCHOLOGICAL FOUNDATIONS

Community-oriented classrooms are supported by developmental systems theory (Bronfenbrenner, 1979; Pianta & Walsh, 1996; Sameroff, 1995), which views development as the result of complex interactions between the individual and his or her environment. Behavior and learning result from the child's integration of skills across various domains of functioning (e.g., cognitive, social, emotional) within the context of and in response to the social environment (Rogoff, 1991; Vygotsky, 1978). Thus, development cannot be viewed in isolation but rather exists as a result of the child's interaction with the social world.

Although different in their emphases, social and contextual theories maintain that children acquire increasingly complex cognitive and social competencies through shared or mediated experiences with significant others. An environment supports development when it provides interesting and challenging experiences in the presence of a competent guide who can nurture the child's involvement and help sustain the acquisition and consolidation of skills. Community-oriented classrooms for young students enhance development by constructing the social context of the classroom so that it adequately builds on children's emerging personal and social abilities. For example, teachers might teach specific social skills each day or include a class meeting in which social concerns are addressed. An important goal of community-oriented classrooms for young students is to provide optimal support for the consolidation of key cognitive, social, and civic skills early in schooling to enhance adaptation to school and successful school learning.

Many theories of child development show the importance of social connectedness to others as a prerequisite for learning. For example, self-determination theory (Connell & Wellborn, 1991; Deci & Ryan, 1985) states that people have three basic psychological needs: to be engaged in meaningful social relationships with others, to have developmentally appropriate autonomy and self-direction, and to be competent in their endeavors. From an attachment perspective, children require caring relationships in order to develop the complex behavioral, emotional, and social-cognitive competencies that help them adapt to school and have good mental health (Bowlby, 1982). Children with positive, caring, consistent caregiving relationships develop both the security and the abilities required for success in any social environment, including school. These competencies include valuing social exchange; trusting the intent of adults; accurately "reading" complex patterns of social behavior; willingly taking positive risks; displaying age-appropriate self-regulatory skills; and developing a sense of worth, self-acceptance, and personal agency. These students look "comfortable in their own skin," get along well with others, feel good about themselves and their accomplishments, and try new things with confidence.

Children without secure relationship experiences face a host of mental health and school adjustment problems, such as being overly aggressive, feeling unsure of their ability to succeed, crying easily when school is challenging, or not having the social skills to play well with others (Greenberg, Speltz, & DeKlyen, 1993; Pianta & Steinberg, 1992). The degree to which schools structure the classroom environment to both meet and enhance psychological and social needs has a critical affect on children's development and adaptation to schooling.

DEVELOPMENTAL TASKS IN EARLY SCHOOLING

Preschool and Kindergarten Development

Schools play important roles in children's development. One important function is to assist children in acquiring abilities that lay the foundation for later school learning and eventual adult employment (Goodlad, 1994). Children 4–8 years old experience rapid developmental change and consolidation of important self-regulatory, social, and academic skills. At the late preschool and kindergarten levels, important developmental tasks include

- Mastering critical preacademic skills

  Controlling attention

  Using multistep problem solving

  Increasing persistence

  Achieving independence

  Mastering task orientation

- Enhancing language and concept development

  Using language to communicate needs and to interact with others

  Mastering basic concepts related to size or position

In addition to enhanced cognitive self-regulation, children show increased abilities to

- Regulate their behavior using language
- Manage their behavior relative to social norms
- Recognize and moderate emotional and social states (e.g., being able to label their feelings, developing strategies to care for themselves when sad or frustrated)

Their social competencies permit cooperative and pro-social interactions with peers and an increased interest in peers and peer acceptance (Bronson, 2000; Hetherington & Parke, 1999).

Classroom environments that optimally support the emergence of these social, emotional, and cognitive competencies will benefit children in later school years. Community-oriented classrooms provide an organization within which peer interactions are democratic and are supported by secure, emotionally vested relationships with adults. For example, students are encouraged to work through difficulties with peers with the support of genuinely caring adults who are committed to the growth of these social competencies in their students.

First- and Second-Grade Development

During first and second grade, children learn to regulate and direct the cognitive skills necessary for learning, including

- Attention and monitoring of mental activities
- Planning and task approach strategies
- Goal setting
- Memory
- Sequencing tasks

Children want to master tasks and acquire basic academic skills, and their behavior is increasingly guided by internalized representations of rules, language, and concepts. They rely less on adult mediation than do children in the preschool and kindergarten period. Children learn to judge their competence by relative ability in various areas (e.g., ability to make friends, academic performance, athletic ability) and are evaluated according to internalized standards for performance and in relation to that of peers. Children become more sophisticated in their language competence and can use discussion in addition to direct experience for learning. They have an emerging ability to take the perspective of others and to use that perspective to guide their behavior. First and second graders show an increasing interest in peers and peer culture and learn to negotiate based on abstract social rules (e.g., fairness).

First- and second-grade classrooms should support children's focus on mastering new skills and motivate them to learn while helping them to develop internal and pro-social behavior standards. These classrooms also should enable students to have positive peer interactions. Community-oriented classrooms accomplish this by

- Creating a supportive classroom climate characterized by positive social interactions between teachers and students
- Teaching the social behaviors necessary for collaborative work, such as listening to, helping, and cooperating with peers
- Promoting a sense of purpose and identity around learning as a primary goal of the classroom community by stressing the importance of learning, personalizing the experiences for individual students, and presenting the material in a way that engages students
- Shaping positive, goal-directed academically oriented attitudes and values within the community such as emphasizing hard work, attention to task, and caring about work
- Focusing on the inherent value of each individual's contribution to the community, regardless of ability or achievement level by reinforcing each student's effort and progress

Civic Development

In addition to helping children gain learning-related skills, the second purpose of schooling is to develop civic-minded, competent, and ethical citizens (Goodlad, 1994). American public schools were founded so that children would learn the ideals of community that support democratic self-governance (Jefferson, 1801/1974). Educated citizens are critical for a representational democracy. John Dewey proposed two primary purposes for schools: to serve the larger community by producing responsible, civic-minded citizens (1916/1970) and to help children develop the ethical, social, and moral reasoning skills to be responsible members of those communities (1909/1975). Thus, an equally important purpose of schooling is to give students experiences of community in which they can practice self-governance and ethical decision making. Community-oriented classrooms teach children specific practices necessary for later involvement in the larger community and the concepts, beliefs, and attitudes (e.g., principles of fairness, equality, and justice) that support democracy and permit a focus on the common good. For example, teachers can encourage students to cooperate with each other rather than compete with each other. Teachers can openly value the contributions of each student and involve students in decisions that affect the classroom community, such as forming classroom rules.

ASPECTS OF THE ENVIRONMENT THAT PROMOTE DEVELOPMENT

Development results from the reciprocal interaction between a child and his or her environment (Bronfenbrenner, 1979, 1999). Children do better when the environment provides opportunities to practice and accomplish developmental tasks in the context of emotional and social support that can sustain the child's efforts at mastery (Pianta & Walsh, 1996). Warmth and coherence are important characteristics of a classroom that supports learning for young students (Good & Brophy, 2000; Stockard & Mayberry, 1992).

The emotional closeness of the classroom is a critical predictor of school outcomes for young students. The supportiveness of others in the classroom, and especially the availability of a secure, emotionally nurturing relationship with an adult, can predict school success in early elementary school (Birch & Ladd, 1997; Pianta & Steinberg, 1992). A warm, supportive environment fosters positive emotional involvement in learning tasks and provides optimum support for the integration of cognition, emotion, and behavior necessary for learning academic material (Bronson, 2000). Students are more likely to be engaged in this type of classroom climate because it communicates to them that their teacher and classmates want them to succeed and can be resources to help them do so.

Equally important is classroom unity (Good & Brophy, 2000). Classroom environments that are predictable and stable and provide consistent, contingent, and accurate feedback are optimal. The degree of organizational and instructional coherence in a classroom establishes the parameters and expectations for learning and helps children acquire a "set" of academic behaviors and attitudes—those that are most compatible with learning in school, such as listening, written and verbal expression, interest, and motivation. This set has strong implications pertaining to the quality of students' learning and their ability to demonstrate their understanding of the material.

Community-oriented classrooms embody these ideals of warmth and coherence because they intentionally develop a supportive web of relationships within the classroom and have a clear, articulated purpose that guides their efforts. The effectiveness of such classrooms is influenced by the degree to which they communicate warmth and support for students and engage in a coherent set of practices that convey meaning and purpose during the school day.

Classroom-Based Practices that Build Community

Community-oriented schools are supported by a belief that children learn in the context of relationships with others (Vygotsky, 1978). These schools structure themselves and their teaching practices so that children form personal relationships with teachers and peers and develop a meaningful commitment to academic work. Of course, behavior in schools is culturally bounded, both according to ethnicity and socioeconomic status and by individual school norms and mores that constitute the school climate. For example, schools in which students generally get along well with each other could be characterized as positive and supportive, whereas schools in which there are frequent fights or conflicts among students could be described as intimidating or threatening. The school climate will potentially have unique effects on students' and teachers' behavior.

Community-oriented classrooms actively shape the culture in the room by maintaining positive and cooperative interactions between teachers and students so that good relationships and a sense of mutual endeavor are fostered. Community-oriented classrooms are sensitive to the unique cultures children bring with them to school because they intentionally develop an inclusive social organization in which each child is valued and is well known to others.

The Centrality of Relationships

Mr. Honda makes it his business to know every student in his kindergarten class well. He likes to create a good relationship with every student. Sometimes, though, he has a hard time getting along with a student. Last week, Max refused to follow any of his instructions and even hit another student when Mr. Honda asked him to join the class at circle time. This week, instead of avoiding Max, Mr. Honda decided to go out of his way to greet Max at the door and ask him how his bus ride was. He picked Max as the special helper at snack time, and he let Max pick the story to read. To Mr. Honda's delight, Max responded to directions better and did not have any incidences of hurting other students.

> Knowing that Mr. Honda was in his corner really made a difference in how Max made it through the day!

Community-oriented approaches emphasize the interdependence among members of the classroom and intentionally develop a strong sense of group membership and affiliation (Goodenow, 1993). The quality of the relationships between individuals is a critical feature of community. The most important relationship in a classroom community for young children is the one forged between a student and his or her teacher, as demonstrated by Mr. Honda and Max. Warm, supportive, caring teacher–student relationships may be related to learning outcomes in important ways. Experiences of social connectedness help children internalize social values and become committed to societal institutions, such as schools (Deci & Ryan, 1985). The development of an academic orientation and intrinsic motivation to learn is promoted by social relatedness to others who share those values. Beyond academic values, a caring relationship with an adult is a well-recognized protective factor associated with resiliency in children and the development of a host of personal competencies that promote school learning (Masten, 1994). Children learn specific skills as well as attitudes and beliefs regarding schooling and learning through their relationships with significant others, including teachers.

Research on effective teaching supports this theoretical premise of the importance of positive teacher–student relationships at school. Among the consistent findings is that achievement is enhanced by high expectations for students coupled with a classroom climate characterized by encouragement and support (Bernard, 1991; Stockard & Mayberry, 1992; Wang et al., 1994). Student perceptions of interpersonal connectedness to others at school and "belonging" to the school culture are associated with academic engagement and psychological well-being (Goodenow, 1992; Wentzel, 1994). Social contextual variables seem to play a role in both learning and affective outcomes of schooling.

Effective teacher–child relationships serve four essential functions in promoting learning and developmental outcomes in early schooling (Pianta, 1999). First, the teacher–child relationship acts as a template for children's emotional experiences in the classroom. The nature of the relationship influences patterns of behavior, expectations, and beliefs about social interactions; these "rules" become stabilized in the context of the relationship. For example, students come to believe that teachers are on their side through repeated, positive interactions with them and then expect their next teacher to be supportive as well.

Second, teachers provide an important source of emotional security that permits the active exploration and risk taking necessary for learning. Close, warm interpersonal relationships permit active "moving out" into the world of school. Students are more likely to try challenging work if they believe their teachers are supportive and invested in their success.

Third, teachers of 4- to 8-year-olds actively shape children's capacity for self-regulation, or the ability to moderate arousal and effectively integrate cognition, emotion, and behavior. The nature of the teacher–child relationship affects the informal and formal teaching of self-regulation because such learning occurs in the context of social relationships. For example, teachers who talk through a problem with a student are modeling effective problem-solving and coaching the student to use language to mediate his or her feelings and actions. Finally, teacher–child relationships influence peer relationships and the development of social competence because children develop a sense of trust and security with adults that they can carry into the world of friendship. Children who have secure, caring relationships with adults develop important social interaction skills in the context of those relationships that they then apply to developing friendships. Of course, children's early relationships with parents and other caregivers influence these experiences and set the stage for their interactions with teachers (Howes & Hamilton, 1992), but teacher–child relationships may build on positive early experiences or may compensate for less than optimal early developmental experiences.

Given the importance of the teacher–child relationship in setting the stage for learning, teachers in community-oriented classrooms adopt different roles and functions from teachers in more traditional schools. First, they nurture caring relationships with students. Relationally oriented teachers express greater warmth and supportiveness toward students and spend more time listening to and talking with students about personal and social issues (Solomon, Watson, Battistich, Schaps, & Delucchi, 1992). These sustaining relationships help children to derive a sense of school as community and to engage in meaningful academic work (Pianta & Walsh, 1996). Teacher caring, warmth, and supportiveness have been found to be associated both with increased academic engagement (Solomon, Watson, Battistich, & Schaps, 1996) and with student satisfaction with school (Baker, 1998b) in elementary school children. Interestingly, when asked to describe the teacher qualities most influential to their classroom experiences, students and teachers consistently focus on the perceived quality of teacher caring and support, not on teacher competency and proficiency (e.g., Rogers, 1994; Witty, 1967).

TEACHER CHARACTERISTICS

Community-oriented teachers share many perspectives and best practices on effective teaching, such as those described by Hamachek's effective teacher (1995), Good and Brophy's proactive teacher (2000), Glasser's quality teacher (1993), Schaps and Solomon's (1990) facilitator teacher, Lickona's moral educator (1991), and Berman and LaFarge's (1993) democratic teacher. All of these models suggest that the following teacher practices enhance instruction while fostering caring relationships and establishing caring classroom communities:

1. Commitment to personal involvement with students and an emphasis on their development as individuals, such as forming and maintaining positive, supportive relationships with students

2. Democratic philosophy, including both fair and consistent practices and shared responsibility for the classroom management with students. For example, students may be expected to help the teacher monitor their own behaviors as well as those of their peers. Students may also be involved with the development and implementation of positive and negative consequences of their behaviors

3. Flexibility, including responsiveness to diversity and the special needs of individuals (e.g., recognizing and supporting different levels of ability among students)

4. Emphasis on active student participation in learning and a teacher-facilitator model of instruction (i.e., by providing students with many opportunities to engage in hands-on activities)

5. Focus on the process of learning, individual progress, and intrinsic motivation, rather than on competitive achievement or an exclusive emphasis on the products of learning. For example, teachers should reinforce students' engagement and effort throughout learning tasks in addition to their final performances or finished products

6. Provision of a psychologically and physically safe, supportive environment in which positive risks are encouraged and mistakes are expected as part of learning, by supporting students' attempts at learning rather than punishing their mistakes

7. High expectations for student behavior and learning, by providing a classroom structure that is challenging, yet reasonable, and expressing confidence in the students' abilities to meet those expectations

Community-oriented teachers are likely to emphasize the primacy of relationships and to promote the interconnectedness of those in the classroom in their practices.

Use of Language

Miss Giovanni paid a lot of attention to the way she spoke in her third-grade classroom. She made sure to say things like, "How are we doing?" and "Our class is right on track!" She tried not to single out any students because she wanted to help the children feel a part of a community and she wanted the students to treat each other with respect and kindness. "I see children working kindly with each other," she said often. At first, it seemed strange to her to keep saying these things, but she moved past this feeling and realized that the students were really responding to it. They even began to mimic her by saying such statements as, "We don't do that in our class!" and "Please be nice!" Miss Giovanni believed that the language helped the students feel closer as a group and allowed them to focus on the fact that they were in this together. She knew that her students believed the class was everybody's responsibility.

Teachers in community-oriented classrooms use language to develop a sense of mutual dependence, to shape the social norms in the classroom toward those that create a sense of community, and to enhance relationships. They look for and point out positive examples of behavior, use praise frequently and effectively, and proactively describe desirable behavior rather than reacting to negative behavior (Good & Brophy, 2000); however, community-oriented teachers also use language that promotes a sense of togetherness within the class. They describe attributes that reinforce the group identity and purpose in the classroom (e.g., "We're hard workers") and behaviors that support the classroom's mission (e.g., "It really helps us stay on track when everyone is paying attention"). They label and reinforce behaviors that contribute to the sense of community within the class, such as instances of kindness or cooperation. Teachers also use language to communicate their care and support for individual students (e.g., "I appreciate your helpfulness," "I'm glad you're here") and for the group (e.g., "I'm pleased that we solved that problem on the playground; you showed a lot of responsibility and caring for each other").

The teacher's use of language is critical to the establishment and maintenance of a classroom community because it creates a shared set of norms that is constructed through social processes. Language is a key mediating variable in shaping group culture, understanding, and perspectives (Schmuck & Schmuck, 1992). Careful and intentional use of language is especially important for teachers of young children. Four- to eight-year-old children's capacity for self-regulation is increasingly negotiated by internalized speech (Bronson, 2000; Rogoff, 1991). Shared language with teachers is critical to the development of this competency and to shaping students' perceptions of themselves as learners. This talk should

1. Convey care and commitment to the child (e.g., "I'm glad to see you this morning Matt," "I look forward to seeing your science project")

2. Help the child to develop a pro-social and academically oriented attitude (e.g., "Rosita, I noticed how well you shared the glue with Jordan," "You really worked hard on your spelling practice today")

3. Communicate that the classroom is a supportive environment for the child to attempt to master tasks (e.g., "Jin Hui, it's okay to try it. I'm sure you'll work hard until you get it")

Utilization of Specific Community-Building Activities

Mr. Valdez started every year with a class-naming unit. He had the students work with partners to brainstorm possible names for the class. Then, he worked with the class to identify the strengths and weaknesses of each name. After evaluating the choices, the students voted on the names. Mr. Valdez liked this process because it gave students a chance to practice problem-solving and the democratic process. Because some students always ended up disappointed, Mr. Valdez used this time to discuss how the class would deal with disappointments and how the students wanted to get along with each other. This year, the class chose "The Stars" because they believed that everyone was a bright light and twinkled in his or her own way. They thought that they could all be the stars of their own learning. The class decorated the room using the star theme, and Mr. Valdez used stars in lesson plans and on graded papers to emphasize the sense of group identity.

Specific community-building activities, such as Mr. Valdez's class-naming activity, help children learn community-based concepts and develop more quickly a sense of community in the classroom. Community-oriented classrooms typically use some form of class meeting (see Developmental Studies Center, 1996b) during which there are community-building activities (e.g., group games or songs), relationship-enhancing activities (e.g., daily greetings), and sharing by individuals. Class meetings also allow opportunities for pro-social behaviors to be taught, practiced, and integrated with academic work (e.g., role playing the resolution of a conflict). Other strategies might include the use of buddies, using between- or within-class peer pairings or small groupings (see Developmental Studies Center, 1996a) to promote friendships between children.

Classrooms might also include attention to the broader community in their missions. This might include home-based activities that help children understand their parents' and caregivers' involvement in the community (see Developmental Studies Center, 1995), or neighborhood outreach and service learning projects (see Developmental Studies Center, 1994). For example, children might learn that some of the older adults in their community are not able to rake their leaves in the fall. The class could then work together to develop strategies to provide this service and carry out the project in the community. Care for one's community and responsible civic behavior are thus modeled as part of the educational process. Teachers are especially likely to use explicit community-building activities early in the school year in order to teach key concepts; however, effective classroom communities use practices that promote togetherness and shared goals throughout the school day, rather than attempting to add on special events throughout the traditional school day, which may not fit seamlessly into the school day. For example, each student in the class may have a rotating daily job in the classroom such as line leader, recess equipment leader, and paper returner.

Teaching Practices

At the beginning of the week, Ms. Smith, a third-grade teacher, had each student set a personal goal for spelling accuracy based on the pretest. On Friday, she would draw a chart. The students would determine whether the majority of the students had met their goals. If so, they would celebrate their achievement. Ms. Smith liked this practice because it gave students individual attention and feedback on their spelling progress but downplayed competition in order to focus on the class's accomplishment. She especially liked the goal-setting part of the activity for the students because it gave them a chance to get excited about their learning. The activity also led to a nice discussion about how to deal with not meeting goals and how the students could coach and mentor each other to do better.

In community-oriented schools, teachers like Ms. Smith maintain their central authoritative role in the classroom, providing structure, direction, monitoring, and feedback to children; however, they use more cooperative and student-directed learning strategies and encourage more active student participation in classroom activities. They ask more questions, elicit more critical thinking and student discussion, use student comments as springboards for discussion, and utilize problem-solving approaches to address student initiated questions and problems (Solomon et al., 1992).

Teachers also purposely mentor students in areas other than academic learning. They directly address social, ethical, and civic behavior as part of their formal curriculum, often through the use of character education, ethics, or social-competence promotion curricula to explicitly teach democratic values and pro-social behavior (see Heartwood Institute, 1995; Lockwood & Harris, 1985; Shure, 1992). They infuse these messages into the academic curriculum (e.g., by using children's literature that includes pro-social themes) and use them informally throughout the day to address interpersonal or classroom problems. For example, if playground equipment is left outside, the teacher may ask the students what classroom rule is being broken. The students may respond that they are not taking care of materials. Then, the students can make suggestions about how the problem can be corrected and take action. There is an intentional focus on shaping the peer culture toward pro-social and supportive interactions. Thus, a cultural norm of mutual respect is established in the classroom, and children acquire important pro-social competencies needed for community involvement.

Grouping practices in these schools may also foster a spirit of community (Wood, 1992). Teachers encourage students to cooperate instead of compete. Schools favor cooperative learning paradigms, promote group or classroom-wide rather than individual projects, and downplay individual testing and competitive grading practices. In addition, these schools use strategies to enhance teacher–student interactions such as multiage grouping (see Developmental Studies Center, 1996b) and block scheduling or other methods (e.g., "school within a school" or "house" strategies) to decrease the number of teachers children work with. For "school within a school" strategies, students and teachers are divided into smaller teams or pods to create closer, more personalized communities within a larger school building. Furthermore, the practice of creating class assignments that keep students and teachers together for several years can be incorporated into school in order to enhance teacher–student interactions (called *looping*).

Discipline in Relationally Oriented Schools

Mrs. Skye, a first-grade teacher, spends a lot of time during her class meetings role-playing how to handle problem situations, especially on the playground. This year, the students have really gotten good at resolving conflicts with less guidance. Yesterday, she saw Michael push Juanita off of the see saw. She was about to run over and intervene when she saw Clark go over to the children and help them to reconcile the matter.

Community-oriented classrooms place a high priority on values that allow students and teachers to work together cooperatively. In this way, the classroom is a model for effective participation in a community. Discipline problems are prevented by

- Teaching students the behaviors necessary to participate successfully in the community (e.g., sharing, taking responsibility for their actions)
- Giving children a legitimate "voice" in the classroom (e.g., allowing students to participate in the development of classroom rules and consequences for keeping or breaking the rules)
- Using discipline infractions as "teachable moments" for community or personal development (e.g., encouraging students to reflect on what classroom rule their behavior breaks and why this rule is important)

Although teachers maintain their central authoritative role in the classroom, they share the responsibility for creating classroom rules with students so that students learn about personal commitment and shared values. This often occurs through the use of democratic class meetings (Developmental Studies Center, 1996a). Within these democratic class meetings, students are able to voice their opinions on what they would like their classroom to be like and contribute to the development of classroom rules and consequences. Rules are based on principles or virtues (e.g., kindness, fairness) and are connected to respect for the community. In this way, children learn the purpose of civic constraints (e.g., importance of being quiet out of respect for others) rather than an arbitrary rule made by adults (e.g., be quiet or you get a check on the board). These schools believe, as Piaget did, that "rules imposed by external constraint remain external to the child's spirit. Rules due to mutual respect and cooperation take root inside the child's mind" (as cited in Lickona, 1991, p. 112).

Conflict resolution is actively taught so that children develop the skills to resolve problems with others (see Committee for Children, 1992; Shure, 1992). Misbehavior is handled in an educational way, using collaborative problem-solving rather than punishment, so that students appreciate a rule's purpose, make amends for wrongdoing, and take responsibility for improving their behavior. In this way, caring, responsibility, and forgiveness are modeled for children within the context of discipline (Lickona, 1991). In general, community-oriented schools do not emphasize extrinsic control strategies such as teacher-delivered reinforcement and punishment systems. They attempt to improve student behavior through increased academic engagement and by enhancing children's interest in school through meaningful academic work and community membership.

Example Applications

Many teachers of young children intuitively use some ideas common to community-oriented approaches. The Child Development Project and the Primary Mental Health Project, for example, systematically use community-oriented ideas to reform school practices.

The Child Development Project

The Child Development Project (CDP; Battistich et al., 1991) is a comprehensive school-reform program for elementary schools. The CDP aims to develop the school as a caring community of learners. It employs intensive staff development to improve the intellectual, social, and ethical development of children. The CDP has six major components:

1. Close and caring relationships among children and between children and teachers, which is fostered through cooperative learning activities and a focus on child development as a function of schooling

2. Challenging, relevant curriculum, based in constructivist learning theory, which provides children with opportunities for self-direction and influence over classroom activities

3. Opportunities to practice and benefit from pro-social values, including curricular approaches (e.g., language arts, social studies, and math applications that teach pro-social values) and modeling of ethical behavior in daily interactions at all levels of the school

4. Developmental discipline that uses democratic processes to involve students in sharing responsibility for creating a caring community in their classroom

5. Close cooperation between families and schools

6. School service programs (e.g., cross-age tutoring, "buddy" programs, and community outreach), so that children have an opportunity to develop altruism and experience connection and caring for others

CDP participation improves children's academic and interpersonal behaviors, attitudes, and motivation (Battistich, Solomon, Kim, Watson, & Schaps, 1995; Solomon et al., 1992). Within CDP schools, a sense of school community influences academic factors via respect for teachers and intrinsic motivation to learn. Children develop excellent social and personal attitudes and behaviors including conflict-resolution skills, intrinsic pro-social motivation, and unselfish behavior. Although the program does not improve all areas of academic performance, children do have better reading comprehension (Battistich et al., 1995). CDP students score just as well on standardized achievement tests as students from schools where CDP is not used (Solomon, Watson, Delucchi, Schaps, & Battistich, 1988) and even score higher on measures of higher-order thinking skills during reading comprehension tasks (Solomon et al., 1992).

CDP students are typically more cooperative and compassionate in their classrooms, more likely to feel accepted by their classmates, more skilled at interpersonal problem-solving, and more strongly committed to democratic values and to school than students from schools where CDP is not used. They are less likely to engage in delinquent behaviors such as stealing, being violent, drinking alcohol, and using drugs (Battistich, Schaps, Watson, & Solomon, 1996; Solomon et al., 1992).

CDP works by affecting teachers' classroom behavior (Solomon et al., 1996). Teachers are warm and supportive; they encourage students to cooperate, to think critically, and to problem solve. They also emphasize pro-social values and avoid extrinsic behavioral control. Teacher behavior affects students' classroom behavior; students are more engaged in learning and interact better with each other. This positive student behavior creates a sense of school community, which in turn leads to positive school-related outcomes, including enjoyment of class, increased motivation to learn, concern for others, and use of conflict resolution skills.

Although the pro-social results of CDP are promising, academic gains are not immediate. The theory supporting CDP emphasizes pro-social and developmental gains as precursors to academic learning; therefore, enhanced academic attainment is eventually expected. Schools that use CDP should be cautious to allow enough time for academic improvement to occur before abandoning the program.

The Primary Mental Health Project

The Primary Mental Health Project (PMHP; Cowen et al., 1996) is a school-based prevention program targeting early elementary children who are at-risk for academic problems. Unlike CDP, which is an educational reform approach, PMHP focuses on students' mental health and seeks to prevent problems by establishing supportive relationships with students who may need extra attention. This specialized intervention service is geared toward children who are not adapting well to school despite the use of a classroom community approach. PMHP focuses on three main objectives:

1. Early detection and screening for school adjustment problems of all students

2. Creation of a new, nonprofessional classroom position (a.k.a., child associate)

3. Implementation of supportive or therapeutic procedures and practices to individual students as needed

PMHP targets children who are experiencing early school adjustment problems and just beginning to show difficulties. In order to effectively screen for students who may need extra attention, PMHP considers teacher reports, parent input, direct classroom observation, and PMHP-developed screening measures. The screening measures focus on identifying children with classroom adjustment problems such as aggression, nervousness, and academic performance problems as well as students who lack school-related resources such as effective learning skills, positive peer relationships, and assertiveness skills. Teacher referrals of children who are aggressive, shy-withdrawn, or have learning difficulties, coupled with the screening measures, identify students who will participate in the program.

PMHP uses nonprofessionals who are recognized for their warmth, care, and experience with children. These adults are called *child associates*. A child associate spends an average of 25–45 minutes per week with a student throughout a supportive relationship centered around children's natural medium of expression—play. Through interactions with the student, the child associate helps him or her to develop a sense of autonomy and security, skills that eventually allow the student to meet a specific set of objectives designed by the student's teacher, child associate, and relevant school professionals. Child associates receive specialized training and on-going supervision from a PHMP professional (e.g., school psychologist, social worker) within the school building, which guides their practicing style. Thus, the amount and quality of support available to students within the building is enhanced and attention is given to promoting their competence in the context of caring relationships with adults. Students also engage in specialized services (e.g., divorce adjustment groups, study skills enhancement, counseling with a school mental health professional) as needed.

Local and state program evaluations and comparison and follow-up studies all support PMHP. Evidence shows that PMHP leads to a decrease in children's maladaptive behavior and an overall increase in children's social competencies (Cowen, Gesten, & Wilson, 1979). The initial gains of students in PMHP continue 2–5 years after students stop participating in the program. PMHP does not require long-term commitment. Shorter-term interventions consisting of two weekly sessions during a 6-week period are as effective as longer interventions consisting of an average of 24.8 sessions during a 5–6 month period.

The PMHP model can be generalized to benefit children in many educational environments, including urban, suburban, and rural school districts. Although the degree of implementation and effectiveness of PMHP differs in various locations, all students participating in the program show significant improvement in classroom adjustment, behavior, and social competencies (Cowen et al., 1983; Farie, Cowen, & Smith, 1986).

CONCLUSION

Community-oriented schooling promotes the social, emotional, cognitive, and civic development of young children. Schooling that builds relationships among students and teachers and fosters a warm, supportive backdrop for learning may help students engage in learning tasks and may support their development as learners. The expectation that children should emerge from public schools as responsible, civic-minded, and competent citizens is not a new idea in education (e.g., Jefferson, 1801/1974) or in child development (e.g., Piaget, 1965). In American schools, however, these values have been downplayed by an emphasis on academic attainment and competition. In community-oriented schools, the development of socially and emotionally competent, ethically minded citizens is not seen as a by-product of effective schooling. Rather, it is equally important as children's academic attainment and is intentionally developed through overt and covert school practices.

REFERENCES

Baker, J.A. (1998a). Are we missing the forest for the trees?: Considering the social context of school violence. [Special section on school violence.] *Journal of School Psychology, 36,* 29–45.

Baker, J.A. (1998b). The social context of school satisfaction among urban, low-income, African-American students. *School Psychology Quarterly, 13,* 25–44.

Baker, J.A., Terry, T., Bridger, R., & Winsor, A. (1997). Schools as caring communities: A relational approach to school reform. *School Psychology Review, 26,* 586–602.

Battistich, V., Schaps, E., Watson, M., & Solomon, D. (1996). Prevention effects of the Child Development Project: Early findings from an ongoing multisite demonstration trial. *Journal of Adolescent Research, 11,* 12–35.

Battistich, V., Solomon, D., Kim, D., Watson, M., & Schaps, E. (1995). Schools as communities, poverty levels of student populations, and students' attitudes, motives, and performance: A multilevel analysis. *American Educational Research Journal, 32,* 627–658.

Battistich, V., Watson, M., Solomon, D., Schaps, E., & Solomon, J. (1991). The Child Development Project: A comprehensive program for the development of prosocial character. In W.M. Durtines & J.L. Gewirtz (Eds.), *Handbook of moral behavior and development: Vol. 3. Application* (pp. 1–34). Mahwah, NJ: Lawrence Erlbaum Associates.

Berman, S., & LaFarge, P. (1993). *Promising practices in teaching social responsibility.* Albany: Educators for Social Responsibility, State University of New York Press.

Bernard, B. (1991). *Fostering resiliency in kids: Protective factors in the family, school, and community.* Portland, OR: Northwest Regional Educational Laboratory.

Birch, S., & Ladd, G.W. (1997). The teacher–child relationship and children's early school adjustment. *Journal of School Psychology, 35,* 61–79.

Bowlby, J. (1982). *Attachment and Loss: Vol. 1. Attachment.* New York: Basic Books.

Bronfenbrenner, U. (1979). *The ecology of human development: Experiments by nature and design.* Cambridge, MA: Harvard University Press.

Bronfenbrenner, U. (1999). Environment in developmental perspective: Theoretical and operational models. In S.L. Friedman & T.D. Wachs (Eds.), *Measuring environments across the life span: Emerging methods and concepts* (pp. 3–31). Washington, DC: American Psychological Association.

Bronson, M.B. (2000). *Self-regulation in early childhood: Nature and nurture.* New York: The Guilford Press.

Committee for Children. (1992). *Second Step: A violence prevention program for children.* Seattle: Author.

Connell, J.P., & Wellborn, J.G. (1991). Competence, autonomy and relatedness: A motivational analysis of self-system processes. In M. Gunnar & L.A. Sroufe (Eds.), *Minnesota Symposium of Child Psychology* (Vol. 22, pp. 43–77). Minneapolis: University of Minnesota Press.

Cowen, E.L., Gesten, E.L., & Wilson, A.B. (1979). The Primary Mental Health Project (PMHP): Evaluation of current program effectiveness. *American Journal of Community Psychology, 7,* 293–302.

Cowen, E.L., Hightower, D., Pedro-Carroll, J.L., Work, W.C., Wyman, P.A., & Haffey, W.G. (1996). *School-based prevention for children at risk: The Primary Mental Health Project.* Washington, DC: American Psychological Association.

Cowen, E.L., Weissberg, R.P., Lotyczewski, B.S., Bromely, M.L., Gilliland-Mallo, G., DeMeis, J.L., Farago, J.P., Grassi, R.J., Haffey, W.G., Weiner, M.J., & Woods, A. (1983). Validity generalization of a school-based preventive mental health program. *Professional Psychology, 14,* 613–623.

Deci, E.L., & Ryan, R.M. (1985). *Intrinsic motivation and self-determination in human behavior.* Norwell, MA: Kluwer Academic Publishers.

Developmental Studies Center. (1994). *At home in our schools: A guide to schoolwide activities that build community.* Oakland, CA: Author.

Developmental Studies Center. (1995). *Homeside activities: Conversations and activities that bring parents into children's schoolside learning.* Oakland, CA: Author.

Developmental Studies Center. (1996a). *That's my buddy!: Friendship and learning across the grades.* Oakland, CA: Author.

Developmental Studies Center. (1996b). *The ways we want our class to be: Classroom meetings that build commitment to kindness and learning.* Oakland, CA: Author.

Dewey, J. (1970). Democracy and education. In S.M. Cahn (Ed.), *The philosophical foundations of education* (pp. 203–221). New York: HarperCollins Publishers. (Original work published 1916)

Dewey, J. (1975). Moral principles in education. Carbondale: Southern Illinois University Press. (Original work published 1909)

Durkheim, E. (1964). *The rules of sociological method* (8th ed.). (S.A. Solovay, Trans.). New York: The Free Press. (Original work published in 1893)

Etzioni, A. (1993). *The spirit of community.* New York: Crown Publishing Group.

Farie, A.M., Cowen, E.L., & Smith, M. (1986). The development and implementation of a rural consortium program to provide early, preventive school mental health services. *Community Mental Health Journal, 22,* 94–103.

Glasser, W. (1993). *The quality school teacher.* New York: Harper Perennial.

Good, T.L., & Brophy, J.E. (2000). *Looking in classrooms* (8th ed.). New York: HarperCollins Publishers.

Goodenow, C. (1992). Strengthening the links between educational psychology and the study of social contexts. *Educational Psychologist, 27,* 177–196.

Goodenow, C. (1993). Classroom belonging among early adolescent students: Relationships to motivation and achievement. *Journal of Early Adolescence, 13,* 21–43.

Goodlad, J.I. (1994). *What schools are for* (2nd ed.). Bloomington, IN: Phi Delta Kappa International.

Greenberg, M.T., Speltz, M.L., & DeKlyen, M. (1993). The role of attachment in the early development of disruptive behavior problems. *Development & Psychopathology, 5*(1–2), 191–213.

Hamachek, D. (1995). *Psychology in teaching, learning, and growth* (5th ed.). Boston: Allyn & Bacon.

Heartwood Institute. (1995). *Heartwood: An ethics curriculum for children.* Pittsburgh: Author.

Hetherington, E.M., & Parke, R.D. (1999). *Child psychology: A contemporary viewpoint* (5th ed). New York: McGraw-Hill.

Howes, C., & Hamilton, C.E. (1992). Children's relationship with caregivers: Mothers and childcare teachers. *Child Development, 63,* 859–866.

Jefferson, T. (1974). Notes on the state of Virginia, with an appendix. In S. Cohen (Ed.), *Education in the United States: A documentary history* (Vol. 2, pp. 747–750). New York: Random House. (Original work published 1801)

Lickona, T. (1991). *Educating for character: How our schools can teach respect and responsibility.* New York: Bantam Dell Publishing Group.

Lockwood, A.L. & Harris, D.E. (1985). *Reasoning with democratic values.* New York: Teachers College Press.

Masten, A.S. (1994). Resilience in individual development: Successful adaptation despite risk and adversity. In M.C. Wang & E.W. Gordon (Eds.), *Educational resilience in inner-city America: Challenges and prospects* (pp. 3–26). Mahwah, NJ: Lawrence Erlbaum Associates.

Ogbu, J.U. (1992). Understanding cultural diversity and learning. *Educational Researcher, 21,* 5–14.

Piaget, J. (1965). *The moral judgment of the child.* New York: The Free Press.

Pianta, R.C. (1999). *Enhancing relationships between children and teachers.* Washington, DC: American Psychological Association.

Pianta, R.C., & Steinberg, M. (1992). Teacher–child relationships and the process of adjusting to school. *New Directions for Child Development, 57,* 61–79.

Pianta, R.C., & Walsh, D.J. (1996). *High-risk children in schools: Constructing sustaining relationships.* New York: Routledge.

Rogers, D. (1994). Conceptions of caring in a fourth-grade classroom. In A. Prillaman, D. Eaker, & D. Kendrick (Eds.), *The tapestry of caring: Education as nurturance* (pp. 78–86). Westport, CT: Ablex Publishing.

Rogoff, B. (1991). *Apprenticeship in thinking: Cognitive development in social context.* New York: Oxford University Press.

Sameroff, A.J. (1995). General systems theories and developmental psychopathology. In D. Cicchetti & D.J. Cohen (Eds.), *Developmental psychopathology: Vol. 1. Theory and methods* (pp. 659–695). New York: John Wiley & Sons.

Schaps, E., & Solomon, D. (1990). Schools and classrooms as communities. *Educational Leadership, 48,* 38–42.

Schmuck, R.A., & Schmuck, P.A. (1992). *Group processes in the classroom.* Dubuque, IA: William C. Brown.

Sergiovanni, T.J. (1994). *Building community in schools.* San Francisco: Jossey-Bass.

Shure, M.B. (1992). *I can problem solve: An interpersonal cognitive problem-solving program.* Champaign, IL: Research Press.

Solomon, D., Watson, M., Battistich, V., & Schaps, E. (1996). Creating classrooms that students experience as communities. *American Journal of Community Psychology, 24,* 719–748.

Solomon, D., Watson, M., Battistich, V., Schaps, E., & Delucchi, K. (1992). Creating a caring community: Educational practices that promote children's prosocial development. In F.K. Oser, A. Dick, & J-L. Patry (Eds.), *Effective and responsible teaching: The new synthesis* (pp. 383–390). San Francisco: Jossey-Bass.

Solomon, D., Watson, M., Delucchi, K., Schaps, E., & Battistich, V. (1988). Enhancing children's prosocial behavior in the classroom. *American Educational Research Journal, 25,* 527–554.

Stockard, J., & Mayberry, M. (1992). *Effective educational environments.* Thousand Oaks, CA: Corwin Press.

Tyack, D., & Cuban, L. (1995). *Tinkering toward utopia: A century of public school reform.* Cambridge, MA: Harvard University Press.

Vygotsky, L. (1978). *Mind in society: The development of higher psychological processes.* Cambridge, MA: Harvard University Press.

Wang, M.C., Haertel, G.D., & Walberg, H.J. (1994). What influences learning? A content analysis of review literature. *Journal of Educational Research, 84,* 30–43.

Wentzel, K.R. (1994). Relations of social goal pursuit to social acceptance, classroom behavior, and perceived social support. *Journal of Educational Psychology, 86,* 173–182.

Witty, P. (1967, May). An analysis of the personality traits of the effective teacher. *Journal of Educational Research,* 662–671.

Wood, G.H. (1992). *Schools that work.* New York: Plume.

Community-Oriented Classroom Practices

Developing Positive Teacher–Child Relationships

Sharon Ritchie

Developing and maintaining a genuine classroom community and the relationships that are central to its success requires a broad view of attachment theory, caring communities, and democratic classrooms, as well as a deep understanding of the day-to-day practices that make those ideas a reality. In a community-oriented classroom, all children are important and unique. Community-oriented classrooms meet the needs of each child without superseding the needs of the entire classroom. It is a safe place where children know that a teacher means what he or she says, that they will be supported if they are having a difficult time, and that there is an expectation that people will be kind and gentle with one another.

This chapter explores both the theory and the practice of a classroom community, examining each fully to provide conceptual understanding of several ideas, including conflict resolution, making plans, building friendships, teacher care, community-oriented skills, individualized responses, coping with anger and frustration, encouraging participation, working with parents, and helping children who need extra attention. At the end of the chapter, a full day in a community-oriented classroom is described. Each idea will hopefully provide you with something to think about, something to practice, new resources to consult, and the motivation to persevere in your attempts to provide children with an atmosphere in which they can build positive relationships, explore their environment, and learn.

CONFLICT RESOLUTION

Children need to know that when problems arise, their teacher will help them, but they also need to learn to solve their problems independently. Teachers hear a lot about how children need to work through their own problems and use their words, but children need a lot of help to actually do this. If you consider how very few adults are truly effective at dealing with conflict, it will become evident that to expect this of 4- to 6-year-olds is often overambitious.

Teaching Conflict Resolution

There are two ways to teach conflict resolution to young children. First, you can employ role playing, in which children are given a role and a scenario. Consider this example:

> Ms. Jackson tells the class that they are going to practice what to do when there are problems on the playground. She tells Dante to grab a ball from Maria. Maria is asked to scream, pretend to hit Dante or run to Ms. Jackson to tattle. Ms. Jackson then asks the children in the class to suggest better ways for the problem to be handled. Based on the answers, Dante will then reenact the scenario asking Maria politely for the ball. Alternatively, Maria may suggest that she and Dante figure out a game to play together.

Although children can be quite good at role play, they are not as skilled when transferring their efforts to actual conflicts. This may be because role play is too artificial and too contained; children are not experiencing the anger, sadness, and impulsivity that accompany a real problem.

Second, you can use genuine conflicts as ongoing opportunities to practice problem solving and resolution. Of the two approaches, this is the most beneficial from a classroom-community perspective. Practicing conflict resolution skills on a daily basis in the context of their own lives provides situations in which problems and feelings are real and children's engagement is more meaningful. Even though it is far easier and more expedient to step in and solve problems for children—it takes a long time for children to successfully work through their problems—they will not learn how to solve their own problems if they do not have consistent practice. Consider this situation:

> Two boys, Tony and Jake, are fighting over a bike. The teacher says to Tony, "Okay, Jake gets to have the bike for 5 minutes. Then, you can have it for 5 minutes." Although the teacher has ended the dispute, the children have not learned how to resolve the problem.

Teachers who are committed to developing community-oriented classrooms must be willing to devote time and attention to the process of conflict resolution. Conflict resolution includes the ability of all involved to express their feelings, the opportunity to hear all viewpoints, and the chance to generate a decision that is agreeable to everyone. In any conflict, feelings are involved, and these feelings must be heard and validated before anything else can be done. Children need to know that their feelings are important. Part of developing a positive relationship between a child and his and her teacher includes the belief by the child that his or her teacher cares about how he or she feels. A teacher who has listened to a child express his or her feelings might reflect "That really made you mad; you really wanted a turn with the truck." When children cannot say how they feel on their own, you can describe their emotions to them, based on their behaviors: "You are yelling, your face is red, and you are stamping your feet. You must be really angry."

Often, when children are upset, it is too stimulating for them to listen to the adults who are talking to them. Waiting until children are calm and can listen and engage in conversation is more effective. A good idea is to start by asking questions such as, "What happened?" Teachers are usually not privy to most of what happened prior to their arrival on the scene. Asking for circumstances can help you arbitrate a situation in a fair and trustworthy manner. Gathering information also can alleviate any discomfort you may feel if you are unsure if you are doing the right thing. Children are not necessarily accurate reporters, but hearing what they have to say will validate their frustration, anger, sadness, or hurt and will help them plan what to do next. You do not have to decide who gets the shovel or the next turn on the computer. Consider how Ms. Riley applies these two concepts in the following situation:

> Ms. Riley hears a commotion and turns to see Angel smack Max with his hand and grab for something that Angel is holding.
>
> "What happened?" she asks with interest and sympathy.
>
> Angel screams, "He took my rolling pin! He took my rolling pin!"
>
> Ms. Riley says, "I see you have a rolling pin Max, where did you get it?"

Max replies, "I had it first, and he hit me."

Ms. Riley says, "I can see that you are both really mad. Angel, even though you are mad, you cannot hit. I don't know who had the rolling pin first, so you guys are going to have to make a plan about it. Tell Max what you want."

"I want the rolling pin. Give it to me!" Angel demands.

Max says, "NO! I want it. I am using it."

Ms. Riley answers, "It looks like you both really want the rolling pin. We need to make a plan about who is going to use it now and who is going to use it later."

Notice that Ms. Riley asked the children to explain what happened first. Then, she validated both of the children's feeling of anger.

After engaging with the children in this way, one of two things will most likely happen. First, one of the boys will give in and say that the other child can use the toy first. In that case, Ms. Riley will praise him for his generosity and assure him that he can have a turn just as soon as the other child is finished. Most often, arguments have far more to do with power and impulsivity than they do with the object in question. Sharing the object becomes much easier after the impulse is quelled and the issue of negotiating power is relieved through problem solving rather than hitting. A second option is that neither of the children will acquiesce. Then, Ms. Riley will not try to solve the problem but instead will say, "It looks like it's too hard for you guys to make a plan right now. Make another choice, and when you think you can make a plan, then we can do that."

Children benefit if teachers come back to the issue later because it is important for children to have the opportunity to reflect on a difficult aspect of their day. While children are on the rug or at the lunch table, Ms. Riley can say, "Remember how Max and Angel were so mad about the rolling pin this morning. They both wanted a turn, and it was really hard to wait." Max and Angel may or may not want to say anything about the earlier problem and that should be their choice. Ms. Riley can conclude by saying, "But they worked it out, and now I see they are sitting next to each other laughing at the lunch table." Teachers don't need to moralize; it is enough to simply restate what happened.

Conflict resolution strategies may not work the first time or every time you use them, but they do provide children with a structure within which to operate. Included in the structure are clear and consistent limits and rules. Children need to know the rules and to know that the rules do not change. Simple rules include

- No name calling.
- No hitting.

- If you are mad, you need to tell someone what you need and how you feel.

Children who experience support, practice, and help when conflict arises will learn to trust that the structure is in place, that you can be a valuable resource for solving problems, and that when a plan is made, it will be followed.

MAKING A PLAN

Children cannot always have what they want at the moment they want it. Teachers can, however, be trustworthy by consistently following through with making a plan to satisfy children's needs and wants. When a child wants a toy that another child has, he or she can be reassured that a plan can be made for him or her to have the next turn. When the children want to play with the tumbling mats but another class is using them, they can make a plan to have them the next day. When a child is eager to share his or her thoughts or wants you to read a book that he or she brought that day and there is simply no time, a plan can be made to read it before lunch.

The consistent teacher earns trust. When you can be trusted to both make a plan and make sure the plan is carried out, children are able to trust that you are a person who means what you say. You make the classroom a safe place for children because the rules and expectations are clear and unchanging, because there is a routine that is followed, and because when plans are changed, there is both an explanation and validation for feelings that may be evoked by the change. The ideas of plans and consistency will be revisited throughout this chapter. They are inherent to developing a safe and respectful classroom community.

BUILDING FRIENDSHIPS

Students need not all like one another, but there should be community expectations that create a respectful atmosphere where people are kind to one another. Vivian Paley (1992) in her book, *You Can't Say You Can't Play* provides some provocative ideas about rejection, sharing, and friendship. Paley introduces a new rule in her kindergarten class: You can't say, "You can't play." When she implements the rule, she realizes that she must follow it as well. She can no longer forbid children to play in an area as a consequence. Also, there can be no more time-out because it is another form of exclusion. The children are pleased that the teacher will have to change, too. The rule is instituted with much discussion and a variety of responses from the children. In essence, children who were systematically excluded before the rule are happier now. All of the children are kinder to each other. It is a book worth reading when considering the complex issues of friendships between young children.

Making friends is an important task for young children. They often barter for what they want by using friendship as a bargaining tool. "I won't be your friend if you don't give me a cookie," they say, or "You can't come to my party if you don't play the game my way." Teachers are enormously important in the negotiation of friendships. By actively supporting children as they develop friendships, you assure them that you are available to help them make friends and work out their problems. You also help children understand that is okay to play with more than one person and to have more than one friend. Children need a great deal of support in understanding that their friend may choose to play with another child but that he or she will come back to play with them another time. Young children who are experiencing jealousy and rejection need validation for those very strong feelings. They need to know too that it is okay to say that their feelings are hurt or that they are angry when their friends play with someone else.

Teasing and name calling can be quite prevalent in classrooms for young children. Children need to know that neither are permitted at any time. The classroom needs to be a safe place for children, and when teachers tolerate teasing and name calling, the room is not a safe place. Gentle reminders such as, "That sounds like teasing. Can you think of something else to say to Aaron?" or "Do we call children names in our classroom?" help children become aware of their behavior and consistently remind them that a classroom community is a respectful place.

In response to the needs of the children to be exposed to many opportunities to make friends, teachers can occasionally create different groupings and pairs that change the dynamics and give students a chance to interact with different children. Children can be paired for art activities or when using the computer. They can sit next to different children at lunch or in their small groups, and they can have a different partner for taking a walk or learning a new dance. If play dates are part of children's lives, you can help facilitate some new friendships by helping parents set up some outside activities.

Many, if not most, early childhood classrooms include children with special needs. Special needs include speech and language disorders, physical disabilities, autism, problems with impulse control and aggression, and so forth. All children need to have friends and all children need to learn to accept diversity. You have the opportunity to help children deal with their fear or hesitation about children who are different from them. There is a tendency to pretend that everyone is the same and to ignore chances to talk about differences. Children need to be able to ask questions without feeling stifled, and they need help to be kind when they are possibly hurting others' feelings.

Children with special needs should have the chance to talk freely about what is different about them and how these things affect them. Their parents can often be very helpful. Many parents are willing to come in and talk to classes about their child: why he or she is in a wheelchair, why he or she is hard to understand, or why he or she has difficulty making friends.

Part of providing new opportunities for new peer interaction involves giving thought to classroom environment and materials. It is important to be clear with children when an activity is appropriate for many participants and when it is okay for it to be private or limited to two or three children. If a child is in an area meant for several children, then anyone willing to be part of the ongoing activity should have access. If one child wishes to reject a participant, then you can help this child either figure out how to accept the new child into play or make a new activity choice.

Think too about the difference between sharing and turn taking. There is a time for sharing areas or materials, but there is also a time for taking turns. If a child chooses to play with something that another child decides she wants, there is a tendency for teachers to impose an arbitrary structure on the object of choice (e.g., "You can have the marble game for 5 minutes, and then it is Patricia's turn"). Consider instead giving the child the power to use the object until she is done. This is not to say that the child should get the marble game every day. If one child has the same toy repeatedly, then you need to help make a plan for many kids to have turns. Children need to know that they can make choices about what to play with. Generally, they are far more ready to relinquish the object when it is their choice.

SHOWING YOU CARE

There are many ways for children to know that you care about them. Consider the following ideas as you think about your relationship with your students.

Greet Children Warmly When They Arrive

Make sure that children feel special and noticed when they come to school. Early morning can be a busy time, and it is easy to forget that each child needs to be welcomed. If you know that a certain child is fond of you, then try to be present when the child arrives. Arrival is also time for separation. Children need to say goodbye to their parents, and each child is unique in terms of readiness to do this successfully. Parents sometimes think that if they slip away unnoticed, then the separation will be easier, so they need help saying goodbye to their children, just as much as their children need help saying goodbye to them. Sometimes parents need to spend a little time with their child—playing or reading a book with them—to ease the transition. Children need to be reassured that their parents will be back for them.

Ask Children About Things that Are Important to Them

You need to know the children in your class. You need to know when a child goes on a special vacation, visits a favorite aunt, or takes a trip to the doctor. You also need to know about things such as a sick grandma or a favorite movie. When you know the children, you can have conversations with them. This lets children know that they are interesting and valuable, and it lets you support children through difficult times. In addition, children have a chance to develop their oral language skills, and you benefit from developing your listening skills.

Children will know that they are being listened to when you are able to restate some of what you have been told; for example, "You're going to your aunt's house after school?" You can then extend the conversation by asking, "What will you do when you get there?" or "I remember last time you baked cookies. Will you do that again?" Children will also know they are being listened to when their feelings are validated; for example, "I hear that you don't want to go to child care today. It is hard when the bus picks you up instead of mommy." Or, "It makes you so mad when your sister rips up your pictures." Sometimes you need patience to let children tell their stories; however, it is worth the time and effort to slow down and listen to a child's perception of the world and what goes on around him or her.

Follow Through

The importance of making and sticking to a plan cannot be overemphasized. Children know that you are trustworthy and that you care about them when they see regular evidence you mean what you say. They know that if you make a plan with them to have a turn with the Tonka Truck, then you will make sure that it happens. They know that if you say you will make vegetable soup for snack time, then indeed you will. They know that if you says it is clean up time, then they need to stop what they are doing and begin to put things away.

Soothe and Care for Children When They Are Sick and Injured

Children need to be treated tenderly. Some children, unfortunately, come to school when they are sick. Often parents must get to work and do not have other options. Optimally, children should be sent home when they are ill, but when they are at school, they need you to care for them. You can say something like, "You are not feeling well. Shall we find you a pillow and blanket and a cozy area to rest?" or "Let's get you some Kleenex and some books, and you can work quietly."

Children perceive their injuries to be quite serious. A tiny scratch that you can barely see can preoccupy a child. There is a tendency to make light of children's "boo boos" and to tell them the injury is nothing and that they will be all right. Children do better when you say, "Oh, that looks very sore. Shall we wash it and find a band-aid?" Children also love to discuss their injuries. Circle time conversation can center around each child's bruise and bump. There is a song that allows each child to highlight their own. "*Bobby* fell down and bumped his *knee*, Ouch, Wouch, he bumped his *knee*. Pick him up on his feet again, *Bobby* fell down, Kaboom!" The italicized parts change as the song moves from child to child and each selects his or her own "owie."

Praise Children in Genuine and Specific Ways

Genuine praise is another way for children to feel known. It is easy to get into the habit of saying "Good job," "That's great," or "That looks pretty," but children will know that the praise is real and directed toward them when it is more specific.

- "Good job. Yesterday, it was so hard for you to clean up, and today, you did it all by yourself."
- "That's great! You made it to the third rung on the monkey bars!"
- "That looks pretty. You used so many different colors. Shall we hang it up so you can show your mom?"

Children who hear specific and genuine praise know that you are paying attention to them.

Respond Noncontingently

Responding noncontingently means teaching children that they are important, valuable, and loveable no matter what behavior they may exhibit. Teachers who link children's behaviors to activities and rewards are telling children that they must be good in order to be valuable and loveable.

- "If you don't sit down and be quiet, then you will not have snack."
- "If you don't put away your blocks, then you will not get a sticker."
- "You cannot be part of the group until you are done crying."

These are threats, and children do not build trusting relationships with threatening adults. There are other ways to respond, such as, "Maria, you are too noisy at the snack table. The other kids can't talk to each other. I am going to pull you away until you can quietly rejoin the group." This statement lets Maria know that her behavior is disruptive, that it bothers the other kids, and that she can make a choice to quiet down and return. Some teachers use stickers and happy faces to control children's behavior, but in a classroom community, children do not clean up their toys or sit quietly in order to get a sticker. They do these things because they are part of a community that takes care of the things in their classroom and respects the rules and routines.

Children do not have to be happy in order to be valued. They need to know that all of their feelings are acceptable but need to be contained in compliance with the rules of *no hitting* and *no name calling*. Children are often excluded when they are crying, sulking, or sad. As stated earlier in the chapter, children's feelings need to be validated. You can say something like, "Chris is so sad today. He had to leave his favorite truck in the car, and he really wanted it." Or, "Marissa has been crying all day. Her mom is on a trip, and she really misses her."

It can be helpful to reframe thinking about children who are not behaving the way you would like. Children who are having a hard time need additional help and support. Their behaviors need to be interpreted as a signal that they need an adult to help them, not to punish, scold, or exclude them. Aspects of a community-oriented classroom that have been discussed earlier in this chapter are the strategies that offer support that children who are oppositional, impulsive, and aggressive require. They need consistent teachers who mean what they say, provide structure, validate angry and sad feelings, help them make friends, support them when they are in conflict, and let them know that they are important and valuable at all times.

TEACHING COMMUNITY-ORIENTED SKILLS

Although teachers are often tireless in their efforts to help children learn their numbers or how to write their names, there is often an expectation that children immediately conform to expectations that include how to sit on the rug or how to walk to the playground. Children need to be taught these skills. When the classroom rules and expectations are taught to children and they have a chance to practice and learn them, then some of the management and discipline problems diminish. When the classroom routine is organized in such a way that it resembles a well-oiled machine—where everyone knows what is expected of them and how to go about doing it—then the teacher has succeeded in teaching the children how to care for the classroom and for each other. Transitions are smooth because children know their responsibilities:

- They know that when the area of the classroom where they were working is clean, they should either wait on the rug for the rest of the class or offer help in other areas.

- They know that when you say it is time to clean up, they can ask if they can save what they are working on instead of putting it away or continuing to work.

- They know that when you ask for quiet, it is a serious request, and it is important to stop talking and to listen.

- They know that when they are walking from one place to another that it can be disruptive and unsafe if they are not calm and quiet.

You are the person responsible for making certain that a classroom runs smoothly. If you begin an activity and do not have all of the materials that you need, then children get restless and noisy while they wait. When children are asked to clean up but many of them keep on playing without your reminding them immediately to stop, then it signals other children that they too can continue to play. When teachers become distracted by other adults, telephone calls, or a long interaction with one child, children too become distracted. Often, children are blamed during these times for not behaving well, when in fact it is the teacher who is responsible. Wait time needs to be minimal, and when it is necessary for them to wait, children need to know the rules, which may include that they must stay seated, that they can talk quietly with one another, and that you will be with them as soon as you possibly can.

Community-oriented skills are also incorporated into structured parts of the day. For example, when working on emergent literacy by discussing the letter of the day, you can have children take turns both talking and listening to other students. Taking turns is a big lesson and a big task for young children to learn. If children are rolling around on the carpet or calling out while other children are trying to have their turn speaking, then the class is not a safe or respectful place. You need to think about how long children are able to participate successfully in activities.

Many teachers like to include a time for sharing. Children are asked to talk about their weekend or their holiday or are allowed to bring something from home. This practice allows individual children a chance to practice talking to the whole group, and it allows them the chance to feel important and valuable. It is also a time when the children who are asked to listen become bored and restless. Teachers often become quite engaged with the individual child, asking good questions and showing interest, but forget how hard it is for young children to stay involved without support. Remembering to observe how the whole class functions during activities where one child is central will help you make good decisions about ensuring maximum participation for all children.

INDIVIDUALIZING RESPONSES

Teachers need to find a balance between supporting self-regulation and helping children who need it. Each child is unique and requires different things from a teacher. Some children require a great deal of attention and thought, whereas others already know that adults are people who can help them solve problems, comfort them when they are hurt or upset, and be available when children need them. Children who move too fast; are too impulsive; or are left out, angry, aggressive, and provocative most likely need extra support from adults in the classroom. Children who are withdrawn or quiet or who avoid adults may also need attention and support.

Support can come in many forms. There is simple proximity: being nearby, standing or sitting behind a child at circle time or table time, placing a hand on a shoulder or a knee. Children who trust adults to be there for them are able to be successful without the constant physical presence of the trusted adult. Children who are not yet so sure of the adults need them to be closer. As a child begins to trust, the adult can move away a little at a time. The contact and reassurance, however, must remain. Try making occasional eye contact when further away, call out to a child to let him or her know you are there, and help the child keep track of where you can be found. When you need to leave the room, go on a break, or pick something up, try to let students know where you are going, when you will be back, and to whom students can go for help while you are gone. Consistency makes a big difference.

Children grow and change over the course of the time teachers spend with them. In the beginning of the year, teachers usually need to be near students—providing support for many children during circle times, playing in the block or pretend area, pushing children on the swings, and guiding children on bikes. It is important to be sensitive to when this is no longer necessary. Teachers need to play different roles as the year goes on. They need to pay attention to when children no longer need them to be so close. Practice moving away, and observe closely how each child copes with the changed proximity. This will give you a lot of information about which children need extra support and which children have developed more self-regulation and, ultimately, more trust.

COPING WITH ANGER AND FRUSTRATION

Mr. Clark's students are enjoying a fun afternoon on the playground. When it is time for them to go back inside, Aaron gets very upset. He cries and screams. The other children look worried and concerned. To ease the transition, Mr. Clark helps Aaron calm down. Another teacher stays with the rest of the class and says, "Aaron is really upset right now. He was having a good time playing and was very disappointed when it was time to come in. Mr. Clark will help him feel better. He will sit with him until he calms down, and then Aaron can come back and be with all of us."

Teachers can use anger and frustration in a classroom to help children and to promote community. A child like Aaron is not a "bad child," just a child who is having strong feelings. Teachers who model support for a struggling child as well as attention to those who are affected by him or her help children see that adults will be there for them if they experience hard times as well.

Paying attention to children's anger and frustration also expands children's repertoire of feelings, helps them move beyond happy and sad, and allows them to recognize that they can have many feelings in each day. When teachers pay attention to children's feelings, they are helping to name the feeling and validate it. Teachers can talk with children about their many feelings and, as they get older, give them more words to describe the feelings. They can learn the difference between frustration and anger, and surprise and fear. They can experience pride, shyness, guilt, and jealousy. Teachers have multiple opportunities each day to talk about feelings and how they change throughout the day.

ENCOURAGING PARTICIPATION

Encouraging participation for all children is important both to the community and to the child. A child who removes him- or herself from the group, hides under the table, prefers to play with toys while the other children are at circle time, or has a tantrum and resists when it is time to join the group is asking for help. Children need to hear again and again that they are wanted in the group and that they need to join in. Children left on their own do not have a chance to learn to relate. They are avoiding relationships and may believe that adults are not useful to them. They need to be brought to the group initially and returned to the group if they leave. These children may benefit from being held on a lap, told they are missed, and included actively in the group. Sometimes it may seem easier to leave them be and to let them make their own decisions about participation, but teachers should keep in mind that it is not helpful to allow children to isolate themselves.

Children also need to know that the community itself can be more important than the needs of an individual child. Too often a child who acts out demands and gets much of a teacher's time, even when the rest of the group is waiting to continue an activity. If a child's nonparticipation becomes aggressive or disruptive, or you notice yourself sacrificing the needs of the whole group for the needs of one child, then the message to the child needs to be: "Everyone else is ready. We are going to go on and hope you will join us when you are ready." Here again, developing a community takes time.

When children at first miss out on group activities, they generally do not care because they have no concept of being a group member. As time goes by, children care more about belonging, and they begin to alter their behavior in order to be included. One child spent 2 years in a preschool where community and being a part of a group were central to the philosophy of the school. When he entered elementary school, he required some extra services. The speech therapist was baffled when he refused to leave the room to go with her. His constant message was "I want to be with the group."

In some cases, teachers should honor a child's choice to be alone. Children do indeed need to have a chance to engage in solitary, productive play. This is not to be confused with aimless wandering or the inability to join into play with others. In a structured day, solitary time can be found during outside time or free choice time. It is important to children to have that choice and to build the skills of being independent and entertaining themselves.

WORKING WITH PARENTS

Community is larger than the classroom. Bringing in parents, having them help determine the vision, and helping them participate in realizing goals is an important aspect of community-based classrooms. Head Start programs have expertise and experience in helping parents feel welcome and in including them in ways that benefit children, teachers, and families. They include parents in decision making, they have monthly meetings and frequent home visits, and they provide multiple opportunities for parents to participate in the classroom. In other programs, an open classroom, a welcoming staff, a full coffee pot, and a variety of ways to participate promote parent involvement.

Parents can be involved in many ways. They can put together home kits for children and parents to check out and work on together. Home kits can include all of the items necessary to conduct a simple science experiment that the child can do with his mother, father, sister, or brother. Kits can include a book with questions the parents can ask the child. They can also contain a simple art project for the family to work on together. Parents can develop a method to lend and check in classroom books to promote reading at home, AND they can work in the classroom, set up the playground, develop materials at home, and so forth. Often, the school is in need of storage cabinets, bookshelves and toy shelves, or a shade structure for an outside area. Sometimes tables are broken, doors don't close properly, or swings have fallen off their chains. Many parents are able to offer their services in this area. Many programs have found that activities such as starting a garden, having a weekend painting day, or asking parents to help build or repair the school can be wonderful opportunities to help the school, to bring families together, and to have a chance for informal conversations.

Ideas for working with parents have been around for a long time, but it is important to give careful thought to how your program works with parents. What do you and your fellow staff members really think about parents? Do you view them as valuable assets who bring cultural richness and new ideas, or do you think of them as people who need a lot of help raising their children correctly? Do you think that parents should take care of the children at home and that you should take care of them at school? Honest consideration of your personal as well as your program's philosophy toward parents can go a long way in determining possible changes. It is clear that no one program can do all things for all children. It is important to identify priorities. If working with parents is high on the list, then extend the energy necessary to include them. If it is not a priority at the moment, tackle that aspect of the program when it comes closer to the top of the list.

Parent participation offers teachers and parents an arena in which to interact, get to know one another, build trust, and develop respect. Being in a classroom can provide opportunities for parents to learn skills from teachers. If parents are struggling with letting their children grow up, setting limits for their children, or helping their children develop friendships and new skills, then being in a classroom for significant periods of time could encourage parents to practice these skills in the home. Working with parents includes helping them be comfortable in the classroom. In the beginning of the year, a potluck dessert or dinner is a welcoming way to bring parents in. In addition, having a classroom scavenger hunt helps parents know where to find the glue, scissors, and books, so that when they come to help in the classroom, they feel as if they can be useful.

Knowing what teachers want is also very helpful for the parents. They need to know what to do if children are having problems. For example, they need to know when they should ask you for help and when you prefer for them to try to help the children themselves first. Knowing up front avoids potential embarrassment and conflict. Just as classroom rules need to be clear for the children, they need to be equally clear for the parents.

Because there is often a hands-off response to parents once their children are in elementary school, the only place to pull the parents into valuing and promoting school for their children may be the early childhood classroom. Many parents are uncomfortable in a school setting; their own lack of success or access to school has possibly made school formidable and intimidating. Parents will build confidence once they are able to talk comfortably with teachers, feel at ease in a classroom, and realize that asking questions is okay. Once this happens, they will be better able to communicate with teachers successfully throughout their child's education experience.

Preschool teachers need the opportunity to work with kindergarten and first-grade teachers to help them value and welcome parents instead of keeping them waiting outside the classroom door. Parents are vitally interested in their children. Elementary and secondary teachers complain endlessly that parents stop coming to back-to-school nights and conferences. Parents are usually blamed, but what role do teachers play?

Think about the frequent mismatch between home and school culture. What if parents believe teachers need to be more or less strict, that children need to do more or less work, or that boys should not be allowed to wear dress-up clothes? What could you do in these situations? Instead of living with the tension that these issues can cause, it is possible for a classroom to be a place to negotiate and discuss views. Teachers should listen to the reasons behind parent's opinions, and parents need help to understand that having a point of view does not always mean getting their way.

HELPING CHILDREN WHO NEED EXTRA ATTENTION

Children who distance themselves from others as well as children who find it difficult for a variety of reasons to comply with rules and expectations are providing signals that they require special attention. To determine children who distance themselves, think of children who look to teachers for comfort, for help, and for companionship. Are there children who do not seem drawn to any teachers? These are children who isolate themselves and may need extra attention. They are usually shy, seemingly compliant, and often sad or quiet.

To help an isolated child, watch him or her carefully, to see who he or she has an affinity toward, and nurture that relationship. Make sure that the preferred person is there each day to say good morning, sits next to the child or offers a lap at circle time, is proactive about transitions, and helps the child enter successfully into play. Make sure you are picking a person who is up to the task of helping this child because it will not help the child to develop a relationship with someone who cannot be consistent, hold to firm limits, be patient, or help the child feel loveable and loved. Reflect on what works for this child, and be conscious of the fact that often an approach may work for a while but does not last. It is also important not to pass this child from one teacher to the next. The child will ultimately interpret this action as rejection.

For children who struggle to get along or who have difficulty complying with rules and expectations, you might first consider whether all interactions with the child have to do with following rules and directions. When children are demanding, it is easy to forget that they need to have a chance to talk about their thoughts and feelings. Often, children who are having a hard time are experiencing intense feelings and need to know that there is a place to express these feelings and a person who will respond to them, help them feel safe, and provide support as they learn more positive ways to get the attention they need. Children need to be consistently reminded of the community rules about no hitting or name calling. They need to know that their anger and frustration is validated and heard, but that they cannot hurt themselves or anyone else. They also need continual practice in conflict resolution; using their words to get their needs met; making a plan, and using the teacher to support them when it is too hard for them to do it on their own.

Consider letting the child be in charge of the conversation. It is important to simply listen. If a child is open to conversation, ask what he or she is building, or drawing, or ask him or her what part to play in a pretend game. You can also ask what children are writing or reading, and why they made a particular choice. What is important is being honest and genuine and interested in children's ideas and experiences.

AVOIDING GETTING TOO ATTACHED

Mr. Ross says, "It is clean-up time. Hector, you need to pick up the blocks." Hector ignores him and continues to play. Mr. Ross repeats his request, and Hector continues to play but starts tossing the blocks across the room.

Mr. Ross says, "Now you have to pick up the blocks that are all the way across the room too."

Mr. Ross knows that Hector is going to have a tantrum if he continues to insist that Hector clean up. He also knows that Hector's father is in prison, that Hector got spanked before school, and that Hector did not bring a lunch today. Mr. Ross leaves Hector to play and goes to circle time with the rest of the children.

Teachers sometimes get too attached to children. Possibly they are trying to meet their own needs rather than the needs of the child. If a teacher needs to feel loved, to be considered the good guy, or to feel like the savior, then the child is not getting what he or she needs. Children need and respond well to structure. Children who experience chaos in their homes may need it even more than others. When a teacher gives into a child, even though the teacher is trying to make that child feel better, the teacher is violating the structure, and this will ultimately confuse the child. Children who constantly test limits are those for whom the limits constantly change. Children need to know that there are rules, that adults are in charge, and that adults will help children when they are having a difficult time. An alternate solution to Hector's situation could be:

Hector continues to throw blocks. Mr. Ross sits down on the floor beside him and says, "I know it is hard to clean up when you are having such a good time. I'll help you clean up."

Hector starts to run away. Mr. Ross pulls him on his lap and, although Hector cries and resists, Mr. Ross holds him until he is calm. Then, they put the blocks away together.

Putting the effort into the difficult situations in the beginning of the year can avoid the likelihood of having them increase or grow worse as the year goes on and the child pushes each limit even further.

Developing a trusting relationship is a process. For some period of time, it will likely be true that a troubled child who begins to form a positive and trusting relationship with you may indeed only respond to you. You may be the only person to whom he listens and follows directions. You may be the only person whose questions the child is willing to answer and whose lap the child is willing to sit on. If you are gone, many of the child's maladaptive behaviors may reoccur. Children make the choice about whom they wish to attach themselves. It takes a while to develop a positive relationship, and even longer to generalize trust to other people. It is a matter of giving the child time, and sometimes it takes a great deal of time.

Being the person to whom a difficult child is attached can be a very difficult task. You will need time to talk about your feelings and to seek ideas and support from other staff members. Carol Cole, a child development specialist with the Los Angeles Unified School District, has developed a support system for teachers working with difficult children. It is called "Going Around the Circle." This system emphasizes regularly scheduled communication between teachers and administrators, as well as access to experts who can offer ideas and help.

Examine the structure and philosophy of your program. Is there an emphasis on keeping children with the same teacher throughout the day? Is there an emphasis on keeping groups of children with the same teacher over multiple years? The relationships between teachers and children are extremely important to children's well being. Children who are secure in their relationships with adults can move further and further away from trusted adult to explore new environments, begin new relationships, and learn new things.

A DAY IN THE LIFE OF A COMMUNITY-ORIENTED CLASSROOM

What might a community-oriented class look like? Consider the following example, which includes arrival, circle time, outside time, center time, small group time, and social studies.

Arrival

When the children arrive in the morning, they need to have the opportunity to reconnect with teachers and the other children. There are many ways to do this. The class can be set up so that children work near one another and near the teachers. There can be many choices for the children, but these activities take place in a designated area rather than scattered throughout the room. In a pre-kindergarten class, there may be tables with playdough, rolling pins and cutters, puzzles, beads and string, easels and paint, and blocks. Things are set up so that several children can engage in the same task at the same time. In classrooms for older children, there could be computers set up with two chairs for each computer. There could also be a letter-writing area, an alphabet area, and an area to complete unfinished homework, all with enough room for multiple users.

During the early morning gathering, you can move amongst children while they are engaging with one another. This should give you time to check in with many of the children, say hello to parents and see if parents have any important news. This can happen verbally or in exchange journals. Exchange journals are simple books that you can write in and send home to the parents if a child has done or said something remarkable during the day. Parents can respond to you or write about important things that are happening in the home that may impact the child in school.

One approach involves gathering "news" from students themselves. When the children enter the classroom, they can choose to go to you and talk about anything that might have happened the night before that they may wish to share. You can write the information for them or support them as they do it themselves. The children then have the opportunity to illustrate their news to share with the class during circle time. This is an early journal strategy that encourages children to share their lives and their feelings and lets them know that everybody's personal life, achievements, and feelings are important. This also helps children get to know one another and value listening to each other.

Another strategy is to ask children as they enter and leave the classroom each day whether they want a handshake or a hug from you. In this way, you are at the door each day for warm greetings and departures and are respectful of children's choices about physical contact.

Circle Time

The early morning gathering can be followed by a more formal circle or rug time. Circle time is traditionally a time to hear a story, sing songs, practice counting, discuss the calendar, and share the upcoming day's events. In terms of building a community, this is a time for children to learn to take turns and to listen to one another. The group can use this time to make decisions about things that affect them all. At the beginning of the year, children can create class rules, discuss personal and classroom goals, and determine how children will solve problems and conflicts. Children can participate in planning how to rearrange the room if they feel that centers are getting too crowded. They can decide together to take an inappropriate computer game off the hard drive, and they can decide what to do with the dead bird that was found on the playground.

Young children are aware of what goes on around them. They can become passionate over too much trash on the yard, a homeless person living on a nearby street, or a child with disabilities who was teased about being different. A group process to hear what children feel about these issues and what they think they might do to resolve them brings a community together. Teachers who dismiss the problem do children a disservice. Using the opportunities that children provide gives children the chance to develop empathy, to be valued for their feelings, and to allow them to work on real problems. Working through issues also offers an opportunity for oral language development. It gives children a reason to write letters and work together to organize a response to a situation. Children may read a class-made book about an important issue to another class or to the whole school. It is not difficult to tie community building into academic pursuits.

Outside Time

Outside time can be problematic as it may be your break time as well as the time children are the least structured and need the most support. Because you may not be present, problems are not always handled in a manner consistent with what happens inside the classroom. In order to set children up for success on the playground, talk about playground rules and expectations each day before going outside. This includes talking about hurting children's feelings, feeling left out, or being teased. Have the person who supervises the yard come in and talk with the class. Let the children get to know him or her and ask questions about rules and consequences. Help children plan what they will do if there is a problem: walk away and ignore it, save it for discussion later, or look for a person on the yard who they trust.

Of course this discussion is very time consuming and will not be something that is necessary everyday throughout the year. Anticipating problems before they begin can go a long way in cutting down the problems overall. Setting up a structure for the children helps them feel that they are safe, that their problems are important and that they can expect to be helped and supported.

Center Time

In most early childhood classes as well as in K-1-2 classes there is a time for free choice or center time. It is important for children to figure out how to manage choices. There are many community lessons built into the idea around choice. Children must negotiate their space, share, and take turns. They must learn to handle disappointment when they do not get their first choice. Choice time offers a rich context for children to practice these skills.

Small Group Time

Small group and independent working times, or times when a teacher is working with one group and the rest of the children are expected to work on their own, is also a time for community building. It is the time for children to learn the importance of being respectful, the need for quiet and concentration, and the appropriate time to interrupt. Children can learn about what resources are available to them when a teacher is not there. One suggestion is to have children prepare a classroom directory where each child advertises his or her own strengths. Children who are looking for someone who is a good speller, an excellent artist, or a computer whiz can consult the directory and learn where to go for assistance. This system allows children to recognize and rely on each other's strengths.

Social Studies

Social studies time is central to community building. Inherent in the work of social studies are diversity issues, cultural issues, controversial issues, gender issues, and so forth. This is a wonderful time to use subject matter as fodder for community building. Children can share their own cultures, as well as their own unique character, whether it be sharing a particular family food or celebration, a way of dressing, or a hair style.

When children are engaged in a social studies activity such as building a community with blocks, they have to think about what it takes to make up a community. They must consider what kinds of jobs are necessary, who needs to make sure that people are safe, who will build the houses and hospitals, where food comes from, and how to get it to people safely. These questions are complex, and talking about them will bring up even more issues: Can girls drive trucks? Can boys take care of babies? Children may perceive that only white people can hold certain jobs, that only people of color can hold certain other kinds of jobs. Social studies provides a chance to talk about their perceptions, about things that are usually ignored, or silenced. When children feel safe being who they are, saying what they think, asking questions, and being listened to and respected, then teachers have achieved community.

Social studies time can also be a time to talk about problems in the community and how to work to solve them. Children in one school were upset at the number of cars that ran a stop sign right outside their classroom window. They set up a videotape and recorded the cars. They then invited the local police to view the video. Police set up a watch and ticketed cars on a regular basis. People started being more careful and the school crosswalk became a safer place. The children learned that they could have some power in changing things in the community.

CONCLUSION

Taking the time to think about the details that develop an ordinary day into days that build community and foster the development of important relationships between children and their teachers and friends is what will make a classroom a very different kind of place. This chapter examines many aspects of a classroom community: conflict resolution, making plans, building friendships, teacher care, community-oriented skills, individualized responses, coping with anger and frustration, encouraging participation, working with parents, and helping children who need extra attention. Teachers who are consistent, who recognize that each child is a unique individual, and who do not sacrifice the needs of one child to the needs of the group are teachers who are well on their way to working within a genuine community of teachers and young children.

Building community-oriented classrooms is not simple. People are complicated, and people in relationships with one another are even more complicated. Building of community means interweaving multiple relationships between children, teachers, parents, and the greater community. Change is slow. Give it time, give it reflection, and don't give up. Change is possible.

There are many people who have given this subject a great deal of thought. Consult the following books for more ideas about developing a community founded on positive relationships.

RECOMMENDED READINGS

Chasnoff, D., & Cohen, H.S. (Producers). (1996). *It's elementary.* [Motion Picture]. (Available from Women's Educational Media, 1-800-343-5540 or http:/www.womedia.org/our/elem.html)

Comer, J. (1997, May). Building schools as communities. *Educational Leadership, 54*(8), 15–19.

Howes, C., & Ritchie, S. (2002). *A matter of trust.* New York: Teachers College Press.

McCaleb, S.P. (1998). *Building communities of learners.* New York: St Martin's Press.

Noddings, N. (1988). An ethic of caring and its implications for instructional arrangements. *American Journal of Education, 96*(2), 215–231.

Oser, F.K., Dick, A., & Patry, J. (Eds.). (1998). *Effective and responsive teaching.* San Francisco: Jossey-Bass.

Paley, V. (1992). *You can't say you can't play.* Cambridge, MA: Harvard University Press.

Early Literacy for Young Children and English-Language Learners

Linda M. Espinosa and
M. Susan Burns

In American society, literacy is essential for school success, civic participation, and abstract learning. Reading ability

> Serves as the major avenue to learning about other people, about history and social studies, the language arts, science, mathematics, and the other content subjects that must be mastered in school. When children do not learn to read, their general knowledge, their spelling and writing abilities, and their vocabulary development suffer in kind. Within this context, reading skill serves as the major foundational skill for all school-based learning, and without it, the chances for academic and occupational success are limited indeed. (Lyon, 1999, p. 1)

Reading and writing allow people to connect to larger social, cultural, and historical knowledge and to communicate thoughts and feelings. Literacy may not be the key to unlocking the content of the soul, but it provides humanity with the means to understand and express the uniqueness and deeper meaning of being human. If an American does not learn to read, he or she has diminished opportunities for a full and satisfying life.

Literacy includes listening, oral language, reading, and writing and is a continuous learning process that begins during infancy. In the first 3 years, oral language development and listening skills play a central role in early literacy development. Books and environmental print are salient contexts for language and listening. Children between the ages of 3 and 7 years learn to use symbols to represent objects or experiences. For example, most children in the United States recognize that golden arches stand for McDonald's.

Because letters and words are essentially symbols that are an abstract representation of something else, children begin to notice print in their environment during the preschool years. Young children learn that certain types of marks (print) represent meanings. Children first think of print as a visual object, then move to the understanding of its symbolic form. They grasp the notion that one object or event may stand for another well before they actually start to read (Marzolf & DeLoache, 1994). Learning that the alphabet is a symbol system for sounds fits into this stream of development.

Children who enter first grade ready to succeed in school typically have had the opportunity to acquire a good deal of knowledge about language and literacy during their preschool and kindergarten years. Long before formal reading instruction is appropriate, many informal opportunities for learning about literacy are available, to varying degrees, in most American homes, preschool programs, and child care environments. This chapter addresses the following questions:

- What are these crucial opportunities for learning about literacy?
- Are they equally available to all children in the United States?
- How do young children's different language experiences affect their development of preliteracy skills and concepts?
- What literacy goals should early educators have for young children whose home language is not English?

STUDENTS WHO MAY NEED EXTRA HELP

In the United States, children from families who do not speak English as their primary language may not receive equal opportunities for learning about literacy. In 1995, approximately 15% of all children ages 5–17 spoke a language other than English at home (U.S. Bureau of the Census, 1995). According to a survey of America's kindergarten classrooms, 9% of kindergarten children were from homes in which English was not spoken (Early Childhood Longitudinal Study, 1999). Head Start reports that 74% of its students speak English, 22% speak Spanish, and 4% speak 1 of 139 other languages (Head Start Bureau, 2000). In many communities, nearly half of the students may come from homes where English is not spoken (Arlington

Public Schools, 1998). Given the continuing immigration trends and the higher birthrates among immigrant groups (U.S. Bureau of the Census, 2000), the number of children arriving at school with no or limited proficiency in English is expected to rise. In fact, the entering kindergarten class in California in Fall 2000 was 70% nonwhite and 33% English-language learners. In addition, almost half (46%) of all children age birth to 5 years in California live in poverty (California State Department of Education, 2001).

Although failure to learn to read adequately is much more likely among impoverished children, nonwhite children, and nonnative speakers of English, data derived from the National Assessment of Educational Progress (1994) reveal an additional cause for concern. Serious difficulties in skillful reading cut across all ethnic and socioeconomic variables. For example, in California, which is a highly diverse state, 59% of all fourth-grade children in 1998 had little or no mastery of the knowledge and skills necessary to perform reading activities at the fourth-grade level, compared with a national average of 44% below basic reading levels (Lyon, 1999). Two comprehensive reports were released in 1998 and 2000 that reviewed and synthesized the considerable research base on early literacy. Both of these reports focused on identifying the risk factors that predispose children to reading difficulties and the instructional approaches that were most effective for preventing reading failure (National Reading Panel, 2000; Snow, Burns, & Griffin, 1998).

Preventing Reading Difficulties in Young Children (Snow et al., 1998) identified five literacy opportunities for young children:

- To experience contexts that promote *enthusiasm* and *success* in learning to read and write and in learning by reading and writing. Think of the sense of enjoyment and emotional warmth shared by children and parents, aunts, teachers, or older siblings when they read with children. These children are gaining the much-needed positive affect and enthusiasm toward literacy that adds to their motivation as they confront struggles in learning to read and write.

- To develop and enhance *language skills, vocabulary and conceptual knowledge*, and *metacognitive skills* needed to meet the demands of understanding printed text. Children develop language skills and gain a sense of themselves as language users. When they are able to communicate their thoughts on complex topics, they are on their way to engaging fully in educational experiences. For example, they can talk about the dinosaurs they saw at the museum and connect that experience to the dinosaurs they see in a book they read in class. Consider also the satisfaction children feel when they get the gist of how to sing the Name Game, a game that manipulates phonological aspects of language. Children acquire conceptual knowledge of the world by having many varied opportunities to visit zoos, museums, and performances, as well as to participate in simple activities such as going to the bakery, shoe store, and food market.

- To acquire an understanding of the *functions of print* and the *utility of literacy*. Children learn that there is important information communicated through print; that text can describe adventure, peoples' feelings, and information people want to know; and that print can make distant experiences personal and vivid.

- To grasp and master the *alphabetic principle* in reading and writing. Children learn how the English alphabet and associated sounds work together.

- To have early *intensified instruction* if they have problems learning to read and write in the early grades. Children must not wait until they experience repeated, long-term failure before they receive appropriate intervention.

Each of these opportunities is summarized next, with an emphasis on the preschool years, kindergarten, and first grade.

PROMOTING ENTHUSIASM FOR READING

Children's exposure to and interest in literacy experiences are influenced by the adults who care for them. Caregivers' literacy attitudes, beliefs, and ability levels affect the literacy opportunities they provide for children in their care and the richness of their literacy interactions with children (Baker, Serpell, & Sonnenschein, 1995; DeBaryshe, 1995; Spiegel, 1994). Parents of prereading children tend either to emphasize literacy as an activity engaged in for purposes of entertainment or as a set of skills to be acquired. Children of parents who emphasize early literacy as a source of enjoyment tend to have a greater orientation toward print along with greater competence in aspects of narrative and phonological awareness than children of parents who approach early literacy as a set of skills (Sonnenschein et al., 1996). An enjoyment orientation is more typical of middle-income parents, whereas lower-income parents are more likely to view literacy as a set of skills to be acquired (Lancy & Bergin, 1992). The socio-emotional context of early literacy experiences relates directly to children's motivation to learn to read later on—enthusiasm about literacy activities is suggested by many researchers as a route to developing children's active engagement in literacy tasks (Baker et al., 1995).

Storybook Reading

Activities such as family storybook reading promote positive feelings about books and literacy (Taylor & Strickland, 1986). The relationship between

parents' behavior and their children's perceived interest in literacy is reciprocal. Parents who believe their children are interested in reading are more
likely to provide abundant print-related experiences than parents who do
not perceive such interest. Parents' interpretations of children's interest in
print, however, are partly a function of their expectations of young children's
capabilities in general. For example, one parent may think a child is interested in reading only if the child asks to have a story read; another parent
may decide a child is interested if he or she is excited when the parent offers to read a story. In the United States, young children are read to fairly
often by their parents. Forty to fifty percent of all families—of all ethnic and
socioeconomic groups—report reading to their kindergartners on a daily
basis (Early Childhood Longitudinal Study, 1999).

Children whose parents teach them that literacy is a source of enjoyment may be more motivated to persist in their efforts to learn to read despite difficulties they may encounter during the early school years. Baker et
al. note that "Parents' descriptions of their children's early efforts to engage
in literacy activities often reflected amusement but also suggest awareness
of the value of such behaviors" (1995, p. 265).

Child Care

In addition to the family, child care programs also provide early literacy experiences that can support young children's interest in learning to read.
Literacy activities often are not at the forefront of planned activities in child
care environments. Neuman (1996) studied the literacy environment in
child care programs in the United States. Traditional caregiving goals, such
as keeping children safe, fed, and clean, were often the main focus of these
programs; yet, many of the children being served were in special need of
early language stimulation and literacy learning. Neuman introduced an intervention that provided caregivers with access to books and training on
techniques for book selection for children of different ages, reading aloud,
and extending the impact of books. Literacy interaction increased in the intervention classrooms from an average of 5 per hour to 10 per hour. Before
the training, classrooms had few book centers for children; after the intervention, 93% of the classrooms had such centers, which enhanced the early
literacy opportunities available to the children.

Children whose caregivers received the training performed significantly better on measures of print (e.g., they understand that it is the print
on the page that is read rather than that the picture is read; Clay, 1979), narrative competence (by pointing to pictures named by a tester; Purcell-Gates
& Dahl, 1991), concepts of writing (e.g., they know that print in English goes
from top to bottom and from left to right; Purcell-Gates, 1996), and letter
names (Clay, 1979) than children in the comparison group. At follow-up in
kindergarten, the children were examined on measures of print (Clay, 1979),

receptive vocabulary (Dunn & Dunn, 1985), concepts of writing (Purcell-Gates, 1996), letter names (Clay, 1979), and two phonemic awareness measures based on children's rhyming and alliteration capacity (Maclean, Bryant, & Bradley, 1987). Of these measures, children in the intervention group performed significantly better on letter names, phonemic awareness, and concepts of writing.

Play

It is of no surprise that play also has a role in children's development of motivation to read, especially when one considers how play encourages young children to reflect on situations through dramatizations of their own invention (Galda & Pellegrini, 1988; Smilansky, 1968; Wolf & Heather, 1992). Play environments that provide choice, control, and appropriate levels of challenge appear to facilitate the development of self-regulated, intentional learning (Badrova & Leong, 1998). Adults intervene in children's play by providing field trips as a source of knowledge, supplying relevant props (e.g., grocery store or library props) to stimulate fantasy, and becoming involved in the play themselves (e.g., suggesting new activities, vocabulary, and rules; Neuman & Roskos 1992).

For play sessions to incorporate aspects of literacy, they need to be at least 20–30 minutes long; otherwise, children cannot create the elaborate scripts that lead to the intentional use of literacy in dramatic play (Christie, Johnsen, & Peckover, 1988). Consider an example of young children establishing and enacting "doctor's office" play. First, the children need ample time to establish everyone's roles. Perhaps they recently read a book about Sam, who has an earache, and are building their dramatic play on this. Someone needs to be Sam; another child, his dad who takes him to the doctor; and another child, the doctor. During this planning, the children decide what items are needed for the play and establish objects to represent those items. For example, a cardboard tube from a paper towel roll might be used to "examine" Sam's earache. A block and a stick might be used as a notepad and pen. Then, the children begin to play the story in detail. All of these steps take time and, perhaps, helpful guidance and support from a teacher.

Print-Rich Environment

Children need book readings and related experiences to develop their background knowledge for the play environment. To support children's writing during play, children need ready access to appropriate materials, such as paper, markers, pencils, and stamp pads (Morrow & Rand, 1991; Neuman & Roskos, 1992; Schrader, 1989; Vukelich, 1994). Even so, the teacher's participation and guidance are pivotal in helping children to incorporate literacy materials into their play (Badrova & Leong, 1998). For example, one study compared children who played in a print-rich center with or without literacy-related guidance from their teacher (Vukelich, 1994). When later tested on their recognition of print, children who had received teacher guidance were better able to recognize the words that had been displayed in the play environment and could do so even when the words were presented in a list without the graphics and context of the play environment (see section Understanding Print later in this chapter).

Play sessions provide a rich context for the development of narratives, which is discussed in the next section on oral language development. Effective play also enhances self-regulatory behavior of young children (Badrova & Leong, 1998). Poor self-regulatory behavior (e.g., activity level, attention, adaptability) is identified as a barrier to children's receptiveness to instruction in the early grades. Torgesen's work cited in the National Reading Panel report provides an example of such a barrier to phonics instruction (National Reading Panel, 2000). He found that kindergarteners with poor self-regulatory behavior were the most resistant to instruction.

DEVELOPING ORAL LANGUAGE

The more children know about oral language before they arrive at school, the better equipped they are to succeed in reading (Snow et al., 1998). Spoken language and reading have much in common. Once words can be efficiently recognized, reading depends heavily on the reader's oral-language abilities, particularly with regard to understanding the meanings of words (i.e., vocabulary), knowledge of narrative, and listening comprehension. Children's ability to efficiently recognize words using sound–letter correspondence is interconnected with phonological awareness (children's understanding that sounds are part of words). Preschoolers' experiences with their own language allow, for example, phonemic sensitivity to develop; the child can then experience alphabetic insight—the key to learning to read an alphabetic language.

Vocabulary, language skills, and knowledge about the world are acquired during interesting conversations with responsive adults. Studies of children's early language development indicate that adult-child influences are reciprocal: children influence the ways that adults behave toward them, and adults influence children's learning experiences and opportunities (Lewis & Feinman, 1991). Talking about books and being involved in shared book reading with an adult, as well as participating in play activities such as those previously mentioned, contribute to children's vocabularies and to their ability to understand stories and other types of text.

Basic to book reading experiences that build oral language skills is that the listener is actively engaged, can develop a good understanding of the text being read, and is exposed to an appropriate number of new words (vocabulary). For parents who need support in providing quality book-reading experiences, parent coaching in holding children's attention, asking questions, interacting with story-relevant comments, and providing feedback to their children have been demonstrated as effective (Edwards, 1995; Whitehurst, Arnold, Epstein, & Angell, 1994).

Conversations at mealtime and in other informal conversations provide opportunities for children to acquire knowledge about word meaning and narratives. As family members and friends recount the day's activities, they give children an experience that is of well-documented value in learning about language and communication (Beals & Snow, 1994; Beals & Tabors, 1995; Blum-Kulka, 1993; Snow & Tabors, 1993). Other means by which adults help children to develop oral language is through singing songs, chanting nursery rhymes and other rhyming games, and storytelling (Baker et al., 1995; Heath, 1983).

Phonological awareness, the understanding that speech is composed of a sequence of sounds (phonemes) that are recombined to form other words, plays a crucial role in learning to read. It begins to develop by about age 3 and improves gradually over many years, in part through experience with rhyming songs, games, and chants, such as the "Teddy Bear" song. Phonological awareness is a product of vocabulary growth, which in turn is a function of exposure to stories and other sources of rich vocabulary input (Weizman & Snow, in press). Phonological awareness can be enhanced through systematic instruction (Byrne & Fielding-Barnsley, 1989).

Play at home and in preschool can increase oral language use. Children interact and use new language as they plan, negotiate, compose, and carry out the "script" of their play (Crenshaw, 1985; Levy, Wolfgang, & Koorland, 1992). In addition, children practice verbal and narrative skills that are important to the development of reading comprehension (Gentile & Hoot, 1983). Constructing narratives makes cognitive demands for recalling and sequencing information (Umiker-Sebeok, 1979), linking references to prior utterances rather than to tangible objects, and disconnecting language from the here and now. It prepares children for the more abstract nature of formal schooling.

Quality of conversation in preschools and amount of one-to-one or small-group interactions are both related to language measures (Phillips, McCartney, & Scarr, 1987). Incidence of cognitively challenging conversation and the use of a wide vocabulary by teachers are correlated with the children's subsequent language and literacy development (Dickinson, Cote, & Smith, 1993). For children from low-income families at age 4, the quality of group book reading experiences is correlated with kindergarten language and literacy measures (Dickinson & Smith, 1994). Given the importance of adult–child interaction, it is disturbing that some children in group care environments may rarely interact with an adult and receive little or no individualized attention (Bryant, Peisner-Feinberg, & Clifford, 1993; Kontos &

Wilcox-Herzog, 1997; Layzer, 1993). The quality and amount of adult–child discourse are important. The amount of cognitively challenging talk that children experience is correlated with the amount of time they talk with adults (Smith & Dickinson, 1994). Modest enhancements of the quality of classroom experiences show positive effects on children's language development skills (Whitehurst et al., 1994).

UNDERSTANDING PRINT

The activities noted in the previous sections that promote motivation and language skills also may constitute opportunities to learn about literate forms, print concepts, and letters (Snow & Tabors, 1993). Adults provide exposure to and explanation of different functions of text, thereby making print meaningful for children in their daily lives. For example, young children learn that print gives people information, such as where milk comes from and how it is processed, how to get to a friend's house, and how to bake a cake. They can learn that print helps people solve problems, such as using written instructions to assemble a toy. They learn that "print tells people what to say when they are reading" (Ballenger, 1999, p. 43). Through exposure to a wide array of books, children learn that print can entertain, amuse, and even comfort people. Through experiences with "writing," children learn to distinguish between drawing and writing. Their scribbling becomes more purposeful, and as older toddlers, they make some scribbles that, to their joy, look somewhat like English writing. In the preschool years, they can be encouraged to write (scribble) messages as part of playful activity.

Adults also draw attention to letters, their symbolic function, and the characteristics of written language (Burgess, 1982; Feitelson & Goldstein, 1986). They point out that the first letter in Ella's name is "E" and that it sounds like /e/. They even compare Ella's nickname to her full name, noting that Eleanor has more sounds in it than Ella. Children's participation in literacy-enhanced socio-dramatic play at home or in child care provides a rich context for learning about print. These experiences are based on the assumption that children have books and other print materials available for play and for interacting with adults and other children. The presence of such items as magnetic refrigerator letters, posters, writing materials for making lists and memoranda, and newspapers and books in the home, as well as adult–child attention to environmental print, have been linked to children's acquisition of an awareness of print (Goodman, 1986).

Though we know that most environments expose children to print, there are differences in the quantity and variety of materials. Neuman's (1996) study of the literacy environments provided for young children in child care environments revealed that before the intervention introduced accessible books to the classroom, children spent major parts of their day in an environment with few literacy materials. Other researchers have found that children's homes differ in the quantity and variety of literacy materials. Shirley Brice Heath (1983), for example, found that the working-class Caucasian, working-class African-American, and middle-class Caucasian families in the southern community she studied had different amounts and types of reading materials.

What do children learn from their print-related experiences? The information presented previously indicates that they learn the functions of print. In addition, they learn the purpose of the marks on the page and a great deal of information about the form of these marks. Preschool-age children can begin to recognize some printed alphabet letters, especially the ones in their own names and frequently encountered words. Many children learn the names of the letters first by singing the alphabet song or other alphabet chants. At age 3 or 4, children begin to attach the names of letters to their shapes. With help, they may soon begin to attend to beginning letters of words they recognize in printed form. Adults sometimes forget that children have to learn the most basic conventions that govern written language, such as the need for spaces between words, that English text is read from left to right and from top to bottom, and that punctuation indicates the end of one sentence and the beginning of the next (Clay, 1975). Young children also learn that the marks on the page represent meanings.

MASTERING THE ALPHABETIC PRINCIPLE

Explicit instruction and practice with sound structures of words usually is part of first-grade instruction though much preparation happens in preschool and kindergarten via phonological awareness activities. Children learn the spelling–sound correspondences and common spelling conventions. They read well-written and engaging texts that are challenging but below their frustration level. Independent readers sound out and confirm the identities of visually unfamiliar words they encounter in the course of reading meaningful text. In first grade, children also learn sight recognition of frequently used words that are irregular in their sound-spelling correspondence.

Children who are at risk for reading difficulties can benefit from explicit phonological awareness training as well as instruction in letter identification and letter-sound correspondences (Ball & Blachman, 1988; Torgeson et al., 1999). There are three levels of phonemic awareness (Muter & Diethelm, 2001): rhyming, implicit phonological segmentation skills, and explicit phonological segmentation skills. An example of an explicit segmentation skill is when children learn to add and take away phonemes while listening to words. Children manipulate small blocks, chips, beads, or any other items to count the number of sounds in a word. The word *row* has two phonemes, *r* and *o*, so the children put out two blocks to represent that word. If they want to then represent the word *oh*, they take one block away and show one block. Next, if they want to represent the word *grow*, they show three blocks, the word *grown*, four blocks.

In phonemic awareness activities, children count the number of sounds in a word, not the number of letters (Burns, Griffin, & Snow, 1999); however, children who have very weak general language abilities may need additional specialized instruction to improve appreciably in reading comprehension. "The goal of phonological training is limited to facilitating the acquisition word-decoding abilities, which are necessary but not sufficient for the development of skilled comprehension" (Snow et al., 1998, p. 251). Fluent reading and comprehension require additional information and skills such as background knowledge, vocabulary, knowledge of word structure, and memory skills, as well as the motivation or desire to read.

As kindergarten and first-grade children write, they use invented spellings that become closer approximations to conventional spelling as they learn the alphabetic principle. Children tend to begin conventional spelling instruction mid-year in first grade and at that point are expected to spell previously studied words and spelling patterns correctly in their final writing products.

FOSTERING READING COMPREHENSION

Reading ability is not just decoding or recognizing words but ultimately is measured by how well one understands or is able to derive meaning from the print material. Children who develop good comprehension skills have extensive background knowledge of the world, a wide vocabulary, a familiarity with the semantic and syntactic structures of the English language, knowledge about different writing conventions that are used to achieve different purposes via text (e.g., humor, explanation, dialogue) and the ability to remember verbal information (Lyon, 1999; Snow et al., 1998). Instructional activities that are designed to explicitly foster the ability to detect and comprehend relationships among verbal concepts and the ability to actively employ strategies to ensure understanding and retention of reading material are essential for comprehension (see reciprocal teaching described later). Children grow in their ability to derive meaning from text initially by interacting with adults around the content of books being read to them, by learning to pay attention to salient narrative elements, and by eventually applying conscious strategies for understanding and using text (Burns, Griffin & Snow, 1999; McGee & Richgels, 1996). By the second grade, children can learn to monitor their own reading process and increase their comprehension.

One approach, reciprocal teaching, has been shown to be effective with children who are at risk for reading failure (Palinscar, Brown, & Campione, 1993). "In reciprocal teaching, teachers give children practice in four strategies: predicting, questioning, summarizing, and clarifying. Children and adults take turns leading discussions about the text" (Burns, et al., 1999, p. 112). Through this process children learn to make inferences about the content of the text and come to conclusions about the meaning of the passages read.

By the third grade, children are increasingly able to read and learn from all variety of text, including both fiction and nonfiction. They can monitor their own comprehension, summarize main points, and discuss details of text. In addition, they can expand their understanding of concepts and ideas by making inferences and using additional print resources. In essence, the child can build a connection between his or her existing knowledge and learn something new from material presented in print. Comprehension is enhanced by continuously interacting with others about aspects of the material before and after it has been read and when this process is not used regularly by a child, it needs to be taught explicitly using methods such as reciprocal teaching, described previously.

EARLY LITERACY FOR CULTURALLY AND LINGUISTICALLY DIVERSE CHILDREN

Children from diverse cultural backgrounds can be distinguished by their ethnicity, social class, or language (Au, 1993). Ethnicity usually refers to one's national heritage, although people usually identify their ethnicity with a country of family origin. Social class refers to one's socioeconomic status (SES) as reflected in parents' occupations and family income. Children from diverse backgrounds may have a first language other than English.

A child's ethnicity, social class, and first language may conflict with the classroom culture. If so, the child may have trouble learning in American classrooms. For example, a young non-English speaker from a lower SES family emigrated from Brazil will be confronted with socio-cultural, linguistic, and emotional challenges in an English-only American classroom that place him at risk for reading difficulties. Although non-English speakers are not familiar with the grammar, meaning, linguistic rules, or phonology of English, they do have prior knowledge of their first language and its use. They have discovered what language is all about and how to communicate in their immediate environment. These children already understand what language is, but they need to understand how the English language works.

Culture and Learning

Culture influences both how children approach learning and how they are socialized into being readers and writers. Whether a child approaches learning as a cooperative task emphasizing group understanding and performance or as an individual achievement is a function of early cultural learning. All cultural groups share attitudes and beliefs about the uses and values of literacy and have preferred literacy practices. For young children, language development and learning about one's own culture are closely linked. "Culture and linguistic identity provides a strong and important sense of self and family belonging, which in turn supports a wide range of learning capabilities, not the least of which is learning a second language" (Garcia, 1991, p. 2).

Families vary in the ways in which they socialize their young children into language and literacy use. Different cultural groups use distinctive methods in their approaches to early literacy. For instance, in most middle-class nonminority families, the mother assumes the major responsibility for socializing the children into literacy; mothers typically talk frequently with their babies, share books, and ask questions that call for labels, clarifications, and descriptions of daily activities. They also expect young children to actively participate and construct their own stories (McGee & Richgels, 1996). In contrast, African-American families are more likely to share the early caregiving responsibilities among family members and close friends (Heath, 1983). Heath (1983), in a carefully documented ethnographic study, revealed that working-class African-American families are more likely to socialize their young children to learn by observing the adults' actions and conversation than by participating in language activities. Thus, children from these backgrounds were less likely to respond according to the teacher's expectations when asked to answer school questions that were phrased in an unfamiliar discourse style.

Early socialization experiences and the accompanying values acquired by young children from culturally and linguistically diverse groups in their home and community environments frequently are not celebrated in school and are not used as the basis for academic learning and socialization. These discrepancies between the literacy culture of home and school result in cultural discontinuity for a child, which makes the child vulnerable (Garcia, 1993; McGee & Richgels, 1996). Children who experience cultural discontinuity between the home and school are more likely to have a negative perception of themselves as learners, readers, writers, and speakers (Garcia, 1993).

Many people have argued for learning and teaching contexts that are socio-culturally and linguistically meaningful for all learners (Au, 1993; Diaz, Moll, & Mehan, 1986; Gee, 1990; Heath, 1986). To improve the continuity between home and school requires culturally responsive curriculum and pedagogy. Culturally responsive approaches include the students' histories, languages, early experiences, and values in classroom activities and instruction that are "consistent with the students' own cultures and aimed at improving academic learning" (Au, 1993, p.13).

Poverty and Learning

Poverty has been shown to correlate with literacy levels at kindergarten entry (West, Penton, & Germino Hausken, 2000). Children from families of lower SES tend to have fewer literacy skills that are prerequisites to learning to read: knowing that print reads left to right; knowing where to go when a line of print ends; knowing where the story ends; the ability to recognize letters, beginning sounds, and ending sounds (Bowman, Donovan, & Burns, 2001). National Council of Educational Statistics data (West, Penton, & Germino Hausken, 2000) revealed that children in homes that receive welfare have fewer books and recordings, and these parents read and tell stories less often to their children. The effects of poverty are partially mediated by the home environment. Duncan, Brooks-Gun, and Klebanov (1994) showed that measures of home learning environment, family social support, maternal depression, and active behavioral coping accounted for one third of the variance that was associated with income at age 5 in IQ scores. Thus, the effects of poverty are more pronounced when additional risk factors in the home are present such as maternal depression and low parental education (Sameroff, 1989).

Children from low-income families who live in low SES communities are also much more likely to have difficulty with literacy than children from low-income families living in middle-class or moderate income communities (Snow et al., 1998):

> Low SES is an individual risk factor to the extent that among children attending the same schools, youngsters from low-income families are more likely to become poor readers than those from high-income families. Low SES is a group risk factor because children from low-income communities are likely to become poorer readers than children from more affluent communities. Because the former are more likely to attend substandard schools, the correlation between SES and low achievement is probably mediated, in large part, by differences in the quality of school experiences. (1998, p. 126)

Literacy for Second-Language Learners

Children who speak a language other than English in their homes have access to language and literacy opportunities in their home and in a variety of preschool and kindergarten environments. It is important to consider ways the various environments support acquisition of the first and the second language and literacy in both those languages when predicting likely outcomes.

English Immersion

Immersion means simply that students learn everything in English. The extreme case of this is called *sink or swim,* but teachers using immersion programs generally strive to deliver lessons in simple and understandable language that allows students to acquire English while having the typical educational opportunities in the preschool or kindergarten curriculum. Sometimes, students are pulled out for *English as a Second Language (ESL)* programs, which provide them with instruction in English geared for language acquisition. The goals of English-only classrooms include development of English, but not development or maintenance of the child's first language.

Bilingual Education

In bilingual classrooms, interaction is divided between English and the child's first or home language. These environments have at least one teacher who is fluent in the child's first language. These classrooms can take a variety of forms: transitional, maintenance of first language, or two-way bilingual programs. The goals might include transitioning into English as quickly as possible, maintaining and supporting primary language development while supporting English acquisition, or promoting second language development for both English speakers and non-English speakers.

Primary Language Programs

All interactions in primary language programs are in the child's first or primary language. In these environments, the teachers must be fluent in the child's home language. The goals include development and support for the child's first language with little or no systematic exposure to English ("Secretary Riley," 1999; Tabors, 1997).

What Type of Program Is Best for Young Children?

The preferred program type for any particular child depends on many factors, including the child's age, motivation to learn English, previous exposure to English, language support at home, and personality (Tabors, 1997); however, research on second language acquisition suggests that effective early childhood programs for language minority students support long-term primary language development. The connections between primary language proficiency and future academic success are well documented (August & Garcia, 1988; Galambos & Hakuta, 1988; Hakuta, 1986). It is not known whether the focus on primary language instruction in preschool constitutes a protective factor for children who will not have the opportunity to acquire initial literacy skills in their native or stronger language. A solid foundation in English oral fluency is highly desirable prior to formal English literacy instruction for children who are not learning to read in their first language (Snow et al., 1998). Thus, attention should be paid to the kind of first-grade classroom instruction available when considering optimal preschool and kindergarten environments.

The long-term goal of most parents and educators is to help children maintain and build the primary language while adding fluency and literacy skills in English, not replacing the first language with English. Cummins (1984, 1986) and Ogbu (1978) argued that children and families who are members of cultural and linguistic minorities also face economic and social discrimination that often alienates them from their own culture. When students whose first language is not English are alienated from their own cultural values and perceive themselves as inferior to the dominant group, they are more likely to experience school failure.

Garcia pointed out the importance of supporting a child's cultural heritage, stating, "Culture and linguistic identity provides a strong and important sense of self and family belonging, which in turn supports a wide range of learning capabilities, not the least of which is learning a second language" (1991, p. 2). In addition to a specific language approach, early literacy educators need to consider the children's cultural background and design a culturally responsive curriculum.

PRIMARY LANGUAGE SUPPORT

Children's primary language can be supported by teachers throughout the day in all kinds of learning situations. In addition, teachers need to provide long-term help to build children's primary language literacy skills. Even when teachers do not speak the child's home language, there are many strategies that would support primary language development:

- Provide bilingual instructional support including paraprofessionals (e.g., instructional assistant, parent volunteers, older and more competent students) if necessary.

- Incorporate children's home languages into the daily classroom activities through song, poetry, dances, rhymes, and counting. Create materials in the children's home languages to represent familiar stories, songs, or poems that will improve early home language literacy.

- Have simple print material in the children's home languages in learning centers. Labeled objects and writing utensils will further support early literacy abilities for non-English speakers.

- Encourage parents and other family members to continue to use the home language during family activities while also supporting early literacy development in that language.

- Loan parents age-appropriate books and stories in the child's home language if available. Encourage parents to engage in playful, interactive reading times in order to motivate children to read.

- Make efforts to learn the students' home languages. Even a few words or phrases will communicate respect and value for the families' languages and culture.

English Language Fluency

Many classroom and instructional approaches are effective for second-language learners (Carey, 1997; Cazden, 1986; Garcia, 1993; Tabors, 1997). The following suggestions synthesize previous research and can apply to all students:

- Allow children to practice following and giving instructions for basic literacy tasks such as turning pages during reading, using pictures to tell a story, telling a story in sequence, and noting the names of main characters in a story.

- Allow for voluntary participation instead of strictly enforced turn-taking and teacher-led reading lessons.

- Have students dictate stories about special personal events.

- Embed all instruction in context cues that connect words to objects, visuals, and movements (Carey, 1997; Tabors, 1997).

- Create a consistent and predictable routine that uses cooperative learning groups, small group interactions, and regular opportunities for English language learners to speak informally with English speakers.

- Make small peer groups to give children opportunities to learn English in nonthreatening, secure environments and promote friendships among children who speak different languages (Johns, 1992). Systematically include a mix of first- and second-language children in organized small group activities.

- Teach English-speaking children in the classroom to act as language resources for second-language learners.

- Modify the second language so that it is comprehensible for young second-language learners. Tabors (1997) recommends that teachers employ techniques such as buttressed communication, repetition, running commentary, and context-embedded talk. To make their speech easy to understand, teachers should speak at a standard speed with some pausing between phrases, use simple short sentences with clear referents, and use more gestures, movements, and facial expressions to help convey meaning (Carey, 1997).

CULTURALLY RESPONSIVE CURRICULUM

All teachers of young children spend considerable time getting to know their students, their backgrounds, their special skills and needs, and some information about their early learning and socialization environments. This is especially important when the linguistic and cultural backgrounds of the teacher and children are different. When collecting information about the specific children in a classroom, teachers should not make assumptions about their cultural background. Racial and ethnic generalizations about particular groups may or may not apply to any particular family or child. All good early childhood teaching starts by finding out who the children are, in order to begin communication and instruction with sensitivity and build on the children's abilities, approaches to learning, and existing knowledge.

By collecting relevant information about the students and families and by spending time talking with parents and other family members, preschool and kindergarten teachers can better understand how to interpret the home language and culture of the children in their classrooms (Tabors, 1997). It is important to learn as much about the families' culture as possible in order to more accurately interpret the meaning on the children's behavior and prevent cultural stereotyping or unrealistic expectations. Culturally responsive teaching systematically integrates the students' values, beliefs, histories, and experiences and builds curriculum around mutual respect and trust (Garcia, 1993).

AREAS FOR NEW KNOWLEDGE

Although we know a lot about early literacy development, there is still a need to determine the effectiveness of specific early reading interventions with specific types of children and how long-term their efforts are. We also need to better understand how to best design literacy instruction for non-English speaking children (e.g., when to introduce English oral instruction, how much English oral proficiency is necessary prior to English literacy instruction, how to adequately assess oral English proficiency, what are the advantages and disadvantages of continuing to support primary language literacy once the child has transitioned to English). This additional knowledge will allow us to identify the types and amount of knowledge teachers of young children need in order to effectively provide early literacy instruction for all children. This, in turn, will help design more effective approaches to staff development.

CONCLUSION

Spoken language and reading have much in common. Children's ability to efficiently recognize words using sound–letter correspondence is interconnected with phonological awareness, which in turn is dependent on knowledge of words. Vocabulary, skills in comprehending and producing extended discourses, and knowledge about the world are acquired as parents, teachers, and peers interact with children having interesting conversations, reading books, telling stories, singing songs, chanting rhymes, and playing— given that these activities take place in a language that young children understand.

Considerable evidence suggests that in preschool and kindergarten classrooms, the teacher's ability to broaden the child's own language through extended, increasingly sophisticated conversations is critical to the preschool years. This contrasts with guidelines for formal reading instruction, in which the evidence is unquestionable that explicit instruction in letters, sounds, and their relationship is helpful to most children, and crucial to some, in first- and second-grade reading instruction (Snow et al., 1998).

Children's homes and early education experiences vary greatly in the quantity and variety of print materials. Children in the United States whose family language is non-English have fewer books in any language in their homes. If American families are monolingual in a language other than English it is important to consider the type of print material accessible to children in their home language. Print material should be available in the families' home language so that children and adults can examine the functions and features of print. When children and families are bilingual, experiences and materials need to be available in both languages so that the children have the experience to develop language and early literacy skills in both their languages.

REFERENCES

Arlington Public Schools. (1998). *Guiding principles and recommendations to promote excellence in educational opportunities for second language learners.* Arlington, VA: Author.

Au, K.H. (1993). *Literacy instruction in multicultural settings.* New York: Harcourt.

August, D., & Garcia, E. (1988). *Language minority education in the U.S.: Research, policy and practice.* Springfield, IL: Charles C Thomas.

Badrova, E., & Leong, D.J. (1998). Development of dramatic play in young children and its effects on self-regulation: The Vygotskian approach. *Journal of Early Childhood Teacher Education, 19,* 115–124.

Baker, L., Serpell, R., & Sonnenschein, S. (1995). Opportunities for literacy learning in the homes of urban preschoolers. In L.M. Morrow, (Ed.), *Family literacy: Connections in schools and communities* (pp. 236–252). Newark, DE: International Reading Association.

Ball, E.W., & Blachman, B.A. (1988). Phoneme segmentation training: Effect on reading readiness. *Annals of Dyslexia, 38,* 208–225.

Ballenger, C. (1999). *Teaching other people's children: Literacy and learning in a bilingual classroom.* New York: Teachers College Press.

Beals, D.E., & Snow, C.E. (1994). "Thunder is when the angels are upstairs bowling": Narratives and explanations at the dinner table. *Journal of Narrative and Life History, 4*(4), 331–352.

Beals, D.E., & Tabors, P.O. (1995). Arboretum, bureaucratic, and carbohydrates: Preschoolers' exposure to rare vocabulary at home. *First Language, 15*(1), 57–76.

Blum-Kulka, S. (1993). "You gotta know how to tell a story": Telling, tales, and tellers in American and Israeli narrative events at dinner. *Language in Society, 22,* 361–402.

Bowman, B.T., Donovan, S., & Burns, M.S. (2001). *Eager to learn: Educating our preschoolers.* Washington, DC: National Academy Press.

Bryant, D.M., Peisner-Feinberg, E., & Clifford, R. (1993). *Evaluation of public preschool programs in North Carolina.* Chapel Hill: University of North Carolina, Frank Porter Graham Child Development Center.

Burgess, J.C. (1982). The effects of a training program for parents of preschoolers on the children's school readiness. *Reading Improvement, 19*(4), 313–318.

Burns, M.S., Griffin, P., & Snow, C.E. (Eds.). (1999). *Starting out right: A guide to promoting children's reading success.* Washington, DC: National Academy Press.

Byrne, B., & Fielding-Barnsley, R. (1989). Phonemic awareness and letter knowledge in the child's acquisition of the alphabetic principle. *Journal of Educational Psychology, 81(1),* 313–321.

California State Department of Education. (2001). *California school readiness initiative.* Sacramento: Author

Carey, S. (1997). *Second language learners.* Portland, ME: Stenhouse Publishers.

Cazden, C. (1986). ESL teachers as language advocates for children. In P. Rigg & D.S. Enright (Eds.), *Children and ESL: Integrating perspectives* (pp. 9–21). Washington, DC: Teachers of English to Speakers of Other Languages (TESOL).

Christie, J.F., Johnsen, E.P., & Peckover, R.B. (1988). The effects of play period duration on children's play patterns. *Journal of Research in Childhood Education, 3*(2), 123–131.

Clay, M. (1975). *What did I write?* Portsmouth, NH: Heinemann.

Clay, M. (1979). *The early detection of reading difficulties* (2nd ed.). Portsmouth, NH: Heinemann.

Crenshaw, S.R. (1985). *A semiotic look at kindergarten writing.* (ERIC Document Reproduction Services No. ED269765)

Cummins, J. (1984). *Bilingual and special education: Issues in assessment and pedagogy.* San Diego: College Hill Press.

Cummins, J. (1986). Empowering minority students: A framework for intervention. *Harvard Educational Review, 56,* 372–390.

DeBaryshe, D.B. (1995). Maternal belief systems: Linchpin in the home reading process. *Journal of Applied Developmental Psychology, 16*(1), 1–20.

Diaz, S., Moll, L., & Mehan, H. (1986). Sociocultural resources in instruction: A context-specific approach. In California State Department of Education, Bilingual Education Office (Ed.), *Beyond language: Social and cultural factors in schooling language minority students* (pp. 197–230). Sacramento: California State Department of Education, Bilingual Education Office.

Dickinson, D.K., Cote, L., & Smith, M.W. (1993). Learning vocabulary in preschool: Social and discourse contexts affecting vocabulary growth. In C. Daiute (Ed.), *The Jossey-Bass Education Series: No. 61. The development of literacy through social interaction: New directions for child development* (pp. 67–78). San Francisco: Jossey-Bass.

Dickinson, D.K., & Smith, M.W. (1994). Long-term effects of preschool teachers' book readings on low-income children's vocabulary and story comprehension. *Reading Research Quarterly, 29*(2), 104–122.

Duncan, D.J., Brooks-Gunn, J., & Klebanov, P.K. (1994). Economic deprivation and early childhood development. *Child Development, 65*(2), 296–318.

Dunn, L.M., & Dunn, L.M. (1985). *Peabody Picture Vocabulary Test-Revised.* Circle Pines, MN: American Guidance Service.

Early Childhood Longitudinal Study. (1999). *America's kindergarteners.* Washington, DC: U.S. Department of Education, Office of Educational Research and Improvement.

Edwards, P.A. (1995). Empowering low-income mothers and fathers to share books with young children. *Reading Teacher, 48,* 558–564.

Feitelson, Z., & Goldstein, D. (1986). Patterns of book ownership and reading to young children in Israeli school-oriented and nonschool-oriented families. *Reading Teacher, 39*(9), 924–930.

Galambos, S.J., & Hakuta, K. (1988). Subject-specific and task-specific characteristics of metalinguistic awareness in bilingual children. *Applied Psycholinguistics, 9,* 141–162.

Galda, L., & Pellegrini, A.D. (1988). Children's use of narrative language in peer interaction. In B.A. Rafoth & D.L. Rubin (Eds.), *The social construction of written communication: Writing research* (pp. 175–194). Westport, CT: Ablex Publishing.

Garcia, E.E. (1991). Caring for infants in a bilingual child care setting. *Journal of Educational Issues of Language Minority Students, 9,* 1–10.

Garcia, E.E. (1993). The education of linguistically and culturally diverse children. In B. Spodek (Ed.), *Handbook of research on the education of young children* (pp. 372–384). New York: Macmillan/McGraw-Hill.

Gee, J. (1990). *Sociolinguistics and literacies: Ideologies in discourses.* London: Falmer Press.

Gentile, L.M., & Hoot, J.L. (1983). Kindergarten play: The foundation of reading. *Reading Teacher, 36,* 46–49.

Goodman, Y.M. (1986). Children coming to know literacy. In W.H. Teale & E. Sulzby (Eds.), *Emergent literacy: Writing and reading.* Westport, CT: Ablex Publishing.

Hakuta, K. (1986). *Mirror of language: The debate on bilingualism.* New York: Basic Books.

Head Start Bureau. (2000). *Celebrating cultural and linguistic diversity in Head Start.* Washington, DC: Commissioner's Office of Research and Evaluation and the Head Start Bureau.

Heath, S.B. (1983). *Ways with words: Language, life, and work in communities and classrooms.* New York: Cambridge University Press.

Heath, S. (1986). Sociocultural context of language development. In California State Department of Education (Ed.), *Beyond language: Social and cultural factors in schooling language minority students* (pp. 143–186). Los Angeles: California State University.

Johns, K.M. (1992). Mainstreaming language minority students through cooperative grouping. *Journal of Educational Issues of Language Minority Students, 11,* 221–231.

Kontos, S., & Wilcox-Herzog, S. (1997). Teachers' interactions with children: Why are they so important? *Young Children, 52,* 4–12.

Lancy, D.F., & Bergin, C. (1992, April). *The role of parents in supporting beginning reading.* Paper presented at the annual meeting of the American Research Association, San Francisco.

Layzer, J.I. (1993). *Observational study of early childhood programs: Final report: Vol. 1. Life in Preschool.* Lanham, MD: Abt Books.

Levy, A.K., Wolfgang, C.H., & Koorland, M.A. (1992). Sociodramatic play as a method for enhancing the language performance of kindergarten-age students. [Special Issue: Research on Kindergarten]. *Early Childhood Research Quarterly, 7*(2), 245–262.

Lewis, M., & Feinman, S. (Eds.). (1991). *Social influences and socialization in infancy.* Norwell, MA: Kluwer Academic Publishers.

Lyon, R. (1999). *Testimony to the Committee on Education and the Workforce, U.S. House of Representatives: Hearing on Title I of the Elementary and Secondary Education Act.* Available from http://156.40.88.3/about/crmc/cdb/

Maclean, M., Bryant, P., & Bradley, L. (1987). Rhymes, nursery rhymes, and reading in early childhood. *Merrill-Palmer Quarterly, 33*(3), 255–281.

Marzolf, D.P., & DeLoache, J.S. (1994). Transfer in young children's understanding of spatial representations. *Child Development, 65,* 1–15.

McGee, L.M., & Richgels, D.J. (1996). *Literacy beginnings: Supporting young readers and writers.* Boston: Allyn & Bacon.

Morrow, L.M., & Rand, M.K. (1991). Promoting literacy during play by designing early childhood classroom environments. *Reading Teacher, 44*(6), 396–402.

Muter, V., & Diethelm, K. (2001). The contribution of phonological skills and letter knowledge to early reading development in a multilingual population. *Language Learning, 51*(2), 187–219.

National Assessment of Educational Progress. (1994). *Reading report card for the nation and the states: Findings from the National Assessment of Education Progress.* Retrieved from http://nces.ed.gov/pubs/94057.asp

National Reading Panel. (2000). *Teaching children to read: An evidence-based assessment of the scientific research literature on reading and its implications for reading instruction.* Washington, DC: National Institutes of Child Health and Human Development.

Neuman, S.B. (1996). *Evaluation of the books aloud project: An executive summary.* Report presented to the William Penn Foundation from BooksAloud!, Temple University, Philadelphia.

Neuman, S., & Roskos, K. (1992). Literacy objects as cultural tools: Effects on children's literacy behaviors in play. *Reading Research Quarterly, 27*(3), 203–225.

Ogbu, J.U. (1978). *Minority education and caste.* San Diego: Academic Press.

Palincsar, A.S., Brown, A.L., & Campione, J.C. (1993). First grade dialogues for knowledge acquisition and use. In E. Forman, N. Minick, & C.A. Stone (Eds.), *Contexts for learning: Sociocultural dynamics in children's development.* New York: Oxford University Press.

Phillips, D.A., McCartney, K., & Scarr, S. (1987). Child-care quality and children's social development. *Developmental Psychology, 23,* 537–543.

Purcell-Gates, V. (1996). Stories, coupons, and the TV guide: Relationships between home literacy experiences and emergent literacy knowledge. *Reading Research Quarterly, 31,* 406–428.

Purcell-Gates, V., & Dahl, K.L. (1991). Low SES children's success and failure at early literacy in skills-based classrooms. *Journal of Reading Behavior, 23,* 1–34.

Sameroff, A.J. (1989). Commentary: General systems and the regulation of development. In M.R. Gunnar & E. Thelan (Eds.), *The Minnesota Symposia in Child Psychology: Vol. 22. Systems and development* (pp. 213–235). Mahwah, NJ: Lawrence Erlbaum Associates.

Schrader, C.T. (1989, June). Written language use within the context of young children's symbolic play. *Early Childhood Research Quarterly, 4*(2), 225–244. (ERIC Document Reproduction Services No. EJ394089)

Secretary Riley supports two-way immersion programs. (1999, May). *Education Week.*

Smilansky, S. (1968). *The effects of sociodramatic play on disadvantaged preschool children.* New York: John Wiley & Sons.

Smith, M.W., & Dickinson, D.K. (1994). Describing oral language opportunities and environments in Head Start and other preschool classrooms. [Special Issue] *Head Start, 9*(3–4), 345–366.

Snow, C.E., Burns, M.S., & Griffin, P. (Eds.). (1998). *Preventing reading difficulties in young children.* Washington, DC: National Academy Press.

Snow, C.E., & Tabors, P.O. (1993). Language skills that relate to literacy development. In B. Spodek & O.N. Saracho (Eds.), *Language and literacy in early childhood education* (pp. 1–20). New York: Teachers College Press.

Sonnenschein, S., Baker, L., Serpell, R., Scher, D., Fernandez-Fein, S., & Munsterman, K.A. (1996). *Strands of emergent literacy and their antecedents in the home: Urban preschoolers' early literacy development.* (Reading Research Report No. 48)

Spiegel, D.L. (1994). A portrait of parents of successful readers. In International Reading Association, *Fostering the love of reading: The affective domain in reading education.* Newark, DE: Author.

Tabors, P.O. (1997). *One child, two languages: A guide for preschool educators of children learning English as a second language.* Baltimore: Paul H. Brookes Publishing Co.

Taylor, D., & Strickland, D. (1986). *Family storybook reading.* Portsmouth, NH: Heinemann.

Torgesen, J.K., Wagner, R.K., Rashotte, C.A., Rose, E., Lindamood, P., Conway, T., & Garvin, C. (1999). Preventing reading failure in young children with phonological processing disabilities: Group and individual responses to instruction. *Journal of Educational Psychology, 91,* 1–15.

U.S. Bureau of Census. (1995). *The Hispanic population in the U.S.* Washington, DC: Author.

U.S. Bureau of Census. (2000). *Population projections of the United States by age, sex, race, and Hispanic origin: 1995 to 2050.* Washington, DC: U.S. Department of Commerce.

Umiker-Sebeok, D.J. (1979). Preschool children's intraconversational narratives. *Journal of Child Language, 6,* 91–110.

Vukelich, C. (1994). Effects of play interventions on young children's reading of environmental print. *Early Childhood Research Quarterly, 9,* 153–170.

Weizman, Z.O., & Snow, C.E. (in press). Lexical input as related to children's vocabulary acquisition: Effects of sophisticated exposure and support for meaning. *Developmental Psychology.*

West, J., Penton, K., & Germino Hausken, E. (2000). *America's kindergarteners: Findings from the Early Childhood Longitudinal Study, K Class of 1998–99.* Washington, DC: U.S. Department of Education, National Center for Educational Statistics.

Whitehurst, G.J., Arnold, D.S., Epstein, J.N., & Angell, A.L. (1994). A picture book reading intervention in day care and home for children from low-income families. *Developmental Psychology, 30*(5), 679–689.

Wolf, S.A., & Heather, S.B. (1992). *The braid of literature: Children's world of reading.* Cambridge, MA: Harvard University Press.

Emergent Literacy Practices in Early Childhood Classrooms

Sharon Ritchie,
Jolena James-Szanton,
and Carollee Howes

4

Literacy can be a difficult subject for early childhood educators. What constitutes appropriate literacy practices for young children and at what age children should be taught to read are questions that require a great deal of thought and dialogue. Some teachers want to model their classrooms after the National Association for the Education of Young Children's (NAEYC) developmentally appropriate practice (Bredekamp, 1987) and may struggle when asked to apply more teacher-directed approaches and rote learning techniques for learning. Other teachers believe that literacy should be taught in kindergarten but feel pressured by parents, administrators, and elementary schools to begin to teach children to read at ages 3 and 4. Still others see children falling behind in school, not learning to read until the third or fourth grade, and feel that an earlier start at reading would have been more beneficial.

Which literacy skills to teach and when to introduce literacy instruction in classrooms is debated across the nation, throughout districts and programs, and even within classrooms where collaborating teachers may have differing practices and beliefs. The debate goes to the heart of what teachers believe is appropriate for young children. A national agenda or a new curriculum may push teachers to change their practices, but these teachers will continue to have their own beliefs about literacy, which are important to examine.

This chapter explores how teachers' and programs' beliefs and intentions about emergent literacy shape or inhibit practices in classrooms and investigates three critical components of pre-literacy practices: the skill and knowledge base for emergent literacy, environments that support children as they learn and grow, and the need for positive teacher–child relationships to frame and organize children's learning.

EXAMINING BELIEFS AND PRACTICES

Because pre-literacy is controversial, teachers need to examine their beliefs and practices and compare how their own philosophy fits with the belief system of their program. Regardless of whether they are fully articulated, the beliefs and intentions of early childhood programs shape the practices in their classrooms (Wishard, Shivers, Howes, & Ritchie, 2001). A program based on the belief that children need to be fluent in English before entering kindergarten will support teachers who use more English in their teacher–child interactions with monolingual Spanish-speaking children. In contrast, a program that emphasizes the importance of children's home languages will encourage teachers to use the children's home languages during instruction. When teachers are better able to talk about their teaching practices and supporting belief system, they are more effective at implementing their practices in the classroom (Kirby & Paradise, 1992).

For the most part, early childhood educators do not have a chance to talk about the issues they face each day. The process of talking about their beliefs about practices helps teachers develop their ideas. A set of helpful questions emerged from work done within teacher focus groups designed to help teachers discuss their teaching practices. These questions may be used during staff meetings to begin examining beliefs but are also helpful for teachers to ask themselves individually (Howes & Ritchie, in preparation). Ask yourself the following questions to help clarify your pre-literacy beliefs and practices.

- How do I define pre-literacy practices?
- Do I use these practices in my classroom? Why or why not?
- How can I find out more about what practices other teachers are using?

After you answer these general questions, ask yourself more specific questions depending on your responses:

- I believe that children should be exposed to literature. What are some ways this could happen?

- I think some practices in classrooms force children to read. What specific practices make me uncomfortable and why?
- I believe that memorizing the alphabet is an inappropriate activity for young children. How did I form this opinion?

It is also worthwhile to think about the following areas and answer the accompanying questions:

1. *Memories of how you learned to read*

    Did reading come naturally, or did I benefit from strategies like learning to sound out letters and words?

    Did my parents read to me often?

    Did I go to the library regularly?

    How did my participation in these activities, or my lack of participation affect my skill and enthusiasm for reading?

2. *Ideas about good practice for second language learners*

    Do I believe that all children should be taught in English, or do I believe that children should learn first in their primary language?

3. *Thoughts about the effect of family participation*

    Do I believe that parents need to participate in a child's education in order for him or her to learn?

    What forms of participation do I find helpful to both children and their parents?

4. *Thoughts about child-initiated versus teacher-initiated learning*

    Do I think children should make the majority of decisions about how they will spend their day?

    What do I think is the job of the teacher in terms of providing stimulating materials and activities from which the child can choose?

    Should a teacher play an active role in how children spend their time (e.g., direct lessons, structure children's engagement in activities). Why? How do children benefit?

5. *Thoughts about daily schedules*

    Do I believe that children should know what to expect each day?

    Do I believe that each day should have a similar format, even if the activities change within the format?

What do I believe are the most important components of each day?

How do the components support the development of the children's literacy skills?

What is the purpose of a less formal structure?

How do I decide on a daily basis what is good for children?

Once you have examined your beliefs, you can focus on particular pre-literacy practices. Practices are defined as the observable behaviors that support or promote your philosophy. Explore the following areas.

Books

How should children be exposed to books in the classroom? Is there a book area in your classroom? If not, what are the barriers to your doing this? Which barriers are in your control and which ones are out of your control? Is there a wide selection of books accessible? Do you read books to children throughout the day? Do books support current classroom activities and themes? Are there additional materials including posters, flannel board stories, and recorded stories and songs? (Questions taken from Harms, Clifford, & Cryer, 1998.)

Writing

How should children experience writing in the classroom? Think about practices that you could develop to support your belief about children learning how to write. Are there a variety of drawing materials such as markers, thick pencils, and paintbrushes available to children? If so, how does using these objects help children move toward writing? Are there materials in the dramatic play areas that children can use to "write" grocery lists, take down orders, or "write" letters to one another? What activities can you provide for children to develop the fine motor skills necessary for writing? For example, are there eyedroppers available in the water table and/or art area so children can use their pincer grasp?

Teachable Moments

How do you define a *teachable moment*? How does your use of teachable moments reflect your philosophy? For example: A child has just finished an art project and she wants the teacher to write her name on it. As the teacher writes her name, she sounds it out. "SA-MAN-THA." In this teachable moment, the teacher linked sounds with letters. Although she may not believe in teaching Samantha how to sit down and write her name, the teacher does believe in responding to a child's interest and initiative. In this way, a child can develop skills without formal instruction.

How do you increase the likelihood of teachable moments? How do you become more aware of what you are doing each day so that you can become more intentional in your practices? Teachers who take advantage of the teachable moments in the day are those who pay close attention to children. They listen when the children talk to them and use that opportunity to help children expand on their ideas. Teachers notice when children are curious or excited about something and are willing to abandon their own agenda to follow the ideas of the children.

LITERACY PRACTICES

In emergent literacy, there is no clear distinction between reading and non- reading; rather, there is a developmental continuum. The ideas presented in this chapter better prepare children for elementary school by promoting their interest in and enthusiasm for oral and written language and the skills that are the foundation for reading and writing. Included in the developmental continuum of writing are the skills and knowledge that are precursors to conventional forms of reading and writing, the environments that support them, and the social interactions that promote them (Bowman, Donavan, & Burns, 2001; Neuman, 1999; Roskos & Neuman, 2001; Shonkoff & Phillips, 2000). As you read, continue to consider your philosophy and beliefs and work to broaden your ideas by including some of the ideas that are presented. Take a few minutes to note your ideas as you move through the material.

- What skills and knowledge do you believe are important for you to have in order to offer children valuable experiences that support their emergent literacy?

- How does your classroom environment support children's learning?

- How do your relationships with the children in your classroom affect their learning?

Skills and Knowledge

The skill and knowledge base of emergent literacy includes the development of oral language, awareness of print, knowledge of letters, and the awareness that language is composed of small sounds that are linked to form words. Skills include following oral directions, developing increasingly complex vocabulary, and the ability to connect stories to life experiences. Children are exposed to many activities and opportunities to develop these emergent literacy skills and knowledge. What may look like play or circle time is really a staging area for literacy practices. As teachers explore their beliefs and intentions about the literacy needs of young children, they realize what they already do to support literacy. A lot of times, it is easier to expand these practices than to start over or to incorporate a completely different practice into the school day.

Consider the events that regularly occur in classrooms:

1. *When children are being read to or are pretending to read*

    Do you have a book corner with a variety of books, both fiction and nonfiction, that rotate on a regular basis to reflect children's interests, classroom themes, and developmental levels (Harms et al., 1998)?

    Is this area inviting and comfortable?

    Do you read to children daily?

    Is there a daily opportunity for children to look at books on their own?

    Are books available in other centers in the room?

2. *When children are telling stories of their own or are describing their lives and activities*

    Do you have the opportunity in whole group, small group, and/or individual time to simply listen to children and the things they have to say?

    Do you have materials that encourage expressive language such as play telephones, and puppets (Harms et al., 1998)?

3. *When children are dictating stories or ideas to teachers who are writing them down*

    When children are drawing pictures, do you take the opportunity to ask them what their picture is about and to write their ideas on their paper?

    When children wish to communicate with someone who is not in the classroom, is writing a letter or a note presented as an option for how they might express themselves?

    Are there examples of teacher-lead and spontaneous dictation in your classroom?

4. *When children are exposed to a print-rich environment*

    Does your classroom have labels to identify the right place to put toys and materials?

Are there word cards, environment labels, name cards, alphabet cards, and templates to help children form letters?

Do children have access to a variety of paper and writing tools?

Does the classroom have alphabet and word puzzles?

Are there writing tools in areas to support play (e.g., grocery lists)?

5. *When children are visually tracing the words to a story, song, or poem*

Are words to favorite songs written for children to follow?

Do you use big books so children can easily see the words in the story?

7. *When children are supported at home*

Do you interact with families to share information on supporting language and literacy learning?

Do you encourage families to build on classroom work at home?

Do you encourage families to take advantage of community resources (e.g., library)?

Do you lend books to families to share with children at home?

Some teachers believe that learning should not interfere with play and creativity. There are dozens of ideas and practices that support literacy without interfering with philosophies that promote child-initiated learning, including nursery rhyme rebuses, song charts, flannel board stories, group writing projects, books on tape, problem-solving and feeling books, name card and sign-in activities, room labels, letter of the week activities, and rhyming books.

Nursery Rhyme Rebus

What Is It?

A rebus is a sentence that is made up primarily of pictures. You can write nursery rhymes and add simple illustrations to replace the important words. For example: Hickory, Dickory Dock, the (MOUSE) ran up the (CLOCK). When you point to the picture, the children know the word that fits into the rhyme. Children can use large pointers to follow the words and pictures as you read aloud.

What Do Children Learn?

Children learn that words have meaning. They associate the picture with the word and practice it over and over. By following the teacher or child who moves his or her finger or pointer across the text and pictures, children learn that print moves from left to right. Their eyes begin to practice the tracking process that is essential to later success with reading.

Song Charts

What Are They?

Song charts are large pieces of paper on which the titles and words to favorite songs are written. These can be hung on large rings so they can be easily flipped through when the children decide what song to sing. Throughout the year as children learn new songs, you can write the words for them and add them to the flip chart. Simple pictures in the rebus style help children remember what the words say. Words to simple and repetitive songs can be written down and the main words can be illustrated.

What Do Children Learn?

In much the same way as using the nursery rhyme rebus, children have the opportunity to track words and to learn that symbols have meaning. In the context of regular preschool activities, this activity adds the literacy component to what is already familiar.

Flannel Board Stories

What Are They?

Flannel board stories are a collection of flannel pieces that correspond to a story and can be attached to a flannel board. Packaged flannel board stories accompany many well-known children's books. For example, *The Very Hungry Caterpillar* (Carle, 1987) is available with accompanying flannel pieces, from the tiny egg right through the blossoming butterfly. You can read the story while illustrating each page by putting the flannel pieces on the board. Children who watch this process a few times will be excited to do it on their own or with friends. If you have both time and talent, you can make your own support materials for books, or for the stories that children make up. These can be stored in individual baggies for easy access.

What Do Children Learn?

Children will spend hours telling and retelling these stories. The flannel figures serve as prompts to help them recall the characters, and the sequence of the story, helping children develop the concept of beginning, middle, and end. This activity also supports vocabulary development as children de-scribe the characters and the story with increasing detail.

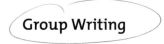

Group Writing

What Is It?

Group writing is a process through which children provide their ideas for sto-ries, class invitations, thank-you notes, or letters to sick classmates or others. You can ask children for their thoughts, then write these thoughts down ex-actly as they are said. When children have returned from a field trip, they can all contribute their ideas about what they liked best. When a classmate is sick for a prolonged period, the classmates can all contribute their best wishes or tell the child about what has been going on in class. When there is a problem, the whole class can contribute ideas about how to solve it.

What Do Children Learn?

Very young children's thoughts are often not complete or even on the topic. Nevertheless, this activity helps children begin to understand that their ideas are important and can be saved for other people to read. Older children begin to see writing as another form of communication. When a girl misses her mother, she can write a note to her. When a boy draws a picture, he can dic-tate the words that explain the story and then "read" it to the group.

Books on Tape

What Are They?

Many commercial stories are available on audiotapes for teachers to buy. These can be used in a learning center where children have headphones and copies of books to read along with the audiotapes. They can also be used in large group settings in which you show one book to all the children who are listening. You and your students can also record your own stories by telling original stories or recording as you read aloud from your favorite books.

What Do Children Learn?

You can use books on tape as an opportunity to demonstrate the importance of reading with expression and inflection. This helps children recognize when a voice is expressing surprise, asking a question, whispering, or shout-ing. Children can add sound effects and illustrate the story on tape so that others can follow along.

Problem-Solving and Feeling Books

What Are They?

Problem-solving and feeling books are children's stories that address the problems and feelings that children experience on a regular basis. For instance, *Are You My Mother?* (Eastman, 1980) helps children identify the feelings of missing their mother. *The Runaway Bunny* (Brown, 1942) addresses a similar issue and helps children know that their mothers will be there for them always. *I Was So Mad* (Mayer, 1997) and *Alexander and the Terrible, Horrible, No Good, Very Bad Day* (Viorst, 1984) address children's anger and frustration at not always getting to have their way.

What Do Children Learn?

Conflicts arise on a daily basis in classrooms, and teachers work regularly to solve problems and develop plans (see Chapter 2). Emotions arise when children are upset with their friends or their teachers, and children need to learn appropriate ways to deal with these feelings. Children who are supported by their teachers learn to talk about what happened and to discuss different ways to solve problems. They learn to talk about the situation after they have solved the problem and to discuss the feelings they experienced during the process. Rereading familiar books in which the characters experience similar problems and feelings helps bring closure to a problem and lets children know that everyone has problems and that these problems can be worked out. This process helps build positive relationships between children and teachers. With your support, children can also write their own stories about angry or sad feelings or about solving problems. These stories can become classroom books made available to other children when they too are struggling with difficult feelings.

Name Card and Sign-in Activities

What Are They?

Name card and sign-in activities are activities that allow children to practice recognizing and writing their names when they arrive at school. Parents regularly sign their children in when they drop them off for the day. It is simple to provide a sign-in for the children, as well. At first, children can identify cards with their names on them. They can be asked to place the card in a special box or on a chart. Magnets or Velcro attached to the back of the cards allow children to attach their name cards to a poster which lets everyone know who is in school that day. Children can also use these name cards to identify where they wish to play in the room during free choice or what class job they will be doing. As children begin to show an interest in writing their names and in holding pencils, you can dot children's names so they can trace them. Eventually, children will become able to write their names without the support of the dots.

What Do Children Learn?

Children learn to recognize their own names in print. In addition, daily practice with writing or tracing their names helps children develop the fine motor strength and coordination necessary to hold a pencil correctly and learn to form the letters. A program called Handwriting without Tears (Olson, 2000) offers a developmental support system for helping children learn to form all letters of the alphabet. Other opportunities for prewriting, include using a computer keyboard or calculator, using alphabet letter puzzles or number puzzles, and incorporating writing or scribbling into play (e.g., writing grocery lists, taking orders). Other support for writing skills includes tracing, using alphabet stamps, and doing motor grasp activities (e.g., stringing beads, using eyedroppers, using small three-dimensional objects).

Room Labels

What Are They?

Room labels are cards with identifying words placed on key objects throughout the classroom. You can write labels for all parts of the classroom. Shelves can be labeled so that children and teachers alike know where the art supplies, dinosaurs, doll clothes, and puzzles belong. The tables, clocks, windows, and doors can all be labeled. The art area, pretend area, block area, and cozy area can be labeled. Often, these labels are accompanied by pictures, which support children as they learn to recognize that the labels have meaning. You can involve children in this process throughout the year. For example, as you are helping children learn what to do in each of the areas in the classroom, you can ask children to name all the materials that they use in the art area and then label them as the children identify them. As the year goes on, you may ask children to identify all the things in the classroom that start with a *C* and then label them as they are identified.

What Do Children Learn?

This practice not only helps keep the room organized by providing clues as to where toys and supplies are stored, but children who have the opportunity to view written words over and over again begin to develop a sight–word vocabulary. The room can be labeled in more than one language to support second-language learners and to let English speaking children know that there are many different languages.

Letter of the Week Activities

What Is It?

Letter of the week activities are a way for you to focus on letters and their corresponding sounds. You can choose one letter/sound per week to focus on and then apply games and activities to that letter and sound. Some teachers go through the alphabet sequentially; others use the first names of the children in the classroom as the guide to what letters children will work on throughout the week. To introduce the letter of the week, you can cut out pictures from magazines and paste them to cards. You can show pictures of objects that begin with the letter/sound of the week and have the children repeat the words. Then, you can hold up pictures of objects that begin with another letter/sound and have the children decide if the objects begin with the letter/sound of the week (Adams, Foorman, Lundberg, & Beeler, 1997). Children can also make their own alphabet collages by cutting out magazine pictures that start with the letter/sound they are concentrating on.

Another activity is Treasure Box. You can present the class with a box labeled with a letter. Children can find things in the classroom that start with that letter/sound to place in the box. This game can also be played in small groups. As children become more comfortable with initial sounds, the game can be expanded to final sounds of words. For example, children can identify objects that end with the /s/ sound.

What Do Children Learn?

With regular practice, children can recite the alphabet, identify beginning sounds of the things in their world, learn that each letter has a corresponding sound, begin to hear that some words sound like others, and begin to develop a strategy for sounding out words. They learn to identify words that begin or end with the same sound and begin to understand that language is made up of sounds that correspond to letters of the alphabet. (Adams et al., 1997). Children listen to the individual sounds that make up a word and pay attention to whether the sounds between words are the same or different. This also helps children become increasingly aware of their environment and supports vocabulary development.

Rhyming Books

What Are They?

Rhyming books are books that include lots of rhyming words. Rhyming helps children to notice the similarities and differences between the sounds of words (Adams et al., 1997). There are a variety of alphabet and rhyming books to choose from. Some excellent examples include *Goodnight Moon*

(Brown, 1947), *The Cat in the Hat* (Dr. Seuss, 1957), *Green Eggs and Ham* (Dr. Suess, 1988), *Eating the Alphabet* (Ehlert, 1989), and *Chika Chika Boom Boom* (Martin, Archambault, & Ehlert, 1986). You can stop after every page and ask the children which rhyming words they heard. You can also ask children to guess the second rhyming word of a pair.

Poetry is also an excellent way to introduce children to rhyme. You can add variety by reciting the poem in a whisper or a loud voice or by having each child recite one word of the poem (Adams et al., 1997). Also consider using rhyming songs like "This Old Man" and "1, 2, Buckle My Shoe."

What Do Children Learn?

Children learn to pay attention to the way words sound, instead of focusing solely on word meaning (Adams et al., 1997). They learn that differences between beginning sounds can make a difference in word meaning (e.g., house, mouse). They learn to generate their own rhymes and increase their ability to remember sounds (Notari-Syverson, O'Connor, & Vadasy, 1998). In addition, they learn that pictures can be used to represent words. Consult curricula such as *Phonemic Awareness in Young Children: A Classroom Curriculum* (Adams et al., 1997) for more information on the benefits of rhyming books.

CREATING A SUPPORTIVE ENVIRONMENT

A supportive environment is essential for literacy learning. Teachers need to create an environment in which children are encouraged to read. When you talk to children about how much you love to read, your enthusiasm will be contagious. You can also create a supportive environment for literacy learning by: reading with emotion, reading nonfiction books, talking about how reading is used everyday, encouraging participation in literacy activities, using pictures, using gestures, repeating ideas, speaking slowly, and offering help with next steps. Other ideas include linking classroom activities to children's lives, thinking about the needs of second-language learners, using older children as role models, using themes, introducing new ideas throughout the year, placing books throughout the classroom, and including parents.

Reading with Emotion

Reading with emotion can be very useful in keeping children engaged, showing children that you enjoy reading, and helping children build a foundation for learning about punctuation. Although you may never actually talk about periods and question marks, children will hear proper sentence structure and grammar. When they are later introduced to punctuation in a formal setting, these early experiences with reading will serve as a foundation for their understanding. While listening to stories, children will also hear the rhyming patterns and alliterations that are so prevalent in children's books.

Reading Nonfiction Books

Too often, early childhood classrooms have only fiction books or stories. This practice overlooks the fact that children enjoy reading factual books as well. There are wonderful books available about animals, frogs and toads, dinosaurs, and people in the community. These books provide children with real information that can help them build their interests and explore classroom themes and lessons in greater depth. Teachers who use nonfiction books to find information when children ask questions are letting children know that books are resources and can provide important information. Some of these books include *The Big Book of Cars* (Lord, 1999), *A Trip to the Doctor* (Linn, 1988), and *Peek at a Pond* (Twinem, 1999).

Talking About How Reading Is Used

Everyday experiences of reading seem like exciting adventures to young children. In order to let children know how useful it is to read and write, consider a variety of topics for conversations with children, either during group time or informally:

- What should I do to make sure that I don't forget what I need at the market?
- I don't know how to make brownies. How will I find out what to do?
- I just got a new game, but I don't know how to play it. What can I do?
- I really want to watch *Rugrats* today, but I don't know what time the show comes on. Where can I look?

These types of discussions let children know the multiple ways that reading supports people in their daily lives.

Encouraging Participation in Literacy Activities

Encouraging children to participate in literacy activities includes noticing and commenting when a child chooses a book, pretends to read to her dolls, remembers the story from the week before, or wants to write a story about a picture he has carefully drawn. Encouraging children also means providing them with the opportunity to participate in activities designed to develop pre-academic skills. You can think of cooking projects and then write out group recipes, develop science projects where children can record their observations, or chat with students at lunch about what they are going to do over the weekend or about their favorite movies. Consider providing motivating materials such as big books, finger puppets, and interesting collections. The goal is to make children conscious of the many literacy activities they are engaged in and enjoying.

Using Pictures

Pictures engage children and hold their attention. They are an excellent way to introduce new vocabulary to children and are often the motivation for long and interesting conversations and good questions. Many teachers have large portfolios of magazine pictures, which they sort according to topic and have at their fingertips for both formal and informal conversations.

When talking about the weather, you may use basic pictures of the rain, snow, and the sun, as well as more advanced pictures of storms, hail, hurricanes, and volcano eruptions depending on the complexity of the conversation. Children not only can discuss what is in the pictures, but they can talk about their own experiences of such weather conditions. Pictures can also be used to discuss the many places where people live. Examples include houses of all kinds: apartments, tenement or project buildings, farms, and tents. Pictures can show children that people live in cities, suburbs, rural areas, deserts, and mountainous regions. There are also wonderful pictures available of animals, from farm animals, to zoo animals, to wild animals that live in Africa. Children can learn about animals that live in the sea and animals that lived long ago. These pictures may lead children to discuss their favorite animals or their own pets.

Using Gestures

Gestures and body language are similar to pictures. They enhance abstract ideas by giving children something concrete to think about. Your gestures and body language can help children understand many concepts such as size. *Big, large, huge, gigantic,* and *loud* can be conveyed through sweeping hand gestures and a loud, deep voice. Songs such as the "Teensy Weensy Spider" can be changed to include gigantic spiders that are sung about in deep, loud voices and using large finger movements. In the same way, *small, tiny,* and *soft* can be conveyed through small hand gestures and soft voices or whispers.

Children can also learn about emotions through gestures and body language. They can learn to recognize a wide range of feelings in themselves and to empathize with the feelings of others. You help children by both using and labeling your expressions to demonstrate happiness, sadness, anger, surprise, pride, and fear.

Repeating Ideas

Children require repetition in order to learn. They enjoy hearing the same books, listening to the same music, and watching the same videos again and again. What might be tedious and boring to adults is continuously entertaining to children. Children often experience themselves as readers after they have memorized a book that they have heard repeatedly. They "read" the story, often imitating the inflections and emphasis that they have heard you use. They use the pictures to help remind them of what comes next. Children learn many other things through repetition as well. They learn to count, to say the letters of the alphabet, to sing songs, and to do finger plays. This method allows information to become part of children's long-term memory so that it is available to children when they need it to help them read and solve problems.

Offering Help with the Next Step

Teachers need to allow children to learn how to solve a problem, rather than simply telling children an answer. To do this, they need to know what type of support a child needs. Does a child need to be given precise words to practice in order to initiate play with a friend or solve a problem, or is he at the point where he needs to be asked open-ended questions such as "What can you do if you want to be part of that game?" or "How do you think we should decide who gets to play with this ball?" If a child gets stuck while trying to say the alphabet or count to a high number, instead of telling the child the next letter or number, think about ways to prompt the child to figure it out on his or her own. Are there alphabet or number sequences on the wall that you can refer the child to? Can you use inflection in your voice and the series of letters or numbers that come before to help the child? (e.g., L-M-N-O- . . .). A rule of thumb is to answer a question with a question to help children expand their thoughts and find out why they think what they do. Doing so will help children develop vocabulary, learn how to articulate their thoughts, and learn what they think and how they think.

Linking Classroom Activities to Children's Lives

Linking classroom activities to children's lives and experiences is an important stepping stone for children's learning because children can use what they know already to make sense of new information. They can also bring information from home that will be new and instructive to other members of the class, including you. When starting on a new project or a new topic, some good questions to ask include:

- Has anyone in the class ever done this before (e.g., baked cookies, gone on a nature walk, planted a garden, visited a bakery)?
- What do you already know about this (e.g., ice, dinosaurs, going to the doctor, building with blocks, going to the library, swimming)?
- When did you feel this way (e.g., sad, happy, scared, angry)?

Thinking About the Needs of Second-Language Learners

The approaches to learning discussed in this chapter easily apply to second-language learners. All of the activities will support children as they work to learn a new language, but another important aspect to working with second language learners is to genuinely value the home languages of children in your classroom by providing books written in their language, highlighting their ability to speak in two languages, having an adult in the classroom who speaks their language (whenever this is possible), and including and validating aspects of their culture that may be different from the cultures of other children in the classroom.

Using Older Children as Role Models

Older children are powerful role models for younger children. Younger children admire children older than themselves and watch them carefully. They strive to do the things that older children do, want to be involved in "big kid" activities, and want to improve their skills to match those of older peers. If older children are available, or if older brothers and sisters occasionally visit the school or child care environment, you might want to think about ways to include them in the school day. In many schools, children from older classrooms visit younger children on a regular basis. They are usually paired with one particular child or a small group of children so that they can begin to know one another and will look forward to the visits. The older children's teachers prepare their students by teaching them how to read books aloud, how to engage young children in stories, and how to ask questions and show storybook pictures. If there are children with special needs in the classroom, the teacher can help them learn that they may need to read more slowly or help them realize that they may have some difficulty understanding what a young child is saying. Older children blossom from the experience of working with younger children, and the younger children typically pay rapt attention to them. Older children are a far greater draw than teachers will ever be! Sometimes, older children spend part of their year writing and illustrating original stories for their young partners. They bring the books and present them to each child at the end of the year.

Using Themes

Another way to support the development of literacy is through the use of themes. One program divided the year into four parts based on the themes of zoo, farm, community, and nursery rhymes. A significant portion of the day focused on the language and ideas of the themes. During the zoo theme, for example, the stories and songs were about zoo animals. In the art area children could cut and paste stripes for zebras and long necks for giraffes. They could build animal enclosures in the block area. During free time, they could act like monkeys, roar like lions, jump through hoops like seals, and talk about what different animals eat. They illustrated their own books about their favorite animal.

By the end of the year, children were well versed in all four themes. They did not get bored because new songs and stories refreshed the classroom on a quarterly basis. New puppets appeared in the puppet area to correspond with the change of themes. The focus of the science area shifted to reflect the new theme as well. The teachers felt organized throughout the year and were able to generate new ideas to keep things fresh for the children as well as for themselves.

Introducing New Ideas Throughout the Year

Do you have the same displays in the classroom in April as you did in September? Do you read the same books, sing the same songs, and provide the same toys and activities all year? If the answer if yes, then you may not be thinking about how quickly children develop and change. In the beginning of the year, children may thrive on sensory materials such as playdough, water play, sand and cornmeal play. A few months later, children may continue to enjoy those activities, but it is good to change the activities in order to challenge them, to offer ways for them to enhance their play, and to help them learn new skills.

Each time children have new opportunities in play, they develop new skills. Many of these new skills promote literacy interest, enthusiasm, and skills. One idea to keep activities fresh is to keep labeled boxes of objects in your storage closet. Some suggestions for box themes include the beauty parlor, pizza kitchen, and office. In the box marked "office" there can be phones, notepads, calculators, paper, envelopes, stamps, pens, and pencils. If you set the box out at free time, children can call in orders, scribble down ideas, punch numbers on the calculator, and address envelopes. All of these activities promote literacy. Children who use these objects will develop new vocabulary around new ideas, learn to use pencils and paper, and begin to imitate writing. They will imitate the use of calculators and possibly develop new interests. A child may pretend to send out for lunch, and the food from the pretend area may become incorporated into the "office" space. Another child may need a guard dog from the animal area for his office.

Listening to children carefully and observing what they talk about and do can provide you with many ideas about what play they would like to engage in. A child might come in one morning chattering eagerly about a visit to a sea museum. Check through the classroom and find all of the things that are available to set up a museum and give tours to his classmates. Another child may talk about a camping trip that she is looking forward to. All of the children can discuss what they know about camping. They can make a tent out of sheets, build a pretend fire, and sing camp songs. Brainstorming ideas with a number of people allows for more creativity and sharing of the workload.

Placing Books Throughout the Classroom

If all of the books are on one shelf or in one area, opportunities to support literacy are being missed. Books on cars and trucks could be located in the block area. Books on colors could be in the art area. In this way, teachers and children have books at their fingertips when they have a question or are looking for new ideas. It is also possible to write books that support the activities. For example, in the block area there could be an illustrated rule book that helps children remember not to build too tall, to be careful of the buildings of others, or to put away blocks neatly. Children can develop the rules, help write them down, and think of ways that pictures will help remind everyone of the rules.

Including Parents

A supportive literacy environment should include careful thinking about ways to include the family and parents. One way of doing this is to set up a classroom lending library. Books can come from the classroom, from school book sales, or from your personal library. The children help choose the books and each book is carefully put inside a sealable plastic bag with a card. The book can be signed out by a parent and can go home to be enjoyed with the family. Other schools have pajama reading nights. Children come back to school in the evenings with their parents, already dressed for bed. The parents read books to their own children or to others in an area set up to be cozy for everyone. There are beanbag chairs, rocking chairs, pillows, and blankets. If the school does not have these things, the children can bring their own blankets or pillows from home.

When literacy is not supported in the home, or when you assume that literacy is not being supported in the home, there are many things to think about. It is important to consider parent's economic situations and work schedules. It is also important to know if parents have difficulty with reading themselves, and if so, you might want to modify your program so that everyone is included and no one is embarrassed. It is very important to remember that parents do care—they just may not all show it in the same way. People's lives are complicated, and making assumptions pushes people apart and further reduces the likelihood of collaboration.

A program called Mother Read addresses literacy and reading on many levels. Parents come together to read children's stories. The books are chosen to reflect multiple cultures, are available in multiple languages, and deal with important childhood themes such as separation, toileting, and nightmares. The parents have opportunities they may not have had as children to explore the ideas in the books and to talk about them in terms of their own children. Parents first get practice reading to one another, then to the children. The parents read to their children within a group setting. Then, the books, along with ideas for additional activities, are sent home so the parents and children can share them there. This goes on for many weeks. Parents address many of their own issues, they think more carefully about what their children need, they are exposed to wonderful books, and at the graduation, they choose their favorite book to take home. Many Head Start programs and many state preschool programs, along with privately funded programs, offer family literacy projects. In addition, many local libraries have storytimes for children of all ages. It is a good idea to know what is available in your area and provide all families with the information.

TEACHER–CHILD RELATIONSHIPS

Teachers have day-to-day contact with children and are influential in how children approach literacy learning. Thinking about and developing positive teacher–child relationships should not be separate from thinking about and developing positive literacy opportunities for children. Children's ability to learn depends on negotiating a trusting relationship with you. If children can trust you, then they will use you to help them learn. Trust between a child and you evolves when

- You are consistent in your responses

- Rules and limits are clear and the a child knows what to expect

- The child knows that he or she can go to you for comfort or for assistance in solving a problem

Children who feel safe at school can move away from you and make the most of the learning environment. They can interact with the toys, games, and books, as well as with their peers. Until children can trust you, move away from you, and begin to explore the environment, they will not learn to read. See Chapter 2 for practical strategies for promoting trusting relationships that foster learning.

CONCLUSION

Teachers both want and need mentoring and opportunities to learn more about the teaching and learning of literacy. This chapter has offered only a short list of practices and ways in which to develop a classroom environment that supports emergent literacy because it is intended to encourage you to think carefully about your thoughts and philosophy regarding literacy. You can start by simply talking with other teachers in your program. You can examine the ideas presented here and see if they work for you. Or, you can meet with teachers from other programs and discuss literacy with them. Create your own framework, use your skills and talents, and carefully think about what you do and why you do it. Remember, the work that happens in classrooms happens because of teachers!

REFERENCES

Adams, M.J., Foorman, B.R., Lundberg, I., & Beeler, T. (1997). *Phonemic awareness in young children: A classroom curriculum.* Baltimore: Paul H. Brookes Publishing Co.

Bowman, B., Donovan, M.S., & Burns, M.S. (Eds.). (2001). *Eager to learn: Educating our preschoolers.* Washington, DC: National Academy Press.

Bredekamp, S. (1987). *Developmentally appropriate practice in early childhood programs serving children from birth through age 8.* Washington, DC: National Association for the Education of Young Children.

Brown, M.W. (1942). *The runaway bunny.* New York: HarperCollins Publishers.

Brown, M.W. (1947). *Goodnight moon.* New York: HarperCollins Publishers.

Carle, E. (1987). *The very hungry caterpillar.* New York: Penguin Books.

Eastman, P.D. (1980). *Are you my mother?* New York: Random House.

Ehlert, L. (1989). *Eating the alphabet: Fruits and vegetables from A to Z.* Orlando, FL: Harcourt.

Harms, T., Clifford, R., & Cryer, D. (1998). *Early Childhood Environment Rating Scale* (Rev. ed.). New York: Teachers College Press.

Howes, C., & Ritchie, S. (in preparation). *Beyond quality: Child care practices in programs for children with difficult life circumstances.*

Kirby, P.C., & Paradise, L.V. (1992). Reflective practice and effectiveness of teachers. *Psychological Reports, 70,* 1057–1058.

Linn, M. (1988). *A trip to the doctor.* New York: HarperCollins Publishers.

Lord, T. (1999). *The big book of cars.* New York: DK Publishing.

Martin, B., Jr., Archambault, J., & Ehlert, L. (Illus.). (1986). *Chicka chicka boom boom.* New York: Simon & Schuster.

Mayer, M. (1997). *I was so mad.* New York: Western Publishing.

Neuman, S.B. (1999). Books make a difference: A study of access to literacy. *Reading Research Quarterly, 34*(3), 286–311.

Notari-Syverson, A., O'Connor, R.E., & Vadasy, P.F. (1998). *Ladders to literacy: A preschool activity book.* Baltimore: Paul H. Brookes Publishing Co.

Olson, J. (2000). *Handwriting without tears.* Los Angeles: Occupational Therapy Association.

Roskos, K., & Neuman, S.B. (2001). In S.B. Nerman & D.K. Dickinson (Eds.), *Handbook of early literacy research.* New York: The Guilford Press.

Seuss, D. (1957). *The cat in the hat.* New York: Random House.

Seuss, D. (1988). *Green eggs and ham.* New York : Random House.

Shonkoff, J.P., & Phillips, D.A. (Eds.). (2000). *From neurons to neighborhoods: The science of early childhood development.* Washington, DC: National Academy Press.

Twinem, N. (1999). *Peek at a pond.* New York: Grosset & Dunlap.

Viorst, J. (1984). *Alexander and the terrible, horrible, no good, very bad day.* New York: Simon & Schuster Children's Publishing.

Wishard, A., Shivers, E., Howes, C., & Ritchie, S. (2001). Child care program and teacher practices: Associations with quality and children's experiences. *Early Childhood Research Quarterly.* Washington, DC: National Association for the Education of Young Children.

Fostering Young Children's Mathematical Understanding

Megan Loef Franke

Children come to school with an amazing amount of mathematical knowledge. They can count, reason about numbers, solve problems, and reason about space. Research has detailed the depth of young children's mathematical understanding and how this understanding develops over time (Baroody, 1989; Clements, Sarama, & Dibiase, 2000; Gelman, 1994). This body of research supports that teachers of young children should acknowledge what students already understand, build on this mathematical knowledge, and view each student as a capable mathematician. Educators of young children have the unique opportunity of linking more informal mathematical learning with school mathematics. This chapter presents current theories, conceptions, and research that provide insight into how educators can start young children on learning trajectories of sound and deep mathematical understanding.

A plethora of books and chapters have been written on how to teach mathematics to young children, ranging from books that lay out a particular

The research reported in this chapter was supported in part by a grant from the U.S. Department of Education Office of Educational Research and Improvement (OERI) to the National Center for Improving Student Learning and Achievement in Mathematics and Science (R305A60007–98). The opinions expressed in this paper do not necessarily reflect the position, policy, or endorsement of the U.S. Department of Education, OERI, or the National Center.

theoretical perspective on young children's learning to those that detail potential practices. The goal of this chapter is to engage teachers in thinking about the direction of current research and the theories that underlie that research. That way, teachers can develop a set of principled ideas to drive their teaching practice.

THEORETICAL PERSPECTIVES

Much of what exists in early childhood mathematics readers or texts draws on the work of Piaget. Piaget's (1954, 1973) work pushed teachers to consider that students come to school with many understandings and that those understandings develop as students engage with their environment. Piaget provided teachers with an image of children as "young scientists" who constantly create and test out hypotheses about their world. He also put forward ideas about what things children can learn at what ages and proposed stages to consider from preoperational to formal thought. He conducted experiments investigating children's abilities to conserve quantity (e.g., Are there more items on a table because of quantity or because the objects spread out farther across the table?). Often, educators cite Piaget's conservation work as rationale for student readiness to learn math.

Piaget's work continues to provide a foundation for how young children engage in and learn mathematics; however, research—particularly in cognitive science—has added more detail to Piaget's theories and conceptions (Chi, Glaser & Rees, 1982; Newell & Simon, 1972; Rumelhart & Norman, 1978). Researchers have learned more about how children learn mathematics and students' developmental trajectories: how children learn to count, add, subtract, multiply and divide, solve fraction problems, and conceptualize geometry and measurement. Across these mathematical domains researchers can also describe the principled ideas that support students' mathematical learning.

Developing Mathematical Understanding

Research on the cognitive aspects of how children learn offers insight about the development of students' mathematical understanding. This insight changes how Piaget's conceptions can be applied to working with young children. Previously, behaviorist learning theorists determined a child's mathematical understanding by analyzing the speed and accuracy of an answer to a particular mathematics problem; however, cognitive research demonstrates that a child's answer is not an adequate indicator of his or her understanding. Two children can solve the same problem in the same amount of time, get the same answer, and understand the problem differently. A child who quickly answers "7" to "3 + 4" does not necessarily understand addition and may only know the number fact and little else about the process of adding. Cognitive science research explains specifically what understanding a problem like "3 + 4" means as well as what generally characterizes understanding. Developing understanding is a dynamic process that takes a very long time and may never be complete (Hiebert & Carpenter, 1992). Mathematical understanding occurs as individuals create a network of connections among their mathematical ideas, a network organized around principled mathematical ideas.

Understanding mathematics from a cognitive viewpoint is based on the number, types, and organization of connections that exist for an individual. Understanding occurs as isolated pieces of information become connected and form increasingly structured and cohesive networks (Hiebert & Carpenter, 1992; Hiebert et al., 1997). A student who understands a math problem possesses multiple connections to information in an intricate web. These connections often grow stronger with continued use; therefore, isolated bits of knowledge are not enough to constitute understanding because connections must be efficiently retrieved. Connections can be conceptualized as organized in some form of a hierarchy.

Let's examine these ideas through the example of "3 + 4." A child could possess a rich web of connections that includes the following information: images of three cats and three cookies, the idea that 3 is a numeral, the knowledge that 3 can be represented by three fingers or by three objects, and the understanding that a counting sequence 1, 2, 3 is associated with the number 3 (see Figure 5.1). If a child is asked to solve the problem "3 + 4," the child might think about the numeral 3, which is in turn connected to a picture of his or her three fingers and the counting sequence 1, 2, 3. Through this process, the child creates his or her solution path. A

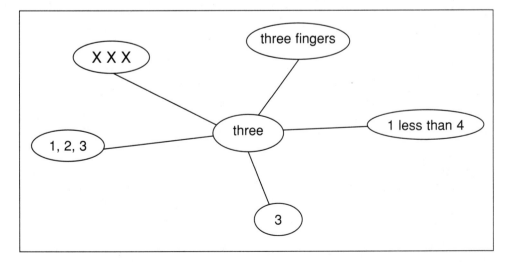

Figure 5.1. Child's web of connections associated with the number 3.

child with many different connections can traverse many different paths and, thus, has many more opportunities to approach and solve the problem (see Figure 5.2). The child is not dependent on a single mode, "3 + 4 = 7," to respond.

This view of mathematics would rarely, if ever, characterize a student as possessing no understanding. Almost always an individual possesses some relevant knowledge. Teachers need to find out what students already know and build on that. Few school-age children understand nothing about the problem "3 + 4." Even young children can quantify the set of 3, showing that they understand that three counters can represent the quantity 3. Rather than focusing on presence or absence of understanding, teachers should focus on the degree of understanding an individual demonstrates.

In the past, mathematical learning involved acquired information. Once information was acquired, understanding could be developed by then making connections with existing knowledge (Nolan, 1973); research has since revealed that incoming information must be connected to some other piece of knowledge in order for connections to continue to be built. Knowledge of a student's existing mathematical ideas is crucial so that the knowledge they are learning is not taught in isolation. In order to help students build understanding, teachers need to provide opportunities for the students to make multiple connections between their mathematical ideas and to think about ideas on multiple occasions so that they can both strengthen the relationships and also build additional connections.

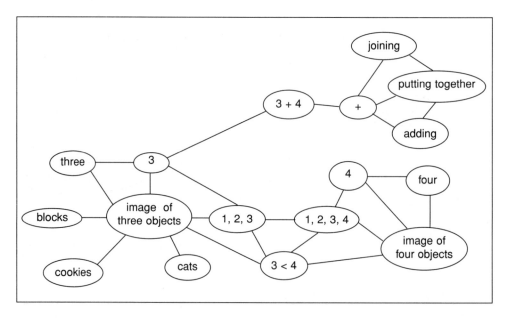

Figure 5.2. Child's solution path.

DETAILING CHILDREN'S MATHEMATICAL THINKING

Cognitive research provides teachers with details about understanding students' developmental trajectories. Mathematics education researchers delineate frameworks of children's developing thinking in various mathematical domains. Researchers have examined children's thinking in **counting** (Gelman & Gallistel, 1978; Steffe, von Glasersfeld, Richards, & Cobb, 1983), **addition and subtraction** (Briars & Larkin, 1984; Carpenter, 1985; Carpenter & Moser, 1982; Resnick, 1982; Riley, Greeno & Heller, 1983), **multiplication and division** (Ball, 1990; Carpenter, Ansell, Franke, Fennema, & Weisbeck, 1993; Greer, 1992; Kouba, 1989; Triosh & Graeber, 1990), **place value** (Fuson, 1990; Fuson & Briars, 1990; Hiebert & Wearne, 1992; Kamii, 2000), and **fractions** (Baker, 1994; Bennett, 1995; Mack, 1990; Post, Harel, Behr, & Lesh, 1991).

Students' mathematical domain-specific developmental trajectories highlight differences in their conceptualizations, show all students as possessing some mathematical understanding, and clarify the principles that make certain types of tasks more difficult than others. The trajectories most relevant for teaching young children include counting; the operations of addition, subtraction, multiplication, and division; place value; and geometry. Although this may seem like a large number of mathematical domains for teachers of young children to address, there are parallels that cross the students' trajectories. Consider the trajectories in students counting and addition/subtraction.[1]

Counting

Developing counting skills and number sense is central to young children's developing mathematical understanding. Much of the mathematics that students encounter throughout elementary school will draw on their understanding of numbers. Often, children begin counting by reciting the number words in sequence (e.g., 1, 2, 3, 4, 5). This type of reciting is called *rote counting.* Students are not required to be able to move objects while they recite the number words or understand anything about number quantities or relationships; however, rote counting is important for developing number sense. Children learn that numbers come before or after each other and that numbers are smaller or larger than one another. They also develop a sense of sequence and pattern.

Rote counting is only the beginning of students' developing rational counting skills. As children learn to rote count, they also begin to connect the counting sequence to sets of objects or *collections.* As young children

---

[1]Counting and addition/subtraction trajectories are elaborated here due to their prevalence in the early childhood curriculum.

begin to count collections, they learn that one counting word corresponds with each object they count (i.e., one-to-one correspondence). They learn that the last number they say as they count the last item in the collection is the total number of objects in that collection. They also learn that counting a collection means continuing to count in sequence until the objects are all counted. Although this may seem simple, young children often begin to count a collection and, in the middle of the counting the collection, decide to start over at 1 rather than continue from the last counting word. As they count, students also begin to notice that when they see two or three or even four objects together they can recognize the quantity without counting. Children develop their rote and rational counting skills in parallel.

As children develop counting skills and a sense of the relative size of numbers, the differences in quantity, and so on, they will begin to make connections among the number words (five), symbols (5), and the quantities (1 1 1 1 1). These connections take time for children to develop. Often, children can count sets and tell their teachers there are five objects in the set, but they do not know what a numeral 5 looks like. This situation should not stop children from counting larger numbers or solving problems. Instead, teachers should provide children with tools to help them make connections to the numeral (e.g., counting strips). Children's understanding of numbers develops as they engage with counting larger quantities and solving problems. Recognizing numerals is not required but is learned through such tasks.

Often, 4- and 5-year-olds can count well into the hundreds. Although a teacher may not feel comfortable asking students to count past 100, there are many advantages to counting past 20. Children have trouble counting in the teens because the number names (e.g., eleven) do not match the written symbols (e.g., 11) in a way that follows the pattern established with numbers less than 10. Children wonder where the words *eleven* or *thirteen* come from, whereas when they hear *fourteen*, they can recognize *four*, which indicates where the number belongs in the sequence. The same is true with *sixteen* or *seventeen*. There are very few sequence indicators in the teens to help children know what number comes next. Contrast that counting sequence with what happens in the twenties (e.g., *twenty-one*, *twenty-two*). This pattern, if extended down to the teens, would go *ten-one*, *ten-two*, *ten-three*. The teen number words make children's job of understanding and remembering the number sequence more difficult. Counting higher than twenty helps students begin to see the number system's pattern, consistency, and place value.

Extending Counting

Teachers often consider counting as primarily developing in 4-, 5-, and 6-year-old children; however, children's counting skills develop all through elementary school. Teachers need to attend to more than children's abilities to count rotely to 100. Some researchers suggest that students will not genuinely see the overall patterns of the number system until they count past 100. They argue that until children count past 100, they do not have the opportunity to think about the relationships among ones, tens, and hundreds and the iteration from ten ones making a 10 and ten tens making 100. Asking children to count past 100 (e.g., count from 80 to 130) often provides insight into the skills and understanding they have developed. For both assessment and development purposes, counting should not stop at 100. Also, teachers should not count solely by ones.

Four-year-olds with the opportunity to engage in many counting tasks learn to count past 100. These children become aware of the quantities that large numbers represent and what 50, 75, or even 150 objects might look like. Early on, children also see value in grouping the objects they count into sets of 2, 3, 5, or 10, especially as they count these large quantities. As they count past 100 and learn to group, children develop an understanding of numbers that provides the basis for operating on numbers (add, subtract, multiply, divide).

Operating on Numbers

Counting and patterns are often considered the core of the early childhood curriculum and the basis for the elementary school curriculum. Although this certainly may be true, counting and patterns are learned to support students in developing the skills and understanding necessary to operate on numbers and solve a variety of problems. Research provides extensive evidence that children as young as 4 years of age can solve quite sophisticated mathematics problems. For instance, Tessa has 8 baskets. There are 4 apples in each basket. How many apples does Tessa have in each of her baskets? The research shows that children are capable of solving a range of problems, and while solving problems develop a number of skills, including more developed counting and patterns skills. Many of the skills teachers hope children will develop already occur as a natural part of solving problems. There is no need to wait until children have sophisticated skills before engaging them in solving problems because children continue to develop their skills as they solve problems. More often than not, when teachers listen to young children solving problems, they realize that children possess many more skills than they realized.

Addition and Subtraction

Research shows that children all across the world solve problems in consistent ways. The strategies children use to solve problems develop at early ages, but these strategies may be quite different from the expected ones. The strategies and the progression of those strategies turn out to be quite robust; we can expect to see the same patterns across many children. First, children model the situation posed in the problem with some physical representation. Then, they move to more sophisticated strategies. Essentially, children's initial strategies follow exactly what the problem says (e.g., the children use counters to do what the problem says, such as "I had 9 and ate 3"). The research describing children's mathematical thinking is reported both in detail and in summaries in a number of different places (Carpenter, 1985; Fuson, 1992). The following is a set of initial ideas for thinking about strategies children use to solve addition, subtraction, multiplication, and division problems.

Researchers studying children's thinking in addition and subtraction outline both a set of problems that characterize the domain itself and a range of strategies that children typically use to solve the various problems. Four basic classes of addition and subtraction problems can be identified based on how children think about solving problems (see Table 5.1). Within each problem class, the problems involve the same type of action or relation. The problems can be characterized as involving 1) joining action, 2) separating action, 3) part–part–whole relation, or 4) comparison situation; however, within each class, different types of problems can be identified based on which quantity is the unknown. The distinctions within and across problem classes are clearest when examining how children solve different problems.

Students use a range of strategies to solve the different addition and subtraction problems. In the following situation, Rachel solves three different problems that most adults would solve by subtracting.

Teacher: TJ had 13 chocolate chip cookies. At lunch, he ate five of those cookies. How many cookies did TJ have left?

Rachel: [She puts out 13 counters, removes five of them, and counts the counters that remain.] There are eight.

Teacher: Good. Now here's the next one. Janelle has seven trolls in her collection. How many more trolls does she have to buy to have 11 trolls?

Rachel: [She puts out a set of seven counters and adds counters until there is a total of 11. She then counts the counters she added to the initial set to find the answer.] Four.

Teacher: That's good. Here's one more. Willy has 12 crayons. Lucy has seven crayons. How many more crayons does Willy have than Lucy?

Rachel: [She makes two sets of counters, one containing 12 counters and the other containing seven. She lines up the two sets in rows so that the set of seven matches the set of 12, and she counts the unmatched counters in the row of 12.] Five more.

Table 5.1. Addition and subtraction problems drawn from research on children's thinking

Joining action

Result unknown:

Anthony had five stickers. His teacher gave him three more stickers. How many stickers does Anthony have altogether?

Change unknown:

Anthony had five stickers. How many more stickers does he have to collect to have 11 stickers altogether?

Start unknown:

Anthony had some stickers. He bought five more stickers. Now Anthony has 11 stickers. How many stickers did Anthony have to start with?

Separating action

Result unknown:

Andrea had eight goldfish. She gave three of her goldfish to Claire. How many goldfish does Andrea have left?

Change unknown:

Andrea won 11 goldfish at the school fair. She gave some of her goldfish to her brother. Now, she has eight goldfish left. How many goldfish did Andrea give to her brother?

Start unknown:

Andrea had some goldfish in her fish bowl. She took eight fish out of her fishbowl, and she still has three goldfish left in the bowl. How many goldfish did Andrea have in her fishbowl to begin with?

Part–part–whole (no action)

Whole unknown:

There are seven girls and five boys waiting in line. How many children are waiting in line?

Part unknown:

There are 11 children playing soccer. Five of the children were boys. How many girls were playing soccer?

Comparison

Difference unknown:

Keisha has 13 toy cars. Tomas has five toy cars. How many more toy cars does Keisha have than Tomas?

Compare quantity unknown:

Tomas has five toy cars. Keisha has eight more toy cars than Tomas. How many toy cars does Keisha have?

Referent unknown:

Keisha has 13 toy cars. She has five more toy cars than Tomas. How many toy cars does Tomas have?

Rachel's solutions to these problems illustrate that children do not think of all addition problems or subtraction problems as alike. Rachel did not take away to solve each of these "subtraction" problems. She chose a different strategy to solve each problem, but there was consistency in her responses. In each case, Rachel directly modeled the action or relationship described in the problem. Rachel did what the problem asked, in the order the problem stated. Specifically, the first problem involved separating 5 from 13, the second involved adding more to the 7 until there were 11, and the third involved comparing two quantities. In each case Rachel's strategy mirrors these relationships. Rachel's strategies reflect the action in the problem and the location of the unknown.

As children engage in solving problems, their strategies develop. Direct modeling strategies, like Rachel's, are replaced initially by counting strategies, which are essentially abstractions of the direct modeling strategies. A counting strategy for Rachel's second problem would be thinking 7 and then counting 8, 9, 10, and 11 and keeping track of the number of units (4) as she counted. Although counting strategies continue to reflect the actions in the problems, they are more efficient and require a more sophisticated conception of number than direct modeling with manipulatives. As Rachel develops in her understanding, she will probably solve the problem by using what she knows about 10 ("7 + 3 = 10"), then adding one more to get 11. She will add these numbers to get the solution ("3 + 1 = 4"). The continued development of more abstract symbolic procedures can be characterized as progressive abstractions of children's attempts to model action and relations depicted in problems. Eventually, Rachel will recognize this problem as a subtraction problem, know "11 – 7" at the recall level, and tell her teacher that she knows this fact.

Rachel would solve multiplication and division problems with parallel solutions to those she used for addition and subtraction. Initially, Rachel would directly model the problem. For a problem like "Maritza has three baskets. She puts three balls in each basket. How many balls does Maritza have in her baskets altogether?," Rachel might draw three large circles on a piece of paper and draw three balls in each basket. To find her answer, she would count all of the balls. Eventually, Rachel would begin to solve the problem without making the baskets and saying to herself, "1, 2, 3, 4, 5, 6, 7, 8, 9." She would keep track of how many groups of three she had counted. Next, she may be able to skip count by threes ("3, 6, 9") or know that 2 groups of 3 equals 6. Then, she would realize that she needs one more group (i.e., 7, 8, 9) to reach her goal. (For more complete descriptions of distinctions among problems and the strategies children use to solve them, refer to Carpenter, 1985; Carpenter, Carey, and Kouba, 1990; Carpenter, Fennema, and Franke, 1997; and Carpenter, Fennema, Franke, Levi, & Empson, 1999.)

The parallel strategy development across the operations indicates that teachers need to think differently about the early childhood and early grades curriculum. First, if a child can directly model a problem, there is no reason why subtraction needs to be taught after addition. The subtraction problems would be no more difficult to solve than the addition problems. Furthermore, the multiplication and division problems are only more difficult because the children have to deal with groups of things, such as the basket of balls (not individual items). Dealing with these groups through direct modeling is not difficult for young children. The evidence on the development of children's mathematical thinking suggests that teachers should not avoid engaging children as young as 4 years old in solving mathematics problems, particularly if they pose the problems so that children can directly model them. The goal here is not to move more sophisticated mathematics to the earlier grades, but to engage children with the ideas that make sense to them and use those ideas to build further mathematical understanding. By ignoring the mathematical understanding that children have before coming to school, teachers communicate to children that their thinking is not important or not correct. Children quickly abandon using that knowledge.

Rather than assuming that children cannot solve any problems when they come to school, researchers now know that children come to school with knowledge that helps them think about how to solve addition and subtraction as well as multiplication and division problems. Researchers also know that there is a sequence to the developmental progression of children's strategies that can help teachers decide which problems to pose and why. Teachers need to realize that, even though individual children may vary in their responses, there are strategies that can serve as benchmarks to help teachers understand what to expect next in the development of children's strategies and mathematical understanding. In many cases, children will use strategies before they have been formally taught to use them. Researchers now have a sense of what children know before they start school, and this information can be used to connect children's existing knowledge to new knowledge.

GUIDING PRINCIPLES

Understanding the development of children's mathematical thinking provides information to help guide the mathematics curriculum for young children; it also points to some underlying principles to guide the teaching of mathematics. These principles can be enacted in a variety of ways depending on the teacher, students, and environment involved. The more a teacher focuses on the guiding principles, the more he or she will come to understand how they play out in his or her context. These principles relate to what it means to engage young children in mathematics and, specifically, to what it means to listen to and build on children's existing mathematical understanding.

Listening to Children's Mathematical Thinking

Listening to children's mathematical thinking requires that teachers have some notion of what to listen for, an understanding of what they might hear, and a way of linking the students' thinking to the mathematical understanding it portrays. Knowing what to listen for can be supported by what is known about the development of children's mathematical thinking; however, teachers also learn about the details of what to listen for as they begin to listen to students in the context of their teaching. Knowing what to expect from children will allow the teacher to understand what a child is trying to say, even if the child is unable to complete his or her thoughts. The teacher will know what questions to ask the child.

If the teacher doesn't know what strategy a child is using to solve a problem, then he or she can only ask the child to repeat his or her thinking. Then, the teacher may have to move on to another child. These options are of limited value. Although a teacher won't always know what strategy a child used or was trying to use, increased knowledge of children's thinking will ensure that the teacher will at least have a sense of the questions that will elicit additional details surrounding the student's strategy.

Listening for Specificity

Theory suggests that it is not sufficient just to recognize that children employ different strategies (Franke, Fennema, Carpenter, Ansell, & Berhend, 1998). Classroom practice that builds mathematical understanding requires teachers to identify the specific strategy a child uses and to articulate how that strategy fits with strategies other children use in solving the same type of problem. For instance, if a teacher posed the problem "70 – 26," the teacher might notice that children solved the problem in different ways: Some children used counters and others used paper and pencil. This knowledge might allow the teacher to predict in a general way what the child would do for a similar problem but would not necessarily help the teacher learn what problem to pose next or predict which strategy might develop next in the repertoire.

One child might model the problem by putting out 70 unit counters, taking away 26 of those counters, and counting those remaining counters. Another child might put out 7 ten blocks, then take away 26 counters by counting from 1 to 26 on the ten bars—eliminating two ten blocks and 6 squares from the third ten block—and counting the remaining units to find the answer. The teacher would be able to make a more specific determination about what to ask next or what problem to pose next if he or she noticed both strategies. Both children used counters, but they used them differently, and the different use reflects the children's understanding of the concept of ten. Neither child was able to operate using tens to solve the problem. The first child did not use tens at all, and the second child used tens to set up the problem but not to find the solution. In this case, a teacher might decide to pose a problem that would stretch the children's thinking and create an opportunity for the children to build knowledge about tens (e.g., "55 – 35," "38 + 20").

Knowing specifics of children's thinking can assist a teacher in figuring out what questions to ask to support children's learning. In the case of the second child, a teacher could ask, "Show me how you used these [pointing to the ten blocks]." This question would focus the child's attention on the ten blocks. The teacher could then say, "What if the problem were 70 take away

20? What would you do?" After solving that problem, the teacher could return to the problem "70 – 26." Knowing children's specific strategies allows the teacher to provide opportunities for children to connect their existing knowledge to new knowledge, and thus develop understanding. Having specific knowledge of children's thinking can allow for specific decisions to be made about how to build on children's mathematical thinking within individual interactions and within the context of the classroom (Carpenter, Reanke, Jacobs, & Fennema, 1998).

By listening to what a child says and reflecting on how it fits with what he or she knows about that child and about children's thinking in general, a teacher can create opportunities for connections to be made among children's existing knowledge or between children's existing knowledge and new knowledge. Teachers' ability to make sense of the child's thinking as well as their ability to consider how to make adjustments to maximize student learning demonstrates how noticing the specifics of students' thinking allows more moves on the teachers' part than focusing on the general surface features of the children's problem-solving strategies.

Listening for Children's Natural Language

One of the most striking consistencies across teachers who successfully create classroom environments where children's mathematical understanding develops is how these teachers discuss their students' solution strategies and how these strategies fit with the development of mathematical understanding (Carpenter et al., 1997; Franke, Fennema, Carpenter, Ansell, & Berhend, 1998). These teachers attend to the language that the children use to describe their problem-solving strategies, use the words they hear children using (e.g., goes around, put together, slide), and connect that informal language to the language of mathematics (e.g., circle, addition). Often, children invent informal names for shapes and mathematical concepts while interacting informally with one another. For instance, children may think of subtraction as "going away" or "flushing." When describing triangles, children may talk about "slanty lines" or "slides." These informal words are meaningful to the child and reveal the child's mathematical understanding. Although these words may not seem mathematical, they carry a great deal of mathematical meaning for the child, so teachers need to pay attention to words children use to talk about mathematics and find ways to connect this more informal language with formal mathematical language.

Representing Mathematical Thinking

Listening to students as a way to foster communication cannot be limited to listening to children talk about their strategies. Often, when solving problems children use some form of external representation. This representation may include (but is not limited to) counters, numerals written to support the solution, or picture drawings. Whatever the representation, it is part of the child's thinking about the problem and serves as a window into the child's understanding of the mathematical relationships in the problem. The representations also provide an opportunity for the teacher to enter into discussion with the student about his or her thinking by providing a context for asking questions that both inquire and scaffold student thinking.

In a combined kindergarten and first-grade classroom, students worked on counting collections. The students not only counted collections such as markers, chair legs, and letters in their first names, but they also recorded their counts on paper. Figure 5.3 shows just a few representations students

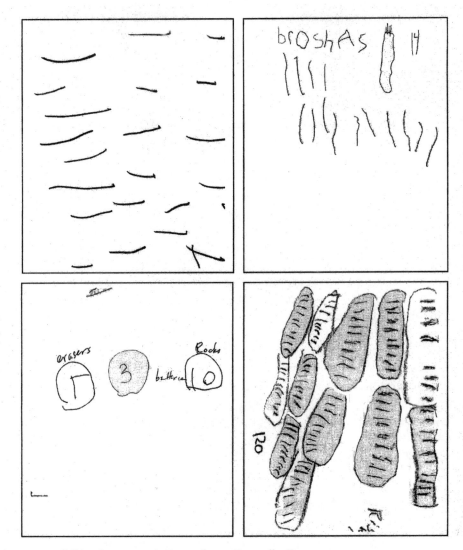

Figure 5.3. Children's representations of counting collections.

in this class produced. The number of objects students counted and the ways they represented those counts varied greatly. The children's representations tell a great deal about how they thought about numbers and how they engaged with counting. The responses in Figure 5.3 range from a child making a mark for each item counted, to labeling those counts with words and numerals, to grouping the objects in ways that reflect their counting. The representations capture not only how many items counted but also the students' abilities to organize, label, group, and represent their collections in multiple forms. The representations provide an opportunity for the teacher to ask questions such as, "So how many did you count altogether? How could we write that down?" or "How could I look at your paper and know how you counted altogether without counting all of them myself? Did you put them in groups?"

Children's representations also serve as vehicles for helping children share their thinking and supporting children in understanding each other's thinking. One child's representation can stimulate other children to make connections and obtain information they may not have otherwise. In the representation of the students' counting collections, students might discuss how some children grouped their collections in tens while others grouped them in twos. They might discuss that some used a numeral to represent the count while others used a quantity. Because the representations a child uses are a window into how the child thought about the problem, students as well as teachers need this information in order to come to some understanding of the child's thinking. Further sharing of these representations can foster discussion of mathematics and extend student understanding.

Communicating

Building communication in the classroom requires that teachers listen to students and that students listen to each other. The *Principles and Standards for School Mathematics* (National Council of Teachers of Mathematics, 2000), as well as other research reports and policy documents, argue for creating mathematical communication in the classroom, but often little is said about how to create this communication. This lack of information creates a perception that developing communication in the classroom is easy; however, because those participating in any conversation must be able to understand at some level what is being said in order for the conversation to be sustained, communicating mathematically can be quite complicated. Therefore, teachers and students must understand and talk about their own thinking and listen, understand, and talk about the thinking of others.

To communicate mathematically, teachers must be able to identify what each child is saying so that the teacher and students can ask questions that stimulate discussion and add to the conversation by building on what was said. Consider a child sharing a rather complicated strategy for solving a problem. One option for the teacher is to thank the child for sharing, then ask another child to share. Another option is to ask the child specific questions about the strategy to try to help the child articulate his or her thinking and enable the other children to figure out aspects of what the child has done. The first option is certainly a viable alternative, but in some cases, it may not lead to the most productive learning for either the child sharing or for the rest of the class. This option also does not foster communication.

The teacher must be able to identify the strategy the child is using in order to make a decision about how to respond and whether to pursue building communication. The teacher must also be prepared for another child in the class to pursue the strategy. Without knowing enough about the child's strategy and thinking about this strategy, the teacher will have a difficult time making a decision about how to pursue what was said and continue to create communication.

Communication in the classroom also requires a restructuring of the mathematics conversation from *teacher to student* to *student to student* with the teacher participating in the dialogue. This requires that the teacher find ways that the students can listen and understand one another. If the teacher does not listen to a child, the other children are not likely to listen either. If the student does not feel as if someone is listening, he or she may not be as likely to explicitly articulate his or her thinking.

Consider this situation: A child began sharing her explanation for a direct modeling strategy for a multi-digit comparison problem. The explanation was long and involved, so after 30 seconds, the teacher had already identified the child's strategy based on what she had said and how she had configured her materials. The teacher told the child that she could see what she was doing and thanked her for sharing her strategy. When the teacher asked to hear another student's strategy, the child said that she was not finished; she needed to share her whole strategy. The teacher watched and listened as the child completed her explanation. Afterwards, the teacher watched other children share their strategies with the class and noticed that the children were not allowed to cut short their explanations because the teacher or another student would ask for more information. The children in the class were learning that they needed to articulate their entire strategy to make sure all of the people in the class had an opportunity to understand.

Children who communicate about mathematics in the classroom do not just learn about mathematics. They learn about effective communication and specifically about articulating their thoughts in ways their audience will understand. As they learn mathematics, they learn to communicate, both of which are critical goals for children. When these concepts are learned together, children can make connections between communication issues and mathematics. Students need to learn how to say what they are thinking and adjust it to fit the context of the situation and the audience. They have to learn to listen to one another and value each other's knowledge. Teachers provide the opportunities that foster children's mathematical communication. Listening to students can enable a teacher to begin to create these opportunities.

Learning from Others

Communication in the classroom not only gives children the opportunity to articulate their way of thinking and feel acknowledged for having their own unique thoughts but also allows children to learn from each other. Research suggests that children and adults develop understanding as they interact within their social environment (Carraher, Carraher, & Schliemann, 1985; Lave, 1988; Saxe, 1991). This means that together the students and teachers construct understanding. The development of understanding in one child affects and is dependent on the understanding of the others the child interacts with. Students not only learn from listening to each other, but they construct understanding that depends on other children. One child may bring one piece of information that elicits a particular piece of information from another child and then feeds back to the first child. For example, when two students are counting collections together, one student may suggest grouping the collection in tens. As they count together, this child will provide support for the other. The other child may suggest that they write the symbol. Together, these students are building understanding of number relations. The understanding that children achieve is dependent on the environment they are placed in. Even within the context of a single classroom during different activities and under differing conditions, children will choose to solve problems in different ways (Ansell, 1995).

Rehearsing Strategies

Listening to children implies that teachers will encourage children to talk about their thinking. There may be advantages to this beyond the teacher learning about the children's thought processes—namely, the development of children's communication skills and the encouragement of the co-construction of mathematical meaning. Children may understand better through the process of telling. As children explain their solution processes, they notice places where what they did does not make sense, then make adjustments. Children may have miscounted, misinterpreted the problem, or miscalculated, but in the process of sharing their explanations, they make adjustments that build on their initial thinking. In a more complex form, children may also realize how they could have created an alternative or more sophisticated solution.

Consider again the child who was able to solve the problem "70 – 26" by initially putting out the ten blocks but then counting by ones to complete the solution. As this child explains his solution, he might recognize that he could have taken away the entire ten block instead of taking away the units one at a time. Describing the strategy in words and actions for others provides another opportunity for the child to think through the problem again, to create connections, and to see patterns in what he or she has done.

CONCLUSION

Teaching young children mathematics is rewarding but challenging. Children reward teachers daily with their inventive and intuitive thinking; yet, children's inventive thinking presses teachers to listen, make sense of, and in some way make use of that thinking in instruction. Together, learning theories and research on the development of children's mathematical thinking provide support for teachers as they attempt to engage their students in learning mathematics. Research suggests that engaging young children in working with pattern blocks and creating patterns is not enough. Young children can successfully count past 100; reason about addition, subtraction, multiplication, and division; and investigate space. This research not only details the development of students' strategies within mathematical domains but also provides principled ideas to help teachers learn in the context of their practice while they explore other mathematical domains.

Listening to children's mathematical thinking is complex, but what teachers hear can drive their immediate interactions as well as their long-term planning. Listening to students' mathematical thinking communicates to the students that they have mathematical ideas worth communicating. So, mathematics instruction should not only be about creating intriguing activities but should also focus on creating opportunities for students to challenge their mathematical thinking. Teachers should find ways to understand how students are thinking and make sense of student thinking in terms of the development of their strategies and the mathematics content. Teachers of young children have the potential to help each student see that he or she is a mathematician.

REFERENCES

Baker, S. (1994). *The development of children's fraction thinking in a first grade classroom.* Unpublished doctoral dissertation, University of Wisconsin, Madison.

Ball, D.L. (1990). Prospective elementary and secondary teachers' understanding of division. *Journal for Research in Mathematics Education, 21,* 132–144.

Baroody, A.J. (1989). Kindergarten's mental addition and single-digit combinations. *Journal for Research in Mathematics Education, 20,* 159–172.

Bennett, T.R. (1995). *Developing an understanding of fractions: An investigative study of student's thinking and cognitive development.* Unpublished doctoral dissertation, University of California, Los Angeles.

Briars, D.J., & Larkin, J. (1984). An integrated model of skill in solving elementary word problems. *Cognition and Instruction, 1*, 245–296.

Carpenter, T.P. (1985). Learning to add and subtract: An exercise in problem solving. In E.A. Silver (Ed.), *Teaching and learning mathematics problem solving: Multiple research perspectives* (pp. 17–40). Mahwah, NJ: Lawrence Erlbaum Associates.

Carpenter, T.P., Ansell, E., Franke, M.L., Fennema, E., & Weisbeck, L. (1993). Models of problem solving: A study of kindergarten children's problem-solving processes. *Journal for Research in Mathematics Education, 24*, 428–441.

Carpenter, T.P., Carey, D.A., & Kouba, V. (1990). A problem solving approach to the operations. In J. Payne (Ed.), *Mathematics for the young child* (pp. 111–132). Reston, VA: National Council of Teachers of Mathematics.

Carpenter, T.P., Fennema, E., & Franke, M.L. (1997). Cognitively guided instruction: A knowledge base for reform in primary mathematics instruction. *Elementary School Journal, 97*(1), 1–20.

Carpenter, T.P., Fennema, E., Franke, M., Levi, L., & Empson, S. (1999). *Children's mathematical thinking: Cognitively guided instruction.* Portsmouth, NH: Heinemann.

Carpenter, T.P., & Moser, J.M. (1982). The development of addition and subtraction skills. In T.P. Carpenter, J.M. Moser, & T.A. Romberg (Eds.), *Addition and subtraction: A cognitive perspective* (pp. 9–24). Mahwah, NJ: Lawrence Erlbaum Associates.

Carpenter, T.P., Reanke, M.L., Jacobs, V.R., & Fennema, E. (1998). A longitudinal study of invention and understanding in children's multidigit addition and subtraction. *Journal for Research in Mathematics Education, 29*(1), 3–20.

Carraher, T.N., Carraher, D.W., & Schliemann, A.D. (1985). Mathematics in the streets and in schools. *British Journal of Developmental Psychology, 3*, 21–29.

Chi, M.T.H., Glaser, R., & Rees, E. (1982). Expertise in problem solving. In R.J. Sternberg (Ed.), *Advances in the psychology of human intelligence.* Mahwah, NJ: Lawrence Erlbaum Associates.

Clements, D.H., Sarama, J., & Dibiase, A. (2000, September). *Report from the Conference on Early Childhood Mathematics Standards* (Invited address). ExxonMobil Annual Conference, Falls Church, VA.

Franke, M.L., Fennema, E., Carpenter, T., Ansell, E., & Berhend, J. (1998). Understanding teachers' self-sustaining change in the context of professional development. *Teaching and Teaching Education, 14*(1), 67–80.

Fuson, K.C. (1990). Conceptual structures for militant numbers: Implications for learning and teaching multidigit addition, subtraction, and place value. *Cognition and Instruction, 7*, 343–403.

Fuson, K.C. (1992). Research on whole number addition and subtraction. In D. Grouws (Ed.), *Handbook of research on mathematics teaching and learning* (pp. 243–275). New York: Macmillan/McGraw-Hill.

Fuson, K.C., & Briars, D.J. (1990). Using a base-ten blocks learning and teaching approach for first- and second-grade place-value and multidigit addition and subtraction. *Journal for Research in Mathematics Education, 21*, 80–206.

Gelman, R. (1994). Constructivism and supporting environments. In D. Tirosh (Ed.), *Implicit and explicit knowledge: An educational approach* (pp. 52–82). Westport, CT: Ablex Publishing.

Gelman, R., & Gallistel, C.R. (1978). *The child's understanding of number.* Cambridge, MA: Harvard University Press.

Greer, B. (1992). Multiplication and division as models of situations. In D. Grouws (Ed.), *Handbook of research on mathematics teaching and learning* (pp. 276–296). New York: Macmillan/McGraw-Hill.

Hiebert, J., & Carpenter, T.P. (1992). Learning mathematics with understanding. In D. Grouws (Ed.), *Handbook of research on mathematics teaching and learning* (pp. 65–97). New York: Macmillan/McGraw-Hill.

Hiebert, J., Carpenter, T., Fennema, E., Fuson, K., Wearne, D., Murray, H., Olivier, A., & Human, P. (1997).*Making sense: Teaching and learning mathematics with understanding.* Portsmouth, NH: Heinemann.

Hiebert, J., & Wearne, D. (1992). Links between teaching and learning place value with understanding in first grade. *Journal for Research in Mathematics Education, 22*, 98–122.

Kamii, C. (2000). *Young children reinvent arithmetic* (2nd ed.). New York: Teachers College Press.

Kouba, V. (1989). Children's solution for equivalent set multiplication and division problems. *Journal for Research in Mathematics Education, 20,* 147–158.

Lave, J. (1988). *Cognition in practice: Mind, mathematics and culture in everyday life.* New York: Cambridge University Press.

Mack, N.K. (1990). Learning fractions with understanding: Building on informal knowledge. *Journal for Research in Mathematics Education, 21,* 16–32.

National Council of Teachers of Mathematics. (2000). *Principles and Standards for School Mathematics.* Retrieved from http://standards.nctm.org

Newell, A., & Simon, H. (1972). *Human problem solving.* Upper Saddle River, NJ: Prentice Hall.

Nolan, J.D. (1973). Conceptual and rote learning in children. *Teachers College Record, 75,* 251–258.

Piaget, J. (1954). *The construction of reality in the child.* New York: Basic Books.

Piaget, J. (1973). *To understand is to invent.* New York: Grossman.

Post, T.P.R., Harel, G., Behr, M.J., & Lesh, R. (1991). Intermediate teachers' knowledge of rational number concepts. In E. Fennema, T.P. Carpenter, & S.J. Lamon (Eds.), *Integrating research on teaching and learning mathematics* (pp. 177–198). Albany: State University of New York Press.

Resnick, L.B. (1982). Syntax and semantics in learning to subtract. In T.P. Carpenter, J.M. Moser, & T.A. Romberg (Eds.), *Addition and subtraction: A cognitive perspective.* Mahwah, NJ: Lawrence Erlbaum Associates.

Riley, M.S., Greeno, J.G., & Heller, J.I. (1983). Development of children's problem solving ability in arithmetic. In H.P. Ginsburg (Ed.), *The development of mathematical thinking* (pp. 153–196). San Diego: Academic Press.

Rumelhart, D.E., & Norman, D.A. (1978). Accretion, tuning, and restructuring: Three modes of learning. In J.W. Cotton & R. Klatzky (Eds.), *Semantic factors in cognition* (pp. 37–53). Mahwah, NJ: Lawrence Erlbaum Associates.

Saxe, G.B. (1991). *Culture and cognitive development: Studies in mathematical understanding.* Mahwah, NJ: Lawrence Erlbaum Associates.

Steffe, L.P., von Glasersfeld, E., Richards, J., & Cobb, P. (1983). *Children's counting types: Philosophy, theory, and application.* New York: Praeger.

Triosh, D., & Graeber, A.O. (1990). Evoking cognitive conflict to explore preservice teacher's thinking about division. *Journal for Research in Mathematics Education, 21,* 98–108.

Classroom Practices that Support Children's Mathematical Ideas

6

Elham Kazemi

Teachers of young children have the unique opportunity to help shape what children think about mathematics. Learning about children's mathematical thinking has inspired many teachers to pay close attention to children's ideas and to create classroom environments that support meaningful learning (Edwards, Gandini, & Forman, 1993; Kamii & Housman, 1999; National Council of Teachers of Mathematics, 2000). Chapter 5 describes a number of principles that can guide the teaching of mathematics. Among these principles is the importance of listening to the details of children's mathematical ideas, encouraging children's informal and natural language, and allowing children to represent and share their thinking with others. Keep these principles in mind while examining the dimensions of classroom practices that can bring them to life.

This chapter describes the features of classroom life that support and develop children's mathematical ideas—how classroom resources, tasks, and conversations can promote understanding. To build children's understanding, teachers need support to continually learn about their students' ideas and about mathematics. Teachers can develop relationships with colleagues that help support their own learning. This chapter also shares some strategies for including parents as collaborators in children's education.

IDEAS FOR STOCKING AND CREATING YOUR CLASSROOM

What kinds of resources and activities are needed for a mathematically rich environment?

Manipulatives

Manipulatives allow children to make representations of what they are beginning to understand. Many classrooms have a good supply of a variety of manipulatives for children to use as they develop their sense of number. Useful materials include a variety of counters, such as commercially available linking cubes and base ten blocks, as well as other objects that can be used as counters, such as beans and pasta. A supply of number lines that extend past 20, measuring tape, hundreds boards, and play money are also valuable as children explore patterns in our number system. Make sure that these manipulatives are easily accessible to children, and give children a choice over which manipulative to use and when to use them.

Choice over these manipulatives is important for several reasons. First, different manipulatives allow for different kinds of explorations with number. Counters that can be easily put into groups of tens, such as linking cubes, can be used as children work on understanding the relationship between tens and ones. Children can build groups of 10 as well as take these groups apart. In contrast, beans do not have that same flexibility. Second, it is useful for children to be able to use more than one manipulative. For example, children can use a number line or a hundreds chart to find where 17 is and what the numeral looks like, but counters can help them think about how big a quantity 17 is. Finally, which manipulative children use can inform you about their understanding. For example, a child's choice to use tens bars instead of just unit cubes to represent and to add two numbers demonstrates his or her developing understanding of how numbers are composed.

A mathematically rich classroom also should have resources that develop children's spatial, measurement, and data-gathering skills. A common collection of commercially available materials include measuring tape, scales, balances, pattern blocks, graph paper, and building blocks. Consider also having materials that children create themselves as they explore their surroundings. For example, to develop a solid understanding of what a triangle is, children should have opportunities to explore essential features of a triangle by making cardboard cutouts or posters of triangles in different sizes and orientations. When children only explore standard, commercially made triangles, they come to believe that a triangle can only look like an equilateral triangle pointing upward (Clements

& Sarama, 2000). Ball (1992) reminded us that manipulatives themselves do not hold meaning. What is important is how children use them and whether children have an opportunity to explore multiple representations of the same idea in order to develop flexible and well-connected understanding.

Representations and Sharing Ideas

In a mathematically rich environment, children should represent and share their thinking. This is important because children need to understand as early as possible that mathematical work involves reasoning, discussing relationships among quantities, and finding ways to express their understanding of different problem situations. Rich opportunities exist throughout the day for children to explore mathematics. Encourage children to keep individual journals to record their thinking through pictures, words, or numbers. You can also place charts around the room recording the strategies of several children for all to discuss and compare, or you can display wall posters of word problems that students have written from their everyday experiences, from literature books, or from a topic they are studying. Provide pencils and paper in the dramatic play area for children to make receipts of restaurant orders, tally up the price of groceries, or survey their friends. Include a place on the classroom calendar for children to tally how many students are present and absent, how many lunches are being bought or brought to school, or how many days have been sunny or rainy.

Consider devoting a classroom center to the writing and sharing of mathematics problems. This center would always be open for children to play at during free time, but evidence around the room wouldn't be limited to the development of number sense. Children develop their spatial sense, for example, by making maps and creating a town in the block area or using measuring tools in the sand box to develop a sense of equivalence.

A mathematically rich environment encourages children to work independently and together to solve and talk about mathematical situations:

- How many people can fit in the dramatic play area at one time?
- How many different ways can we sit on the rug so that everyone can see the story?
- About how many books do you think fit on one shelf in the library?
- Let's count by fours as we line up to go out for recess.
- If we have 26 juice boxes, do we have enough for everyone?
- How much taller is Maria than Juan?
- How big is your foot?

All of these questions help students to realize that mathematics is practical and can be applied to their everyday lives.

SPECIFIC MATHEMATICAL TASKS

In the early years of school, children develop a sense of number. They explore what it means to join, pull apart, and group numbers. Although it is too early (in many cases) to introduce formal mathematical language, teachers can encourage and build on children's informal language to understand mathematical relationships. For example, young children may not yet know how multiplication is represented symbolically, but they can try to solve word problems that include grouping, such as three plates with two cookies on each plate, by modeling the action in the problem. In addition to a sense of a number, young children develop spatial skills while building, mapping, and measuring. They further learn to question and organize their experiences through investigations with data.

Counting Collections

Counting collections is a simple task that can be repeated numerous times across the year and varied easily. The goal is for children to find and count a collection; it can be anything found around the room: bottle caps, raisins in a box, blocks, or books on a shelf. At first, the task can simply be to count the collections. As children repeat this task, variations can be included. You can ask students whether they can make a representation of their count on paper and observe how the students' representations change over time. You can also encourage students to find different ways of grouping or skip counting. Ask students to estimate their count first and then verify the estimate. How close are their estimations? Students can monitor whether their estimations get better as the year progresses.

It is also important to sit with a group of children as they count and ask questions that help expand their number sense. If a child has reached 20, you can ask

- How many more do you need to get to 25?
- How many tens are there in 20?
- What was the number before 19?

The advantage of counting collections is that this open-ended task allows children at different ability levels to find an entry point into the activity. At the same time, it allows the teacher to vary the task enough to challenge children as their abilities develop.

Drawing on Everyday Experiences

Many teachers take advantage of the smallest moments during the school day to infuse mathematics: transitions, lining up, taking attendance or the lunch count, and passing out materials. Such times provide continued opportunities for children to rehearse their rote counting and to begin to see patterns and relationships among numbers. Children who know that there are 20 students in the class work hard to figure out how many are left if two people are absent. Some may count all of the students to see how many people are present. Others might look up at the number line and count two back. Still others may try starting with different numbers and counting until they find the right number. As you listen to children's strategies, you can assess what mathematics strategies they are using. You can also encourage students to try out each other's strategies.

Children's everyday games can be another source for mathematical investigations. Penner and Lehrer (2000) described first- and second-graders' investigations about a game of "Mother May I?" In this game, one child is *Mother* and the rest of the players line up and try to move toward and tag Mother. As the players ask permission to move, Mother responds by telling them how to move—by taking baby steps, giant steps, turn steps, or foot-to-foot steps. The children realized that when they formed a line opposite Mother, they did not all start at the same distance away from her. Some of them had an unfair advantage in getting to Mother first. The children explored other geometric models such as triangles, squares, and circles to see which one would provide a fair playing space. Because young children have a strong sense of fairness, this question provided the motivation for an extended investigation of geometric properties.

Listening to children's thinking does not mean reinventing the curriculum. Although you must be purposeful in choosing and facilitating tasks, much of the mathematical work in which children engage can be drawn from their own experiences. Consider ways to "mathematize" the stories that children tell about themselves. Children often come to school telling stories about what they did over the weekend: a party they went to, a new toy they got, or something they saw on television. Such stories can be the inspiration for mathematical problems. For example, if Antonia brings in pictures of her new puppy, encourage the children to make up mathematical stories about the puppy:

- If her puppy eats two biscuits every afternoon for 3 days, how many biscuits will he have eaten altogether?

- Antonia had eight socks. When she came home, she saw that her puppy had chewed up two of them. How many socks does she have left?

Mathematizing children's own stories is a wonderful way to develop relevant and engaging problems, especially if you feel commercially-made resources do not reflect and connect to the students you teach.

Creating Data Displays

Young children can explore data collection and analysis using simple charts. They can begin by working with daily surveys. Initially, daily surveys may take the form of simple yes–no questions. (Economopoulos & Murray, 1998). A chart divided into two columns labeled *yes* or *no* can display the day's survey question:

- Do you like raisins?
- Do you have an older sister or brother?
- Do you like working on the computer?

Ask children to record their names under the appropriate column and to describe what they learned from the survey.

This kind of task can elicit a number of different mathematical ideas. Children can make comparisons between the number of students responding yes or no. With continued experience, they might become dissatisfied with the two categories and want to make further distinctions. Perhaps some people like carrots a lot, whereas others only like them a little bit. Or maybe some people like carrots only if they are cooked, whereas others like them raw. Such observations will help children learn that an important part of data collection is writing questions that everyone will interpret in a similar way and providing choices that will capture the range of possible responses. Children's analysis of these surveys can also spur action. Perhaps a survey on the kinds of food children like would provide data on which snacks to purchase for an upcoming field trip. In this way, children can also learn about the purposeful nature of data collection.

You can also guide students' experiences with more open-ended questions, such as "What do children like to play at recess?" In contrast to the yes-no questions described previously, children will need to develop a plan for collecting the data and make choices about how to organize and represent the data. This kind of task can allow you to assess how children make sense of a more complicated data set. For example, each child could survey the class to find out what game each person played that day at recess. After the survey is completed, you can invite the children to find a way to represent the data on paper. Your observations of what the children do can provide a window into their emergent understandings about representing and classifying data.

Before children make their representations, they will need to decide how to organize the data. One child might put soccer and basketball together under the category of "team sports" while another might keep each activity distinct. Some might organize data into two categories: playing together or playing alone. Once they have their categories, their representations will differ as well. Some children may choose to draw pictures of the different activities and the number of people associated with that activity. Others may begin to create symbols for each category. The remaining children may begin to organize the data into columns or rows.

The diversity in children's displays may provide you with a vehicle for facilitating conversations in which children compare and make sense of each other's displays. They can talk about their choices, both in grouping and displaying their data, and the observations they made about the data. They can discuss which displays were easier for others to understand as well as how different displays helped them see a different dimension of the data. Such activities can help children begin to appreciate the way they can communicate ideas graphically.

Data investigations can also be naturally connected to children's scientific work. Collecting and analyzing data is a powerful tool for answering scientific questions, generating new questions, and making predictions. For example, children often grow plants and vegetables at school. They could collect data about whether plants grow faster in the sunshine or shade with smaller or greater amounts of water. Another example can be drawn from children's everyday experience with painting. Paintings are often hung up or put outside to dry before children can take them home. They can collect data to determine how much quicker their work will dry if it is put outside and whether it makes a dramatic difference. Children could collect data on when they get hungry or sleepy in the morning to determine when it is the best time to take their morning snack or nap. Through all of these ways, children can explore and develop their skills working with data.

Creating Problems from Children's Literature

You might be wondering if you need a particular curriculum to best support children's thinking or if you have to reinvent everything on your own. As many of the tasks described here demonstrate, coming up with problem situations for children to explore mathematics does not have to be time-consuming or linked to any particular curriculum. You can use whatever resources are available to draw out children's ideas, including children's literature. Books can inspire a variety of problem situations, ones that involve number, data, or geometric sense. They also provide a way for teachers to link mathematical investigations to contexts and themes with which children are familiar. For suggested books and activities, see Burns (1992, 1995), Griffiths and Clyne (1991), and Moyer (2000) as well as other resources listed at the end of this chapter.

Books do not need to have obvious mathematical themes in order for teachers to draw them into mathematics lessons. In *Aunt Flossie's Hats (and Crab Cakes Later),* two girls visit their Aunt on Sunday afternoons (Howard, 1991). They treasure the stories Aunt Flossie tells as they play with her many hats. After reading this book, children can design their own special hats. They can create a timeline of the memories each hat in the book inspired. In addition, they can solve a variety of word problems (or create their own) such as the following:

- Sarah went to the closet to get Aunt Flossie's hats. There were three shelves, and on each shelf, she found four hats. How many hats did she find?

- Aunt Flossie had collected 15 hats. How many more does she need to have 20 altogether?

- Sarah tried on four hats, and I tried on five hats. How many hats did we put on altogether?

Children's literature provides inspiration to vary the kind of problems that students attempt to solve—ones with joining and separating actions, as well as ones that involve grouping.

Aunt Flossie's Hats (and Crab Cakes Later) can be the source of interesting data investigations, too. Children can survey one another to find out how many hats each person in the class has. They can play with different ways of organizing the data. Perhaps one child will make a list. Another might create piles or sections on a page for everyone with the same number of hats. After collecting the data, the children could talk about the patterns they see in their data. In this way, children begin to appreciate how to collect, organize, and interpret data.

Noticing Children's Mathematical Reading

Children's interests in reading and storytelling can provide rich opportunities for them to discuss number, location, shape, size, and spatial relationships. Ginsburg and Seo (2000) described the kinds of mathematical ideas that are at play even as preschoolers start to explore books. They described the activities of three children as they pretended to read a book together. The children gave each other directions about how to hold the book and whether the book was at the right orientation and angle. The children noticed a lot of pumpkins drawn on one page and stretched their arms further and further apart as they wondered how much "a lot" was. As they continued to read, they rated how scary the book was. Their talk around the story brought out mathematical ideas about perspective-taking, orientation, and relative and absolute magnitude.

In *Feisty Females: Inspiring Girls to Think Mathematically* (Karp, Brown, Allen, & Allen, 1998), the authors encourage teachers to do second readings of literature with their students and to ask them, "What mathematics do you find in this book?" In each chapter of *Feisty Females,* the authors describe how this process of mathematizing literature provokes various mathematical investigations. For example, they describe an investigation related to the book *Wilma Unlimited: How Wilma Rudolph Became the World's Fastest Woman* (Krull, 1996), which tells about the childhood difficulties of the Olympic star Wilma Rudolph. When the children were asked to find the mathematics in the book, they identified a number of events in the book that allowed them to think about magnitude, such as the length of Wilma's races, her 50-mile bus ride to the hospital twice a week when she was battling polio as a child, and her premature birth weight of 4 pounds. The authors also describe a more prolonged investigation the students engaged in as they compared each others' birth weights and childhood diseases, discovering that measles and mumps were infrequently experienced and polio was not at all. Thus, they had opportunities to relate their findings to the discovery of various vaccines.

MATHEMATICAL TALK

Teachers want to make their classrooms engaging and inviting places for students to learn, and they work hard to create tasks that are motivating and fun. In supporting the development of children's mathematical ideas, it is crucial to pay attention to the way mathematics is treated in classroom conversations. The idea of engaging children in what Wood, Cobb, and Yackel (1991) called *genuine conversations* about mathematics means taking students' ideas seriously.

During the first month of school, you set the norms of how children will talk and listen to one another. You should help students learn that you are interested in their thinking and ask them to explain how they figured something out. For some children, asking, "Why did you do that?" may signal that they did something wrong. It is important to convey that you are interested in how students reached their answers, not just the answer itself. It is important to emphasize and practice what happens when someone shares his or her thinking—what should other students be doing? How do students respond respectfully after listening to someone else's thinking? Encouraging children to ask one another questions when they are confused or when they miss an explanation can demonstrate to students that they have an important and active role to play during discussions.

Eliciting and Building Student Thinking

Listening to children's ideas begins with asking them to share their thinking and listening to them until they complete their explanations. Several strategies can begin the same way but end differently, so it is important not to prematurely assume how the child figured something out. A child may start counting up from 4 to 11 to find the difference between the two numbers but may have different ways of keeping track of that count. The following example from a first-grade class shows the way one teacher routinely asked students to share their thinking:

> Ms. Frances: Can someone circle today's date on the calendar? [Sue marks a ring around 17]. Okay. Our field trip to the aquarium is on the 21st day of the month. How many more days before we go? [Children spend a minute or so figuring out the problem. Ms. Frances waits until about half the hands are raised, then calls on Pat.]
>
> Pat: There are four days before our trip.
>
> Ms. Frances: How did you figure that out, Pat?
>
> Pat: I counted 17 [pause], 18, 19, 20, 21 [Holds up a finger with each count.] So the answer is 4.
>
> Ms. Frances: Good job, Pat. Did anyone else solve the problem another way?
>
> Mike: Well, I know that 17 plus 3 is 20, and 1 more than 20 is 21, so 3 and 1 is 4.
>
> Ms. Frances: Good thinking. Did anyone solve the problem another way? [Children explain the various strategies they used to solve the problem. Most of the time, Ms. Frances just listens.] Four days before our trip. Is that more or less than a week away? [Class discusses using the calendar, counting, and comparing 4 and 7 to decide on the answer.] (Carpenter, Carey, & Kouba, 1990, pp. 125–126)

As discussed in Chapter 5, it is important to ask questions until you understand the details of their students thinking. Notice that Ms. Frances created a problem from an everyday routine—in this case, the calendar activity—and then asked Pat to explain his thinking. Pat seemed very comfortable telling and showing her what he did. Many children may need support to develop clear explanations. For example, Pat may have only stated that he counted and ended his explanation there. If Pat had not given a complete explanation, Ms. Frances could have asked him to explain how he counted. She could have initiated discussions with her class about what counts as a complete explanation. Knowing how Pat counted is important because it reveals something about his mathematical understanding. In this case, we learn that Pat can count on from 17. He didn't need to count out 17 to begin with, and he has a way to keep track of his count so that he can remember how many numbers are between 17 and 21. When a child says, "I can't explain," "I just knew it," or "I did it in my head," you can follow up by asking questions like, "What numbers were you thinking of in your head?" "Where did you start?" or "If you had to explain it to someone else who really didn't understand, what would you say?".

Another strategy is asking multiple students to explain their strategies. Thus, you convey that you are not only interested in the answer but also in the many possible paths to finding the answer. This will also give you the opportunity to hear more than one child's thinking so that you can assess what the students understand. Although students often feel compelled to follow a strategy when the teacher models it—even if they don't understand it— students are less likely to adopt a peer's strategy if they don't understand how it works. Sharing the intellectual work across the class conveys to the children that their ideas are taken seriously (Kazemi & Stipek, 2001).

Ms. Frances also listened carefully to a number of different strategies. She was listening for the range of strategies in her classroom. Mike's strategy is more efficient than Pat's. Instead of counting up by ones, he is able to use landmarks, like 20, to move from 17 to 21. As Ms. Frances listened to her students, she might note which children use which strategies, how comfortable they are with those strategies, and whether children understand why each other's strategies work. These observations are important because she can use them to push her students' thinking. For example, there may be a number of students who are comfortable with Pat's counting-by-ones strategy but have not yet tried to make their counts more efficient like Mike's. She could ask the children to compare those two strategies and explain why each worked. Then, she could pose a new problem and challenge them to try Mike's strategy. These kinds of conversations and tasks can facilitate children to reflect on the mathematical processes they are using, develop a repertoire of strategies, and be able to make choices about efficient ways to solve problems.

Teachers should use the previous problem to create the next one so that they are building from a context that the children already understand. For example, at the end of the Ms. Frances's exchange with her students, she asked them whether they were more or less than a week away from the field trip. She introduced a different kind of problem situation, one that involved comparison, and allowed the students to really think about the problem situation and not just apply an operation they have been practicing. Comparison problems can often be hard for children (Carpenter, Fennema, & Franke, 1996). By listening to the children's ideas, Ms. Frances can assess how students' understandings are developing.

Encouraging Children to Look for Patterns

Teachers of young children know that children love to make observations of the world around them. Many people would characterize mathematics as a language of patterns. As children develop number sense, they develop the ability to reason quantitatively. While many early childhood programs include much work with geometric patterns, it is important to remember that children can also explore numerical patterns. Does the following scenario seem familiar? Alex, a 5-year-old, has discovered a pattern comparing her age to the age of her brother, Paul, who is 2 years younger.

> Alex: When Paul is 6, I'll be 8. When Paul is 9, I'll be 11. When Paul is 12, I'll be 14 . . . [she continues until Paul will be 18, and she will be 20].

> Adult: My word! How on earth did you figure all that out?

> Alex: It's easy. You just go "three-FOUR-five" (clapping on the four). You go "six-SEVEN-eight." You go "nine-TEN-eleven." (Clements, 2001, p. 271)

By conveying a curiosity about numbers and praising children when they discover new relationships and patterns, you can encourage students to make mathematical observations about the world around them. Following Alex's discovery, her teacher could ask her as well as other children in the class if they could find similar patterns between Alex's age and an older or younger classmate. Teachers can help bring children's informal mathematical ideas to an explicit level of awareness (Clements, 2001).

Responding to Students' Mistakes

When students stumble or use an incorrect strategy to solve a problem, teachers have wonderful opportunities to explore and develop their students' ideas. Although instinctively you may want to step in and show the student the right way to do the problem, by letting the student correct his or her own mistake you can learn a lot about when and why students stumble. It is just as important to find out how a child is thinking when a mistake is made as when a correct solution is reached. Perhaps a child is consistently miscounting or skipping over a number. Perhaps a child is applying a comfortable, well-understood strategy to a wholly new problem situation. Or a child didn't quite understand what was happening in the problem. Maybe a child will find the inconsistency on his or her own just by being asked to explain. In classrooms that honor children's thinking, children must know that they are asked to explain their thinking at all times and not just when they are correct or incorrect.

ASSESSMENT

Whether making informal or formal observations, assessment is a tool for teachers to develop more detailed knowledge of their children's understanding and to document that knowledge in a way that will enable them to make instructional decisions and to communicate with parents and colleagues (Webb & Coxford, 1993). Setting up fruitful mathematical tasks and facilitating mathematical conversations clearly are important elements of being a mathematics teacher, but continually weaving assessment into instruction enables a teacher to reflect on children's activities and children's talk. Otherwise, teachers can set up engaging tasks but not be as aware of the mathematical growth that children are making.

One of the criticisms of the mathematics reform movement has been that children have a lot of fun in class but may not learn a lot. Purposeful and planned assessment strategies can enable you to have a rich record of your children's mathematical growth. Jan Mokros and her colleagues (1995) suggested that you keep in mind the following questions as you monitor children's mathematical work:

1. Do students come up with their own strategies for solving problems, or do they expect you to tell them exactly what to do? What do their strategies tell you about their mathematical understanding?

2. Do students understand that there are different strategies for solving problems? Do they articulate their strategies and listen to others' strategies?

3. Do students choose tools and materials that help them with their work? Do they use these materials and tools effectively?

4. Do students have ideas about how to record their work, or does writing and drawing about what they have done seem difficult for them?

Because children's ideas can develop in remarkable ways in the early years, your role in documenting that evolution is critical. Many of the skills that you use to document children's emergent literacy skills can be used to document their mathematical ideas, including the use of anecdotal records, interviews, and portfolios of student work.

Keeping Anecdotal Records

Anecdotal records are informal observations made while children are working on an activity. You may have a particular topic or issue to look for as children are working, such as how children are keeping track of their counts or how children are writing down their strategies. Typically, anecdotal records are made as teachers monitor or interact with children and the teacher is struck by something the child did. You can keep track of your records in a variety of ways, such as using electronic files for each child or using a three-ring binder with a tab for each child. Some teachers keep a clipboard with Post-it notes or peel off labels. When they notice something they want to remember, they quickly scribble it down and then file those notes in a folder or binder at the end of the day (Strickland & Strickland, 2000).

You can use these brief observational notes to follow up with children at appropriate times. Parents and administrators will also appreciate the detailed examples that you can provide at conference time with such a system in place. James St. Clair, a teacher in a bilingual kindergarten, used anecdotal records within a demanding schedule (St. Clair, 1993). He jotted down observations of children's mathematical activities on index cards to include in their portfolios. One of his observations reads:

> 11/15: While making a clay pizza with meatballs, two children approached Eduardo with a clipboard and three jars of beans, asking him to estimate the number in each jar. I had filled the three jars with beans, which had 15, 25, and 50 beans in them. Eduardo estimated 14, 30, and 50. I was impressed! (1993, p. 67)

St. Clair could also record how Eduardo made those estimations. What kind of strategy was he using? Keeping a record of such observations can allow you to see growth in children's mathematical thinking over time. St. Clair (1993) noted that his informal observations also allow him to see children in a variety of contexts, especially when they are not aware that they are being observed and are not trying to perform for someone else. You can regularly review your anecdotal records to reflect on what you see your students learning. A review of the records can also help you notice which students have not been observed lately and make it a point to watch children who might have been overlooked. The power of using anecdotal records is the ability to review concrete moments recorded over time, to discover patterns in students' responses to tasks, and to make judgments about the kind of learning taking place in the classroom.

Using Interviews

Interviewing a child provides a more in-depth look at his or her mathematical understanding. In order to be able to conduct interviews with children, you have to be creative in the way you use classroom time. Interviews typically last 10–15 minutes. Thus, you might need to conduct interviews during independent reading time, play time, or center work when the other children are busy and do not have to rely on you to facilitate the activity. To create an interview, the teacher should identify three to five tasks that can be posed to each child. Together, the tasks should provide information about the student's current level of understanding. The goal of the interview is to elicit the child's thinking, not to teach a new skill to the child.

The Teacher's Guide to Flexible Interviewing in the Classroom (Ginsburg, Jacobs, & Lopez, 1998) is a good resource for explaining how to structure and interact with children in an interview. If the interview is meant to tap children's current understanding of number, the following tasks might be posed:

1. Count a collection of 50 objects. Listen to the child's oral count and ask the child to write the numbers.

2. Pose a word problem and document the child's strategy.

3. Ask the child to make up a word problem for a particular number sentence such as $7 + 5 = ?$ or $7 + ? = 12$.

You can pose the same set of interview questions several times throughout the year. For example, with the first task, you could document a child's ability to count the same collection three or more times across the year. Using this task as a focused assessment tool over the course of the year can allow you to document a child's growth in rote counting, symbolic representation, and knowledge of skip counting or grouping.

Children develop their problem-solving strategies from directly modeling the action, to using counting on or counting back strategies, to putting together and pulling apart numbers based on relationships children have learned about our number system. To document growth in children's strategies, you can pose a similar kind of problem at three points across the year. Even though children might be able to successfully solve the problem at each of the three points, documenting the strategy students use can provide evidence of progressively sophisticated thinking. Asking children to solve a word problem as well as to generate one can provide evidence for the ways in which children are making sense of the problem situation and symbolic notations.

Collecting Portfolios of Student Work

Collecting portfolios of students' work is another way to record students' growth. However, be strategic about which pieces of work to include in a child's portfolio. Keeping everything is not helpful because the sheer volume becomes overwhelming to review and interpret. Instead, think about the main mathematical ideas you are working on during the school year and the various mathematical strands (e.g., number, measurement, data analysis). For each of those strands, keep pieces of student work that show early understanding, developing understanding, and fluency (at the standard appropriate for the grade level). Children create all sorts of explanations of their thinking through the pictures they draw and the statements that they write as they solve mathematical problems. St. Clair (1993) called this work *recordings*, and he described how he encouraged children to write or draw about the work that they were doing.

> The process of recording forces children to consider what they have done and how they might represent it. Often the recording is a cooperative activity that has kids discussing how they shall express what has happened. Then, as children describe their recordings to their classmates, they develop their skills as communicators. (1993, p. 70)

As St. Clair suggests, students' work might also show growth in young children's ability to articulate their ideas. Often, however, what young children draw or write is not self-evident. You can jot down brief descriptions of the child's thinking or direct quotes that may prove helpful later when reviewing the portfolio with colleagues, parents, or administrators.

In addition to pieces of work selected by you, children may be encouraged to select one or two pieces for each parent conference that conveys what they are most proud of in their mathematical work. This activity can promote exchanges between parents and children about mathematics, encourage self-awareness in children, and promote pride in their work.

EQUITY

Understanding mathematics is within the reach of every child. Classrooms should convey a fundamental respect for children's ideas. Listening closely to children's ideas, tying mathematical work to children's experiences, and creating a social climate that promotes respect removes stereotyping of children based on ability, gender, or ethnicity. Without equitable opportunities, other dimensions of the classroom do not function as well (Hiebert et al., 1997).

Research on classrooms that promote widespread and equitable participation demonstrate that the teacher plays a critical role in shaping a classroom where all children have opportunities to develop their mathematical thinking. An equitable classroom requires teachers to be sensitive to tasks that are both relevant and engaging to students and to be flexible in how children express their thinking. Teachers should be sensitive to giving all children a voice in the classroom and inviting children to continually work on creating an environment that is both safe and challenging. The norm-building that occurs at the beginning of the year is a crucial way to create a socially and intellectually nurturing environment. You can explicitly talk with students about how to participate in classroom discussions, what to do when someone gets stuck or confused, how to react if someone gives an answer, and how to respectfully disagree with someone. Children can learn ways to phrase questions to one another, such as, "I'm not sure I understand why you did ___?" or "I got stuck here, and I wonder if someone can help me," or "I don't feel like everyone's listening to my ideas," instead of "You're wrong!" and other statements that can stifle rather than promote productive discussions.

It is important to regularly monitor which children are participating in activities and how they are participating. By tape recording whole group discussions and listening to them later or observing individual and group problem solving, teachers can pay attention to the way everyone in the classroom, including teachers, is interacting with one another. The nature of children's participation can be incorporated into anecdotal notetaking as well. If there are children with special needs in the class or who seem to struggle with mathematical ideas that most others in the class are comfortable with, it is important for the teacher to monitor whether children are respectful of their ideas. Can you find evidence of those children participating in substantive ways in classroom discussions or are they mostly overlooked? Are some children regularly called on only to provide yes or no answers or brief fill-in-the-blank responses whereas others have more opportunities to provide explanations and conjectures? These kinds of patterns of interaction can often go unnoticed unless you regularly take the time to monitor both the degree and kind of participation in the classroom.

In addition to monitoring the kind of social and academic interactions children are having in the classroom and paying attention to who participates and how, you need to also regularly assess whether the physical environment of the classroom and the content of the curriculum reflect the children in the classroom. Many of the suggestions provided previously in the chapter, including mathematizing children's stories, making links to children's literature, and creating problem situations out of children's everyday experiences, are strategies you can use to make sure that the mathematics curriculum reflects the diversity of children's experiences in the classroom.

COLLABORATION WITH COLLEAGUES

Developing classroom practices that support children's thinking is hard work, especially because most teachers were not taught the way students are taught now. When you were a student, "math" may have consisted of a series of worksheets that asked you to restate and practice examples you had seen the teacher present. You may not have been asked to explain your thinking and may have gone through school without a solid understanding of how mathematical ideas are related. It makes sense that many teachers are not comfortable with mathematics and do not think of themselves as mathematical thinkers. Yet, learning about children's thinking is an intriguing journey that allows you to continually deepen and expand your knowledge of children's ideas, mathematics, and teaching.

Teaching is a learning profession, not simply a telling profession (Darling-Hammond & Sykes, 1999). Teachers have long criticized the culture of isolation that characterizes much of their work. Many schools are experimenting with ways to increase professional dialogue and collaboration among teachers. It is crucial to be creative in finding time to talk with colleagues about the teaching and learning of mathematics. You might arrange with the librarian to allow you to leave your class in the library while you visits a colleague's classroom. The purpose of these classroom visits is to talk with your colleague's students as they work on mathematical problems and to spend some individual time with children. Your colleague might return the favor by visiting your classroom once a week to do the same thing. You might leave notes for each other as you learn new things about each other's students, and in this way, you continue the conversation about children's thinking.

A teacher working in a year-round school might spend some of his or her time off substituting in other classes in her own school. He or she might visit classrooms and talk with colleagues about how they teach mathematics. Principals can devoted a staff meeting once a month for teachers to share the mathematical work their students are doing around a particular theme. During these meetings, teachers can note the strategies that their students are using and together try to make sense of their students' understanding. Teachers of young children often have the advantage of having parents or other adults in the room with them. Extra hands may allow teachers to find those precious moments to talk with a student individually or to try out something new with a small group of students.

There are also a number of case-based materials available to teachers who would like to work together with more structured materials to learn more about children's ideas (see Barnett, Goldenstein, & Jackson, 1994; Schifter, Bastable, & Russell, 1999). No one strategy will work for every teacher. You can set up reading clubs, video clubs, or other study groups to investigate a puzzle of practice that you face (Loucks-Horsley, Hewson, Love, & Stiles, 1998). Whether you find a partner to talk with or a group, it is energizing to learn with colleagues who have the same questions and passions as you.

WORKING WITH PARENTS

Many teachers wonder how best to include parents in the education of their children. Portfolios of students' work provide a powerful mechanism to communicate with parents about their children's development and to provide examples of the kinds of mathematical work that occur in the classroom. You can walk parents through their child's portfolio, point out work where you noticed significant gains, relate observations and questions their child had as he or she worked in class, and provide a story about what skills you would expect their child to learn next. Many parents may have never had such a detailed conversation about their child with a teacher and will appreciate how much you know about their child's thinking and growth.

Working with parents is certainly not limited to conferences. You can send home a new idea every week focused on a mathematical idea, especially at the beginning of the year, to help parents develop some new routines at home and an appreciation for seeing the world with mathematical eyes. Whether at an open house, a parent breakfast, or a class celebration, you can use the work students are generating to invite parents to be curious about the way their children are solving problems. Many parents may have questions about whether their children are developing the necessary skills they need in order to be successful in mathematics, and they might worry that they are not seeing the kinds of routines and activities they remember experiencing as a child. These concerns can be addressed, in part, by your ability to talk about a child's mathematical growth through the systematic record keeping described earlier in the chapter.

You may also want to take advantage of existing parent gatherings (e.g., open houses) or to create new opportunities for parents to come together to talk specifically about mathematics. Many schools have established mathematics nights. During these special occasions, you may find it helpful to organize a mathematics activity that parents and children can engage in together. Doing mathematics together is one way that you can help parents appreciate and recognize the mathematics that children are doing and provide suggestions for how to engage in mathematical conversations with their children. Engaging parents in mental math activities can also draw out the various ways in which adults flexibly compose and decompose numbers. These experiences can be tied back to the ways in which you are working with the children in the classroom.

Parents often question teachers about how they should work with their child at home. Parents also may be unsure about what it means to draw out their child's thinking. Certainly, they cannot be expected to develop the same level of expertise as teachers. Parents can, however, engage in activities with their children at home that will nurture children's natural curiosity about mathematical ideas. Many of the examples used in this chapter can provide direction for parents of young children. For example, one of the messages you can give parents is, "Count everything!" They can count the number of stoplights between home and school or the number of cans in the cupboard. They can count the number of trees on their block or the number of lamps in the house. When dinner is being served, children can count whether they have enough plates and cups for everyone. As parents read with or to their child, you can encourage them to create mathematics problems. To develop spatial and visualization skills, parents can help their children draw a map of their room, house, or block. They can look for different kinds of triangles in the house. You can even suggest simple cards games such as Go Fish, War, or Concentration that build children's sense of number.

One of the central ideas in developing good relationships with parents is helping them see the abundant ways in which they can draw out mathematics in the everyday experiences they have with children. Working with their children at home does not have to be limited to worksheets they complete together.

CONCLUSION

Teaching young children mathematics is an exciting endeavor. Children have such profound ideas, and you can draw out, reflect on, and build these ideas.

Creating classrooms that honor and build children's mathematical ideas is both challenging and rewarding work. The work begins with a simple invitation, "Tell me how you figured that out." Once you begin listening to children's ideas, your curiosity inevitably grows. Being a successful mathematics teacher is not just about generating engaging activities; it is a continuous process of making sense of children's ideas and experimenting with ways to elicit and build their ideas. Begin or continue this journey! Learn more about students, and develop classroom practices to facilitate deep and connected mathematical understandings.

RESOURCES FOR INTEGRATING CHILDREN'S LITERATURE INTO MATHEMATICS LESSONS

Bauermeister, E., & Smith, H. (1997). *Let's hear it for the girls: 375 great books for readers 2–14*. London: Penguin Books Ltd.

Burns, M. (1992). *Math and literature (K-3): Book one*. Sausalito, CA: Math Solutions Publications.

Griffiths, R., & Clyne, M. (1991). *Books you can count on: Linking mathematics and literature*. Portsmouth, NH: Heinemann.

Karp, K., Brown, E.T., Allen, L., & Allen, C. (1998). *Feisty females: Inspiring girls to think mathematically*. Portsmouth, NH: Heinemann.

Sheffield, S. (1995). *Math and literature (K-3): Book two*. Sausalito, CA: Math Solutions Publications.

Thiessen, D., Mathia, M., & Smith, J. (1998). *The wonderful world of mathematics: A critically annotated list of children's books in mathematics* (2nd ed.). Reston, VA: National Council of Teachers of Mathematics.

Welchman-Tischler, R. (1992). *How to use children's literature to teach mathematics*. Reston, VA: National Council of Teachers of Mathematics.

Whitin, D.J., & Wilde, S. (1992). *Read any good math lately?: Children's books for mathematical learning, K-6*. Portsmouth, NH: Heinemann.

Whitin, D.J., & Wilde, S. (1995). *It's the story that counts: More children's books for mathematical learning, K-6*. Portsmouth, NH: Heinemann.

REFERENCES

Ball, D.L. (1992). Magical hopes: Manipulatives and the reform of math education. *American Educator, 16*(2), 28–33.

Barnett, C., Goldenstein, D., & Jackson, B. (Eds.). (1994). *Fractions, decimals, ratios and percent*. Portsmouth, NH: Heinemann.

Burns, M. (1992). *Math and literature (K-3): Book one*. Sausalito, CA: Math Solutions.

Burns, M. (1995). *Math and literature (K-3): Book two*. Sausalito, CA: Math Solutions.

Carpenter, T., Carey, D., & Kouba, V. (1990). A problem-solving approach to the operations. In J.N. Payne (Ed.), *Mathematics for the young child* (pp. 111–132). Reston, VA: National Council of Teachers of Mathematics.

Carpenter, T.P., Fennema, E., & Franke, M.L. (1996). Cognitively guided instruction: A knowledge base for reform in primary mathematics instruction. *Elementary School Journal, 97,* 3–20.

Clements, D.H. (2001). Mathematics in the preschool. *Teaching Children Mathematics, 7,* 270–275.

Clements, D., & Sarama, J. (2000). Young children's ideas about geometric shapes. *Teaching Children Mathematics, 6,* 482–487.

Darling-Hammond, L., & Sykes, G. (Eds.). (1999). *Teaching as the learning profession.* San Francisco: Jossey-Bass.

Economopoulos, K., & Murray, M. (1998). Mathematical thinking at kindergarten. In S.J. Russell, C.C. Tierney, & J. Mokros (Eds.), *Investigations in number, data, and space.* Palo Alto, CA: Dale Seymour Publications.

Edwards, C., Gandini, L., & Forman, G. (1993). *The hundred languages of children: The Reggio Emilia approach to early childhood education.* Westport, CT: Ablex Publishing.

Ginsburg, H.P., Jacobs, S.F., & Lopez, L.S. (1998). *The teacher's guide to flexible interviewing in the classroom: Learning what children know about math.* Boston: Allyn & Bacon.

Ginsburg, H.P., & Seo, K. (2000). Preschooler's mathematical reading. *Teaching Children Mathematics, 7,* 226–229.

Griffiths, R., & Clyne, M. (1991). *Books you can count on: Linking mathematics and literature.* Portsmouth, NH: Heinemann.

Hiebert, J., Carpenter, T.P., Fennema, E., Fuson, K.C., Wearne, D., Murray, H., Olivier, A., & Human, P. (1997). *Making sense: Teaching and learning mathematics with understanding.* Portsmouth, NH: Heinemann.

Howard, E.F. (1991). *Aunt Flossie's hats (and crab cakes later).* New York: Clarion Books.

Kamii, C.K., & Housman, L.B. (1999). *Young children reinvent arithmetic: Implications of Piaget's theory* (2nd ed.). New York: Teachers College Press.

Karp, K., Brown, E.T., Allen, L., & Allen, C. (1998). *Feisty females: Inspiring girls to think mathematically.* Portsmouth, NH: Heinemann.

Kazemi, E., & Stipek, D. (2001). Promoting conceptual understanding in four upper-elementary mathematics classrooms. *Elementary School Journal, 102,* 59–80.

Krull, K. (1996). *Wilma unlimited: How Wilma Rudolph became the world's fastest woman.* Orlando, FL: Harcourt.

Loucks-Horsley, S., Hewson, P.W., Love, N., & Stiles, K.E. (1998). *Designing professional development for teachers of science and mathematics.* Thousand Oaks, CA: Corwin Press.

Mokros, J., Russell, S.J., & Economopoulos, K. (1995). *Beyond Arithmetic: Changing mathematics in the elementary classroom.* Palo Alto, CA: Dale Seymour Publications.

Moyer, P.S. (2000). Communicating mathematically: Children's literature as a natural connection. *Reading Teacher, 54,* 246–255.

National Council of Teachers of Mathematics. (2000). *Principles and standards for school mathematics.* Reston, VA: Author.

Penner, E., & Lehrer, R. (2000). The shape of fairness. *Teaching Children Mathematics, 7,* 210–214.

Schifter, D., Bastable, V., & Russell, S.J. (1999). *Developing mathematical ideas.* Palo Alto, CA: Dale Seymour Publications.

St. Clair, J. (1993). Assessing mathematical understanding in a bilingual kindergarten. In N.L. Webb & A.F. Coxford (Eds.), *Assessment in the mathematics classroom* (pp. 65–73). Reston, VA: National Council of Teachers of Mathematics.

Strickland, K., & Strickland, J. (2000). *Making assessment elementary.* Portsmouth, NH: Heinemann.

Webb, N.L., & Coxford, A.F. (Eds.). (1993). *Assessment in the mathematics classroom.* Reston, VA: National Council of Teachers of Mathematics.

Wood, T., Cobb, P., & Yackel, E. (1991). Change in teaching mathematics: A case study. *American Educational Research Journal, 28,* 587–616.

Understanding Multicultural and Anti-bias Education

Aisha Ray

Schools play a complex and contradictory role in the United States: They are supposed to provide equal opportunities for socially marginalized children but often reflect and reproduce social inequalities (Bowles & Gintis, 1976; Haney, 1993; Jones-Wilson, 1990; Ogbu, 1978; Rist, 1970; Sapon-Shevin, 1993; Strickland & Ascher, 1992). At the heart of this contradiction lies a challenge to American preschool and elementary educators to respond effectively and fairly to cultural, racial, gender, sexual preference, ethnic, and ability diversity. These issues are important because they are linked to low educational achievement of a disproportionately large percentage of children, especially African American, Native American, Latino, Asian American, Pacific Islander, impoverished and immigrant children, as well as children who are not proficient in Standard English and those with disabilities. In addition, young children of privilege who grow up in areas that are not culturally and economically diverse need to develop acceptance of diversity and willingness to challenge bias, prejudice, and privilege.

DIVERSITY IN AMERICA

Educating young children to embrace and value diversity is essential for the economic advancement and social and political stability of American

135

democracy (Banks, 1972). The United States has always been a pluralistic nation—multicultural, multiracial, multiethnic, multilingual, and socially stratified (One America, 1997). Early childhood educators particularly need to address the issues of cultural, racial, and ethnic diversity because the demographics of American society are changing. Historically, race, social class, and ethnicity have been used to maintain the social, political, and economic privilege in the hands of European Americans at the expense of marginalized groups (Aronowitz & Giroux, 1993; Miron, 1999; Takaki, 1994). The American population, however, is becoming significantly younger and nonwhite (Maharidge, 1996). In addition, the nature of American families is changing—a majority of mothers work outside the home, a significant proportion of all families are headed by single parents, and in many families, both parents work. Consider the following facts:

- The majority of immigrants to the United States come from Central America, Asia, the Caribbean, and South America (U.S. Bureau of the Census, 1999).

- In 1999, one quarter of all 3- to 9-year-old children had parents who were born outside the United States (U.S. Bureau of the Census, 1999).

- More than one third of 3- to 9-year-old children are African American, Latino, Asian American, and Pacific Islander (U.S. Bureau of the Census, 1999).

- Children who are racially and culturally diverse are the majority in the 25 largest U.S. school districts (Gay, 1995).

- It is estimated that if current demographic trends continue, by the year 2020, the population younger than 18 years old will be 48% nonwhite and Spanish speaking, and by mid-century, the majority of Americans will live in ethnically diverse families (McAdoo, 1993).

- Child poverty in America continues to disproportionately affect racial and ethnic minority children—37% of African American children and 34% of Latino children under the age of 18 live in poverty, whereas only 11% of Caucasian children younger than 18 live in poverty (National Center for Children in Poverty, 2000).

Twenty years from now, the present population of 4- to 8-year-old school children will be adult citizens. Will their educational experiences in preschool and primary classrooms give them the necessary foundation to be reflective citizens who respect differences and resist bias based on race, class, or ethnicity? Current preschool and primary school practices need to adequately address this question. New initiatives are needed to ensure that educators are prepared and able to educate children for the challenges of a truly diverse society.

THEORIES ON DIVERSITY EDUCATION

Before discussing specific practice and learning issues, multicultural and anti-bias education needs to be placed in a broader theoretical perspective. If tolerance for diversity can be organized as a curriculum and taught to 4- to 8-year-old children, two questions need to be addressed:

1. What evidence from research and theory supports the assumption that significant differences exist between groups in the United States because of culture, race, or ethnicity?

2. What theoretical rationale and evidence supports the claim that young children can learn about multiculturalism and anti-bias?

Do Substantive Cultural, Racial, and Ethnic Differences Exist?

Culture is defined as "the prism through which members of a group see the world and create shared meaning" (Bowman, 1989, p. 2). It is a dynamic social construction that adapts to collective experiences and ecological conditions, yet not all members of a culture express or adhere to all core values, norms, and behaviors all of the time or to the same extent. For example, African Americans who are classified as one "racial" group are often defined as having one culture despite considerable evidence that cultural discontinuities exist among African Americans (Anderson, 1999; Gwaltney, 1980; Shimkin, Shimkin, & Frate, 1978). Research suggests that social class (Anderson, 1999; Landry, 2000; Pattillo-McCoy, 1999), geography, and national origin (Kasinitz, Battle, & Miyares, 2001; Shimkin, Shimkin, & Frate, 1978; Stepick, Stepick, Eugene, Teed, & Labissiere, 2001) among other factors influence the culture of African Americans.

Child rearing is the process through which cultural knowledge, including meaning, identity, language, values, beliefs, norms of behavior, morality, and role prescriptions are transmitted intergenerationally. This process is intended to develop the normative competencies appropriate for a given culture (LeVine, 1974, 1980; Whiting & Edwards, 1988). Research has documented that distinct cultural traditions exist among racial and ethnic groups within the United States—African American (Boykin & Toms, 1985; Young, 1974), Hawaiian (Tharp, 1994), Hmong American (Walker-Moffat, 1995), Mexican American (Delgado-Gaitan, 1994), Navajo (Tharp, 1994), and Caucasian Americans (Heath, 1992; Whiting & Edwards, 1988), among others.

Americans commonly equate race or ethnicity with culture (Derman-Sparks & Phillips, 1997; Smedley, 1997); however, scholars generally agree that race is a biologically unsupported construct (Gould, 1981; Torres, Miron, & Inda, 1999). The social inequalities that exist between identified racial or ethnic groups are the consequence of social, economic, and political circumstances (Smedley, 1997). Ethnicity is derived from individual or ancestral origins in a specific country; for example, Italian Americans trace their ethnic identity to Italy.

Personal cultural, ethnic, and racial identities can be complex. For example, a child of Dominican parents living in New York may identify as Black, Latino, and Dominican, and a child of Sioux and Irish parents living on the Rosebud Reservation may identify with one parent's culture and not the other. Furthermore, gender, sexual preference, and disability may also contribute to the construction of complex identities. Over time, people's understanding of their own cultural, ethnic, and/or racial identity may change. The separation of ethnicity and culture permits distinctions among fourth generation Mexican-Americans, first generation Columbian immigrants, and second generation Puerto Ricans (Wardle, 1996).

Theoretical models that attempt to explain child development without accounting for cultural context are prone to biases in interpretation of child behavior or outcomes (Harkness, 1980). Harkness suggests that interpretation of behavior outside of its cultural context is especially problematic when the researcher and the subjects do not share the same cultural frame of reference. This observation is particularly important when assessing the relationship between home culture and school culture. Teachers may have cultural traditions different from those of the children in their classrooms.

When children and teachers with different cultural orientations meet in classrooms, poor educational outcomes or conflicts may result (Gonzalez-Mena, 1997). For example, non-Native American teachers' inability to recognize the collective nature of Pueblo Indian children's home culture has been identified by researchers as a factor that may inhibit learning (Sunia & Smolkin, 1994). Furthermore, Boykin and Bailey (2000) identified three African American cultural themes (i.e., communalism, movement-expressiveness, and verve) present in children's home environment and influential in developing their learning styles. Research (see Boykin & Bailey, 2000) suggests that instructional practices that incorporate African American themes are related to improved performance of African American children on tasks such as problem solving and inferential reasoning. Conversely, the failure to utilize knowledge of children's home culture may contribute to poor academic outcomes and limited school success.

Cultural differences are rarely trivial. They often involve fundamental aspects of meaning (e.g., the individual's rights versus the group's), interpersonal communication (e.g., norms of personal space), and concepts of power and authority (e.g., norms related to gender; Gonzalez-Mena, 1997; Greenfield & Cocking, 1994). Irvine (1990) described these encounters as lacking "cultural synchronization" and suggests that they may help to account for the relatively poor performance of economically disadvantaged children. Researchers have suggested that some cultural traditions may be more compatible with the expectations, structure, and teaching strategies present in U.S. schools and may account for the greater school success of children for whom the cultural fit between home and school is relatively seamless (Gay, 1991; Hale-Benson, 1982; Ogbu, 1978).

In addition, the organization of schools, teaching practices, and instruction may reinforce and reproduce cultural inequalities that disadvantage children from culturally diverse backgrounds. For example, teaching practices and educational policies that do not support non-English and non-Standard English as children's home language may be a key contributing factor to the academic underachievement of immigrant children who live in poverty in American classrooms (Adger, Christian, & Taylor, 1999; Delgado-Gaitan, 1994; Delpit, 1998; Fillmore & Meyer, 1992). Similarly, educational policies aimed at discipline and punishment of children disproportionately have a negative influence on the educational outcomes of students living in poverty, racial minority students, and males (Ferguson, 2001; Skiba, Michael, Nardo, & Peterson, 2000).

Giroux (1996) suggested that all educational environments are social institutions in which knowledge is organized and produced through processes of exclusion and inclusion. These processes are embedded in and reflect historical, political, and social arrangements that generally benefit groups with power and privilege. Curriculum and teaching practices are areas in which groups representing competing societal interests (e.g., advocates of bilingual versus English-only education) have struggled over what knowledge will be taught, which "voices" will be heard or silenced, and ultimately how social power and advantage will be distributed in society. It is argued that through instructional practices, curricula, and assessment practices (e.g., testing, tracking, discipline) schools reward and privilege certain groups of children over others thereby reproducing inequality (Aronowitz & Giroux, 1983; Bowles & Gintis, 1976; Haney, 1993; Ogbu, 1978; Rist, 1970; Sapon-Shevin, 1993).

In summary, substantial research evidence supports the notion of cultural differences in American ethnic and racial groups. Schools may not be able to successfully educate culturally, racially, and ethnically diverse children when there is mismatch between home and school cultures (Watson-Gegeo, 1992). Schools and teachers need to understand the diversity of their students' home cultures (Delpit, 1988; Irvine, 1990; Ladson-Billings, 1994).

Child Development

In preschool and the early primary grades, multicultural and anti-bias education (via the social studies curriculum) combines *process,* learning to think critically and to be reflective about one's self, with *content,* the child, family, neighborhood, and larger community (Dodge, Jablon, & Bickart, 1994). The Constructivist theories and the Interpretive Approach to socialization attempt to explain young children's development during this time.

Constructivist theorists argue that, regardless of age, children actively construct knowledge and meaning that reflects their cultural context (Cole, 1991; Piaget, 1969; Rogoff, 1982, 1990; Vygotsky, 1978). Children organize knowledge, modify constructs they have already formed when confronted with new contradictory experiences and information, and synthesize old and new constructs into more elaborate and complex concepts and meanings (Piaget, 1969; Vygotsky, 1978). Together with more mature cultural experts—namely parents, teachers, and older children—young children co-construct knowledge about their world. Hence, child development occurs in the context of interpersonal and community interactions because the child is never isolated from other people or removed from dynamic cultural processes (Rogoff, Baker-Sennett, Lacasa, & Goldsmith, 1995).

Building on Vygotskian and Piagetian theory, the Interpretive Approach to socialization asserts that the child is not just a constructor of knowledge created along with older cultural experts, but an innovator, appropriator, and reproducer of culture (Corsaro & Miller, 1992; Gaskins, Miller, & Corsaro, 1992). Through their participation in cultural routines (e.g., going to school), young children create social knowledge and skills that are independent of adults (Corsaro & Rosier, 1992). They do not simply learn adult culture; rather, through interaction and negotiation, they contribute to adult culture and ultimately transform it.

Between 4 and 8 years of age, children absorb an enormous amount of knowledge about themselves and their world. In relation to understanding diversity, children construct knowledge in two important areas: 1) *self*, including ethnic and racial identity, and 2) *morality and positive justice*. In addition, children move from a rudimentary to a more elaborate understanding of

- Human similarities and differences
- Common basic needs of people (e.g., food)
- Concepts of time and place (e.g., past, present, future)
- Interaction of people with their environment (e.g., climate)
- Human interdependence (e.g., roles, rights, and obligations of family members; Dodge et al., 1994)

Knowledge of Ethnic and Racial Identity

Young children contend with contradictory and complex information and experiences related to their identities and those of individuals and groups representing distinct cultural, ethnic, racial, linguistic, gender, faith, and social class communities. Yet, between the ages of 4 and 8, most children develop a complex and layered understanding of themselves and others (see Coles, 1964, 1977).

Young children construct notions of the values and biases associated with social categories. For example, by the time young children enter kindergarten they recognize racial differences (Bigler & Liben, 1993; Hirschfeld, 1995; Spencer, 1982). When asked to sort dolls and pictures into racially identified groups, 4-year-old children are able to do so. Around 4 years old, children also are aware of their own ethnic identity and society's evaluation of it. By 6 years old, children recognize class differences (e.g., people who look impoverished in comparison to wealthy) and economic inequalities (Leahy, 1981, 1983). These findings suggest that young children learn the prominence of social categories, such as race and class, and begin to attach meaning to them.

Environment plays a powerful role in shaping children's attitudes toward these social categories. Spencer and Horowitz (1973) demonstrated that 3- to 5-year-old African American and European American children's preference for white objects could be altered and sustained over time if they participated in training sessions in which they were rewarded when they chose black objects and images. In addition, Native American children expressed a greater preference for Native American dolls when the researcher spoke to them in their own language (Annis & Corenblum, 1987). The degree to which young children of color internalize the negative evaluations others may hold about their racial, cultural, or ethnic group continues to be an unresolved issue in research (Akbar, 1985; Cross, 1991; Spencer & Markstrom-Adams, 1990).

Knowledge of Morality and Justice

In the process of developing a sense of self and of their place in the world, young children also learn the moral standards of their family, community, and society. Preschool children tend to believe that adults impose social rules and judge an act as "bad" if these rules are broken (Piaget, 1932/1965). For example, young children in a preschool program may evaluate another child's behavior, such as hitting, as "bad" because the teacher stated that it is so. Additional research suggests that children between the ages of 5 and 7 are unable to separate their own interests from those of others and base their judgment of whether an action was good or bad on its outcome (Kohlberg, 1984). For example, a 5-year-old may want another child's cookie and may assume that others also have the same desire. If the child takes the cookie by force, he or she may judge the action as "good" because the outcome coincides with his or her desire.

After age 7, children tend to evaluate moral issues in terms of their own self-interest but recognize that other individuals may have different views. As children grow older (around age 10) they are more likely to base their judgments of good and bad, and right and wrong on *autonomous moral reasoning* (Piaget, 1932/1965). In doing so, children recognize that individuals can independently arrive at different positions on social rules, can test their views against those held by others, and will apply the rules to all parties once individuals agree on the rules.

Damon (1975, 1977, 1980) examined young children's reasoning about *positive justice,* or how decisions are made about fairly dividing resources and rewards. Before age 4 or 5, children tend to reason that if they want something, then they should have it. Their explanations are related to their desires, and they tend not to offer objective justifications for their wishes. Typically, a child younger than 4 years might say, "But I want that toy, so I should have it." In contrast, 4- to 5-year-old children are likely to focus on their desires, but justify them based on some observable characteristic (e.g., age, gender). For example, "I should get it because I'm a boy." Between ages 5 and 7, children make decisions on the basis of strict equality (i.e., everyone should be treated fairly). They may say, "Everyone should get one cookie because we should all get the same." Children develop a notion of reciprocity in action between ages 6 and 9. This means that if people do good or bad things, they should receive a reward or punishment equal to their deed. For example, a child might state, "Miesha should get twice as many cookies as Maria because she did twice as much work." Around age 8, children begin to recognize that individuals may have a right to more than an equal share if there is a compelling reason (e.g., poverty, physical disability), or if they contributed more to the outcome, but these children continue to have difficulty weighing competing factors. For example, an 8-year-old might explain that a poor child should receive more birthday gifts because he has less than a wealthier child.

In conclusion, 4- to 8-year-old children have a developing sense of fairness and justice that is concrete and is tied increasingly to notions of equality. In addition, they have constructed categories of race and ethnicity for themselves and for others. These categories reflect general cultural notions of the physical characteristics that define race. Moreover, attitudes and beliefs that children hold about racial characteristics may be altered by intervention strategies designed to teach them to think differently about race.

LEARNING DIVERSITY IN PRESCHOOL AND PRIMARY CLASSROOMS

Scholars suggest two critical characteristics of successful schools and teaching practices for culturally, ethnically, and racially diverse students: *curricula* that embrace, respect, and build on the experiences, abilities, and knowledge children bring to the classroom, and *culturally relevant instruction* that is relationship based and uses students' cultures and home languages to enhance educational achievement (Delpit, 1998; Fillmore & Meyer, 1992; Hale-Benson, 1982; Ladson-Billings, 1994).

Research indicates that when many children of color enter school, educational practices and teacher expectations can negatively influence child outcomes (Delpit, 1988; Edmonds, 1979; Fillmore & Meyer, 1992; Hale-Benson, 1982; Irvine, 1990; Ogbu, 1990; Winfield, 1986). American preschool and elementary classrooms are intergenerational meeting grounds of diversity (Darling-Hammond, Pittman, & Ottinger, 1987). A multicultural social studies curriculum that uses culturally relevant teaching strategies offers a tool that teachers may use to help young students understand and appreciate their own and others rich cultural traditions, behaviors, and beliefs. It also serves as a way for teachers to learn about and respect the diverse backgrounds of students and families.

Educators agree that the purpose of multicultural education is to help children from diverse backgrounds receive equal educational opportunities and to help children develop positive attitudes, behaviors, and expectations toward people who differ from them in terms of culture; race; ethnicity; religion; social class; or physical, psychological, or mental ability (Banks, 1993; Boyle-Baise, 1999). It is intended to convert a relatively mono-cultural early childhood social studies instruction into one that embraces the many voices and perspectives present in American society.

Banks and Lynch (1986) suggest that the development of truly multicultural education requires the transformation of the entire school environment. They describe eight characteristics that are essential for a transformed multicultural school:

- Staff who hold anti-racist values and beliefs
- Democratic attitudes and values
- Norms and values that legitimize cultural and racial diversity
- Assessment and testing procedures that promote social class and ethnic equality
- Curriculum and teaching materials that incorporate multiple and diverse cultural perspectives
- Appreciation of language diversity (including children's home language)
- Culturally responsive teaching and motivational practices that are effective with students from diverse cultural traditions
- Equal status within the school for students from all ethnic, cultural, and social class groups
- Teacher and student knowledge and use of skills necessary to combat racism and other forms of bias

Anti-bias education (Derman-Sparks & the ABC Task Force, 1989; Spencer, 1998) shares the same goals as multicultural education but addresses the responses individuals have to racial, cultural, gender, disabilities, and other sources of diversity. Phillips (1989) argued that exclusionary or discriminatory behavior results from individuals' biased reactions to cultural and racial difference. Anti-bias curriculum is intended to intervene with children to help them to develop reactions to difference that do not lead to biased attitudes and unjust behavior. It incorporates the development of skills and abilities in children so that they are able to respond to and resist prejudice in themselves and others. In addition, the curriculum is designed to teach children to "construct a knowledgeable, confident self-identity; to develop comfortable, empathetic, and just interaction with diversity; and to develop critical thinking and the skills for standing up for oneself and others in the face of injustice" (Derman-Sparks et al., 1989, p. ix). Both approaches aim at transforming society through changing the way that American children think about themselves and others in relation to diversity. They deliberately encourage students to learn about the sources of inequality, the common interests shared by all human beings, and the aspects of culture and heritage that make groups unique.

Banks (1993) identified four approaches to curriculum that promote diversity and justice:

1. The *Contributions Approach* essentially adds cultural heroes (e.g., Martin Luther King, Cesar Chavez) to the preschool and elementary curriculum. The school curriculum and teaching practices (e.g., democratic values of teachers, school norms, values that legitimize multicultural education) remain mono-cultural. A version of the Contributions Approach, the *Heroes and Holidays Approach* is distinguished from it in that multicultural content is limited primarily to heroes, holidays, and events (e.g., Cinco de Mayo, African American History Month). It leaves the remainder of the mono-cultural school curriculum untouched. It also may exclude children whose cultural heroes and holidays are unfamiliar to teachers.

2. The *Additive Approach* adds cultural content, including themes and perspectives, to the curriculum but does not alter the characteristics of school philosophy or practices. Often, this approach adds an ethnic or cultural unit or book to the existing classroom. A common practice in preschool and primary classrooms is the inclusion of books, stories, and music that reflect the cultural traditions of children. This is a commendable practice, but it is just a starting point to address the goals of transformative multiculturalism and anti-bias education. Banks suggests that often this approach does not sufficiently alter the mono-cultural perspective in the schools because the ways in which materials are presented and interpreted do not reflect multiple perspectives. An example is the treatment of the Thanksgiving holiday in many kindergarten classrooms. Native Americans occupy center stage in the Thanksgiving story, but they are viewed exclusively from the Pilgrims' point of view. Children

do not discuss how Native Americans may have felt about the settlers or what might have motivated Native Americans' responses to Europeans (Banks, 1993).

3. The *Transformation Approach* alters the fundamental assumptions of the curriculum. It reconfigures the curriculum so that children can learn themes, events, circumstances, and problems from a variety of perspectives. In relation to the Thanksgiving example used previously, teachers and children listen to stories and interpretations of the contact of Native Americans and Pilgrims from the perspective of each group. They talk about the difference between the way each group describes events, they discuss apparent differences in the two perspectives, and they discuss parallels in their own lives when they and others have had different perspectives on the same event. Through offering multiple perspectives, curriculum materials, and thoughtful discussion of complex events, the teacher moves the classroom toward truly transformative multicultural and anti-bias education. (See for further elaboration Banks, 1996; Gay, 2000; Haberman, 1995; Ladson-Billings, 1994; and Scheurich, 1998.)

4. The *Personal-, Social-, and Civic-Action Approach* involves all of the aspects of the Transformation Approach but includes expectations that children will make decisions and act in relation to problems, issues, and ideas they have encountered in lessons they have studied. Banks (1993) concedes that 4- to 6-year-old children may be less able than older children to respond to racial, ethnic, or cultural issues consistently, but teachers can help young children examine issues of diversity that are within their immediate experience, such as making friends with children in their classrooms who are different from themselves and talking about themes of exclusion or bias in books, stories, or television programs with which they are familiar.

Classroom practice in the majority of American schools does not appear to extend beyond the multicultural moments of Contributions, Additive, and Heroes and Holidays Approaches (Miller, 1998). Teachers are one of the most important factors in creating multicultural and anti-bias practice and instruction, but implementing Transformation and Personal-, Social-, and Civic-Action Approaches may be a challenge for many teachers and teacher educators (Banks & Lynch, 1986; Derman-Sparks et al., 1989; Phillips, 1989; Gay, 1986).

Teachers' own attitudes, thinking, and behaviors regarding cultural, racial, and ethnic diversity may limit their ability to implement multicultural and anti-bias educational practices (Gay, 1986; Knapp, 1995; McAllister & Irvine, 2000; Moulty, 1988, in Grant & Secada, 1990; Sleeter, 1993). For example, after studying 140 high-poverty elementary school classrooms in 15 schools, Knapp (1995) identified two dimensions of teachers' instructional responses to the diversity of children in their classrooms. *Constructive* teachers believe that all children can learn regardless of home culture characteristics. *Nonconstructive* teachers assume that students' backgrounds determine their educational outcomes.

In addition, the degree of responsiveness that teachers exhibit in dealing with student differences is important. *Active* teachers believe that they understand the cultural backgrounds of the children they teach and use teaching strategies and curricula that support their beliefs. *Passive* teachers, however, do not respond to differences because they do not perceive differences or do not recognize them as significant in the child's educational performance. The researchers caution that active responses should not be perceived as automatically positive. Active teachers can incorrectly assume that they understand children's home culture, and as a result, may develop teaching strategies based on erroneous assumptions. Using the dimensions of constructive/nonconstructive and active/passive, Knapp identified five patterns of teacher responses to classroom diversity:

1. *Active nonconstructive teachers* have low expectations and overtly negative stereotypes of children from certain cultural and class groups. Specifically, they believe that because of background characteristics (e.g., living in public housing), some children cannot succeed in school. Teachers frequently act in ways that deliberately limit children's opportunities to learn (e.g., ignoring children, assigning the bulk of instruction of children to a teacher aide, not calling on children when they raise their hands). They explain their behavior toward particular groups of children by stating that they don't want to embarrass children by exposing their ignorance to the class or frustrate them by assigning work they cannot complete. Teachers' low expectations and negative educational practices often lead to poor educational outcomes for children, which in turn reinforce teachers' original assumptions and practices.

2. *Passive nonconstructive teachers* do not appear to hold overtly prejudiced attitudes toward the children in their classrooms, but through missed opportunities, ignorance of children's home culture, lessons that are irrelevant to children, and misunderstandings of children's behavior, these teachers limit children's opportunities for learning. Because they want to avoid overt discrimination and controversy, passive nonconstructive teachers appear to teach a mono-cultural curriculum that may not be immediately relevant to children from diverse cultural backgrounds.

3. *Passive constructive teachers* are similar to passive nonconstructive teachers in that they do not exhibit negative attitudes toward student diversity. They differ in three important ways—they have basic knowledge of their student's backgrounds, they have high expectations for their students regardless of their backgrounds, and their instructional practices utilize student's personal experiences and home culture. But, although these teachers often provide opportunities for students to share their experiences, they do not actively respond to the issues raised by the chil-

dren's contributions or incorporate them into classroom instruction. For example, teachers may permit children to talk about activities they engage in with their families (e.g., telling traditional stories), but do not incorporate stories from children's home cultures into classroom instruction.

4. *Active constructive teachers* hold high expectations for children and believe that background characteristics (e.g., poverty, poor family literacy) can be overcome through educational intervention. They assume that effective teaching requires the use of children's backgrounds and cultural heritage, and they celebrate the diversity of their students. These teachers deliberately convey to children that their background is an asset and not a problem in achieving educational objectives. For example, through the use of literature, poetry, and folktales, teachers weave together home and school pre-literacy and literacy activities into a seamless curriculum. They engage in positive discussion with children about the positive role their families and communities play in their lives.

5. *Proactive teachers* share all of the behavior and values of active, constructive teachers in that they celebrate the cultures of the children in their classrooms, and they incorporate into their teaching specific strategies intended to overcome aspects of their students' backgrounds that may impede their educational achievement. They deliberately develop instructional practices that use students' strengths, and in order to enhance learning, they consciously alter teaching methods in response to student's cultural characteristics. For example, proactive teachers of children from cultures that value cooperative effort in the achievement of group goals, such as Pueblo children (see Sunia & Smolkin, 1994, for a description of proactive teaching in Pueblo classrooms), will incorporate into instructional practices many opportunities of peer teaching and learning. Similarly, proactive teachers of African American children from low-income families will utilize instructional practices that reflect cultural practices prevalent in children's homes (e.g., communalism, meaning an emphasis on social interconnectedness and interdependence; movement-expressiveness, denoting an environment rich in rhythm, dance, and physical expression; and verve, or heightened stimulation; see Boykin & Bailey, 2000, for a fuller explanation of these factors.)

Knapp (1995) found a relationship between teachers' active or proactive use of children's home culture and children's academic achievement in writing and mathematics. Teachers who deliberately used children's home culture as a vehicle for helping them make meaning of curriculum content appeared to contribute to the development of knowledge and skill building. These findings suggest that teachers' active use of children's cultural backgrounds may positively affect educational outcomes.

Teachers' attitudes toward issues of diversity, privilege, and inequality may influence their capacity to embrace multiculturalism and anti-bias instruction. Moulty (1988, in Grant & Secada, 1990) reported that almost 40% of preservice teachers 1) did not believe that institutionalized racism influenced the experiences of minorities; 2) were not aware of how teachers' and students' beliefs, values, biases, and stereotypes might influence learning and teaching; and 3) did not believe that educators could significantly affect how teaching professionals think about learners in a diverse society. An additional factor—namely, the efforts of teacher educators (i.e., teacher college classes on multiculturalism, in-service training) to change teachers' stereotyped attitudes toward racial, ethnic, and cultural diversity—has had only moderate success (Webb-Johnson, Artiles, Trent, Jackson, & Velox, 1998), and there is a dearth of longitudinal studies that assess whether positive interventions have lasting effects on teaching practices. This is not to imply that many preschool and primary teachers are not committed to multiculturalism and anti-bias education in principle (see, for example, Berriz, 2000; Cruz-Janzen, 1998), but it does suggest that for many teachers, active examination of their own socialization regarding racial, ethnic and cultural biases, and racial and class privilege is difficult (Sleeter, 1993).

SUGGESTIONS FOR FUTURE AREAS OF WORK

A substantial gap exists between multicultural and anti-bias practice and theory (Gay, 1995; Wardle, 1996). Much work remains before the transformed multicultural school (Banks & Lynch, 1986) and anti-bias teaching and learning (Derman-Sparks & Phillips, 1997) are fully incorporated into U.S. schools. Some research and practice issues might move the field of multicultural and anti-bias education forward if addressed:

1. Teacher preparation and the role of teacher education institutions
2. In-service and supervisory support to new and veteran teachers in the field
3. Research that supports the value of multicultural and anti-bias education for child outcomes
4. Parent and community involvement in and attitudes toward multicultural and anti-bias education

Teacher Preparation

A body of research, conducted with scientific rigor, needs to be developed to determine effective undergraduate and graduate teacher training regarding diversity. This research should examine

- Necessary knowledge base, practice, and support needed by student teachers in order to enter the field as competent practitioners of multicultural and anti-biased education
- Content undergraduate and graduate education programs should teach regarding diversity
- Nature of student teacher supervision around issues of working effectively with diverse populations during practicum experiences
- Knowledge base, personal self-reflection, experiences, and values related to diversity of the faculty in undergraduate and graduate schools of education

Results from research on multicultural education preservice teacher education indicate methodological shortcomings (i.e., instructors of courses commonly evaluate their own work) and mixed results (see Grant & Secada, 1990; Ladson-Billings, 1995; Grant & Tate, 1995). An effective program of research should be designed, funded, and executed that helps to illuminate which student teacher training strategies, practices, and faculty characteristics are most effective in developing multicultural literacy and effective practice.

Support

Teachers who are already committed to and are implementing multicultural and anti-bias approaches in their classrooms need support to effectively continue their work. Researchers need to determine these supports, as well as practices these teachers think are effective in teaching children tolerance of diversity and anti-bias values and behaviors. Some new and veteran teachers may resist multicultural and anti-bias education, or be unable to move beyond Contributions and Additive Approaches to institute diversity education practices in their classrooms. Qualitative and quantitative research that helps to identify both the source of resistance and ways to address it in training, mentoring, or supervision would be enormously beneficial.

Value

There is a dearth of research, especially longitudinal research, on actual multicultural and anti-bias classroom practice that demonstrates its effectiveness over time in making young children more tolerant, less biased, and more proactive against bigotry and inequality. The field would benefit by systematic analysis of what teacher qualities, teaching practices, child characteristics, and curriculum most effectively achieve the goals identified by advocates of multicultural, anti-bias pedagogy.

Parent and Community Involvement

The literature on multicultural, anti-bias, and diversity education is relatively silent on the role of parents, families, and communities. Indeed, they appear to be the forgotten contributors to multicultural and anti-bias instruction. When parents are mentioned, they are often cast as the source of children's biased attitudes, but few studies attempt to assess parents' knowledge of and commitment to the goals of multicultural and anti-bias education, parents' views of bias and prejudice and ways to eliminate them, parents' views of what schools should do to eliminate biases and promote diversity, and parents' interests in aligning with teachers and schools to advance multicultural and anti-bias education (Barta & Winn, 1996). Systematic investigation of these little understood areas would help to identify ways in which teachers and schools might work cooperatively with parents to support the education of children who are able to live as effective and reflective citizens in a diverse society.

CONCLUSION

The development of transformative multicultural and anti-bias educational practice in American preschools and early elementary classrooms remains a compelling challenge to both schools and society. In the foreseeable future, will we as a nation successfully prepare children for a world increasingly comprised of the rich diversity of human cultures, languages, talents, and abilities? Will we be able to adequately prepare teachers who understand and incorporate into instruction children's home cultures, strengths, and characteristics? Will we develop pedagogy that is truly multicultural and assures the educational achievement of all children, and will we organize schools that proactively embrace diversity, are democratic and transformative, and reproduce equality (not inequality)? It is clear that the answers to these difficult questions rely on more than improved teaching and teacher preparation. But teaching and teachers do and will continue to play a critical role as frontline practitioners in the struggle for a truly transformative multicultural and anti-bias educational practices and pedagogy.

Both the research and practice literature (Fillmore & Snow, 2000; Irvine, 1990; Knapp, 1995) consistently indicate that teacher characteristics (e.g., professional training, cultural self-awareness, attitudes toward children's home cultures and languages) are key factors in children's school success. In addition, models of teachers who engage in transformative multicultural and anti-bias instruction and practice are available to guide our future work (see Banks, 1996; Knapp, 1995; Ladson-Billings, 1994). Our challenge as early childhood educators is to recognize, embrace, and work for the essential goal that lies at the heart of this work—the creation of a future for children, families, and schools that is free of bias and discrimination based on race, ability/disability, language, gender, sexual preference, ethnicity, and social class, and is truly inclusive and democratic.

REFERENCES

Adger, C.T., Christian, D., & Taylor, O. (Eds.). (1999). *Making the connection: Language and academic achievement among African American students.* Washington, DC: Center for Applied Linguistics.

Akbar, N. (1985). Our destiny: Authors of a scientific revolution. In H.P. McAdoo & J.L. McAdoo (Eds.), *Black children: Social, educational, and parental environments* (pp. 17–32). Thousand Oaks, CA: Sage Publications.

Anderson, E. (1999). *Code of the street: Decency, violence, and the moral life of the inner city.* New York: W.W. Norton & Company.

Annis, R.C., & Corenblum, B. (1987). Effect of test language and experimenter race on Canadian Indian children's racial and self-identity. *Journal of Social Psychology, 126,* 761–773.

Aronowitz, S., & Giroux, H.A. (1993). *Education still under siege.* Westport, CT: Bergin & Garvey.

Banks, J.A. (1972). Imperatives in ethnic minority education. *Phi Delta Kappan, 53*(5), 266–269.

Banks, J.A. (1993). Multicultural education for young children: Racial and ethnic attitudes and their modification. In B. Spodek (Ed.), *Handbook of research on the education of young children* (pp. 236–250). New York: Macmillan/McGraw Hill.

Banks, J.A. (Ed.). (1996). *Multicultural education, transformative knowledge, and action: Historical and contemporary perspectives.* New York: Teachers College Press.

Banks, J.A., & Lynch, J. (Eds.). (1986). *Multicultural education in western societies.* Austin, TX: Holt, Rinehart and Winston.

Barta, J., & Winn, T. (1996). Involving parents in creating anti-bias classrooms. *Children Today, 24*(1), 28–31.

Berriz, B.R. (2000). Raising children's cultural voices. [Electronic version]. *Rethinking Schools, 14*(4), 1–6. http://www.rethinking schools.org/Archives/14_04/bil144.htm

Bigler, R.S., & Liben, L.S. (1993). A cognitive-developmental approach to racial stereotyping and reconstructive memory in Euro-American children. *Child Development, 64,* 1507–1518.

Bowles, S., & Gintis, H. (1976). *School in capitalist America.* New York: Basic Books.

Bowman, B.T. (1989). Educating language-minority children. *ERIC Digest.* Urbana, IL: ERIC Publications.

Boykin, A.W., & Bailey, C.T. (2000). *The role of cultural factors in school relevant cognitive functioning: Description of home environment factors, cultural orientations, and learning preferences* (Report No. 43, U.S. Department of Education, Washington, DC).

Boykin, A.W., & Toms, F.D. (1985). Black child socialization: A conceptual framework. In H.P. McAdoo & J.L. McAdoo (Eds.), *Black socialization: Social, educational, and parental environments* (pp. 33–52). Thousand Oaks, CA: Sage Publications.

Boyle-Baise, M. (1999). Bleeding boundaries or uncertain center? A historical exploration of multicultural education. *Journal of Curriculum & Supervision, 99*(3), 191–216.

Cole, M. (1991). Culture and cognitive development. In M.E. Lamb & N. Bornstein (Eds.), *Developmental psychology: An advanced textbook.* Mahwah, NJ: Lawrence Erlbaum Associates.

Coles, R. (1964). *Children of crisis: A study of courage and fear.* New York: Dell Books.

Coles, R. (1977). *Children in crisis: Vol. 5. Privileged ones: The well-off and the rich in America.* New York: Little, Brown and Company.

Corsaro, W.A., & Miller, P.J. (1992). Editors' notes. In W.A. Corsaro & P.J. Miller (Eds.), *New directions for child development: No. 58. Interpretive approaches to children's socialization* (pp. 1–4). San Francisco: Jossey-Bass.

Corsaro, W.A., & Rosier, K.B. (1992). Documenting productive-reproductive processes in children's lives: Transition narratives of a Black family living in poverty. In W.A. Corsaro & P.J. Miller (Eds.), *New directions for child development: No. 58. Interpretive approaches to children's socialization* (pp. 67–92). San Francisco: Jossey-Bass.

Cross, W.E., Jr. (1991). *Shades of black: Diversity in African-American identity.* Philadelphia: Temple University Press.

Cruz-Janzen, M.I. (1998). Culturally authentic bias. [Electronic version]. *Rethinking Schools, 13*(1), 1–4. http://www.rethinkingschools.org/Archives/13_01/bias.htm

Damon, W. (1975). Early conceptions of positive justice as related to the development of logical operations. *Child Development, 46,* 301–312.

Damon, W. (1977). *The social world of the child.* San Francisco: Jossey-Bass.

Damon, W. (1980). Patterns of change in children's social reasoning: A two-year longitudinal study. *Child Development, 51,* 1010–1017.

Darling-Hammond, L., Pittman, K.J., & Ottinger, C. (1987). *Career choices for minorities: Who will teach?* Washington, DC: National Education and Council of State School Officers Task Force on Minorities in Teaching.

Delgado-Gaitan, C. (1994). Socializing young children in Mexican-American families: An intergenerational perspective. In P.M. Greenfield & R.R. Cocking (Eds.), *Cross-cultural roots of minority child development* (pp. 55–86). Mahwah, NJ: Lawrence Erlbaum Associates.

Delpit, L. (1988a). The silenced dialogue: Power and pedagogy in educating other people's children. *Harvard Education Review, 58,* 280–298.

Delpit, L. (1998b). What should teachers do?: Ebonics and culturally responsive instruction. In T. Perry & L. Delpit (Eds.), *The real Ebonics debate: Power, language and the education of young children* (pp. 17–27). Boston: Beacon Press.

Derman-Sparks, L., & the ABC Tack Force (1989). *Anti-bias curriculum: Tools for empowering young children.* Washington, DC: National Association for the Education of Young Children.

Derman-Sparks, L., & Phillips, C.B. (1997). *Teaching/learning anti-racism: A developmental approach.* New York: Teachers College Press.

Dodge, D.T., Jablon, J.R., & Bickart, T.S. (1994). *Constructing curriculum for the primary grades.* Washington, DC: Teaching Strategies.

Edmonds, R. (1979). Effective schools for the urban poor. *Educational Leadership, 37,* 15–24.

Ferguson, A.A. (2001). *Bad boys: Public schools in the making of Black masculinity.* Ann Arbor: University of Michigan Press.

Fillmore, L.W., & Meyer, L.M. (1992). The curriculum and linguistic minorities. In P. Jackson, (Ed.), *Handbook of research on curriculum: A project of the American Educational Association* (pp. 626–658). New York: Macmillan/McGraw Hill.

Fillmore, L.W., & Snow, C.E. (2000, August 23). *What teachers need to know about language.* Center for Applied linguistics. Available on-line: http://www.cal.org/ericcll/teachers/teachers.pdf

Gaskins, S., Miller, P.J., & Corsaro, W.A. (1992). Theoretical and methodological perspectives in the interpretive study of children. In P.J. Miller & W.A. Corsaro (Eds.), *New directions for child development: No. 58. Interpretive approaches to children's socialization* (pp. 5–24). San Francisco: Jossey-Bass.

Gay, G. (1986). Multicultural teacher education. In J.A. Banks & J. Lynch, (Eds.), *Multicultural education in Western societies* (pp. 154–177). Austin, TX: Holt, Rinehart and Winston.

Gay, G. (1991). Culturally diverse students and social studies. In J.P. Shaver (Ed.), *Handbook of research on social studies teaching and learning: A project of the National Council for the Social Studies* (pp. 144–156). New York: Macmillan/McGraw Hill.

Gay, G. (1995). Bridging multicultural theory and practice. *Multicultural Education, 3*(1), 4–9.

Gay, G. (2000). *Culturally responsive teaching: Theory, research and practice.* New York: Teachers College Press.

Giroux, H.A. (1996). *Fugitive cultures: Race, violence, and youth.* New York: Routledge.

Gonzalez-Mena, J. (1997). *Multicultural issues in child care* (2nd ed.). Mountain View, CA: Mayfield Publishing.

Gould, S.J. (1981). *The mismeasure of man.* New York: W.W. Norton & Company.

Grant, C.A., & Secada, W.G. (1990). Preparing teachers for diversity. In W.R. Houston (Ed.), *Handbook of research on teacher education* (pp. 403–422). New York: Macmillan/McGraw-Hill.

Grant, C.A., & Tate, W.F. (1995). Multicultural teacher education through the lens of multicultural education research literature. In J.A. Banks & C.M. Banks (Eds.), *Handbook of research on multicultural education* (pp. 145–166). New York: Macmillan/McGraw-Hill.

Greenfield, P.M., & Cocking, R.R. (1994). *Cross-cultural roots of minority child development.* Mahwah, NJ: Lawrence Erlbaum Associates.

Gwaltney, J.L. (1980). *Drylongso: A self-portrait of Black America.* New York: Random House.

Haberman, M. (1995). *Star teachers of children in poverty.* West Lafayette, IN: Kappa Delta Pi.

Hale-Benson, J.E. (1982). *Black children: Their roots, culture, and learning styles* (Rev. ed.). Baltimore: The Johns Hopkins University Press.

Haney, W. (1993). Testing and minorities. In L. Weis & M. Fine (Eds.), *Beyond silenced voices: Class, race, and gender in United States schools* (pp. 45–73). Albany: State University of New York Press.

Harkness, S. (1980). The cultural context of child development. *New Directions for Child Development, 8,* 7–14.

Heath, S.B. (1992). *Ways with words: Language, life, and work in communities and classrooms.* New York: Cambridge University Press.

Hirschfeld, L.A. (1995). Do children have a theory of race? *Cognition, 54,* 209–252.

Irvine, J. (1990). *Black students and school failure.* Westport, CT: Greenwood Publishing Group.

Jones-Wilson, F.C. (1990). The state of African-American education. In K. Lomotey (Ed.), *Going to school: The African-American experience* (pp. 31–51). Albany: State University of New York Press.

Kasinitz, P., Battle, J., & Miyares, I. (2001). Fade to Black?: The children of West Indian immigrants in Southern Florida. In R.C. Rumbaut & A. Portes (Eds.), *Ethnicities: Children of immigrants in America* (pp. 267–299). Berkeley: University of California Press.

Knapp, M.S. (Ed.). (1995). *Teaching for meaning in high-poverty classrooms.* New York: Teachers College Press.

Kohlberg, L. (1984). *The psychology of moral development: The nature and validity of moral stages* (Vol. 2). New York: HarperCollins Publishers.

Ladson-Billings, G. (1994). *The dreamkeepers: Successful teachers of African American children.* San Francisco: Jossey-Bass.

Ladson-Billings, G. (1995). Multicultural teacher education: Research, practice, and policy. In J.A. Banks & C.M. Banks (Eds.), *Handbook of research on multicultural education* (pp. 747–759). New York: Macmillan/McGraw-Hill.

Landry, B. (2000). *Black working wives: Pioneers of the American family revolution.* Berkeley: University of California Press.

Leahy, R.L. (1981). Development of the conception of economic inequality: I. Descriptions and comparisons of rich and poor people. *Child Development, 52,* 523–532.

Leahy, R.L. (1983). Development of the conceptions of economic inequality: II. Explanations, justifications, and concepts of social mobility and change. *Developmental Psychology, 19,* 111–125.

LeVine, R.A. (1974). Parental goals: A cross-cultural view. *Teacher's College Record, 76,* 226–239.

LeVine, R.A. (1980). Studies in anthropology and child development. In C.M. Super & S. Harkness (Eds.), *New directions in child development: No. 8. Anthropological perspectives on child development* (pp. 71–86). San Francisco: Jossey-Bass.

Maharidge, D. (1996). *The coming white minority: California, multiculturalism, and America's future.* New York: Vintage & Anchor Books.

McAdoo, H.P. (1993). Introduction. In H.P. McAdoo (Ed.), *Family ethnicity: Strength in diversity* (pp. ix–xv). Thousands Oak, CA: Sage Publications.

McAllister, G., & Irvine, J.J. (2000). Cross cultural competency and multicultural teacher education. *Review of Educational Research, 70*(1), 3–24.

Miller, H.M. (1998). Victims, heroes, and just plain folks. *Reading Teacher, 51*(7), 602–605.

Miron, L.F. (1999). Postmoderism and the politics of racialized identities. In R.D. Torres, L.F. Miron, & J.X. Inda (Eds.), *Race, identity, and citizenship: A reader* (pp. 79–100). Malden, MA: Blackwell Publishers.

National Center for Children in Poverty. (2000). *Child poverty in the United States: Young child poverty fact sheet.* (July 2000). Available on-line: http://cpmcnet.cpmc.columbia.edu/dept/nccp/ycpf.html

Ogbu, J. (1978). *Minority education and caste: The American system in cross-cultural perspective.* San Diego: Academic Press.

Ogbu, J. (1990). Literacy and schooling in subordinate cultures: The case of Black Americans. In K. Lomotey (Ed.), *Going to school: The African-American experience* (pp. 113–131). Albany: State University of New York Press.

One America. (1997). The advisory board: The President's initiative on race. Available on-line: http://www.whitehouse.gov/Initiatives/OneAmerica/advisory-plain.html

Pattillo-McCoy, M. (1999). *Black picket fences: Privilege and peril among the Black middle class.* Chicago: University of Chicago Press.

Phillips, C.B. (1989, January). Nurturing diversity for today's children and tomorrow's leaders. *Young Children,* 42–47.

Piaget, J. (1965). *The moral judgment of the child.* New York: The Free Press. (Original work published in 1932)

Piaget, J. (1969). *The child's conception of the world.* Totowa, NJ: Littlefield, Adams & Co.

Rist, R.C. (1970). Student social class and teacher expectations: The self-fulfilling prophecy in ghetto education. *Harvard Educational Review, 40,* 411–451.

Rogoff, B. (1982). Integrating context and cognitive development. In M.E. Lamb & A.L. Brown (Eds.), *Advances in Developmental Psychology* (Vol. 2). Mahwah, NJ: Lawrence Erlbaum Associates.

Rogoff, B. (1990). *Apprenticeship in thinking: Cognitive development in social context.* New York: Oxford University Press.

Rogoff, B., Baker-Sennett, J., Lacasa, P., & Goldsmith, D. (1995). Development through participation in sociocultural activity. In J. Goodman, P.J. Miller, & F. Kessel (Eds.), *New directions for child development: No. 67. Cultural practices as contexts for development* (pp. 45–64). San Francisco: Jossey-Bass.

Sapon-Shevin, M. (1993). Gifted education and the protection of privilege: Breaking the silence, opening the discourse. In L. Weis & M. Fine (Eds.), *Beyond silenced voices: Class, race, and gender in United States schools* (pp. 25–44). Albany: State University of New York Press.

Scheurich, J.J. (1998). Highly successful and loving public elementary schools populated mainly by low-SES children of color: Core beliefs and cultural characteristics. *Urban Education, 33*(4), 451–491.

Shimkin, D.B., Shimkin, E.M., & Frate, D.A. (Eds.). (1978). *The extended family in Black societies.* Hawthorne, NY: Mouton de Gruyter.

Skiba, R.J., Michael, R.S., Nardo, A.C., & Peterson, R. (2000). *The color of discipline: Sources of racial and gender disproportionality in school punishment.* Bloomington: Indiana Policy Center, Indiana University Press.

Sleeter, C.E. (1993). How white teachers construct race. In C. McCarthy & W. Crichlow (Eds.), *Race, identity, and representation in education* (pp. 157–170). New York: Routledge.

Smedley, A. (1997, September). American Anthropological Association Statement on "Race." *Anthropology Newsletter* Retrieved August 13, 2000 from http://www.aaanet.org/stmts/racepp.htm

Spencer, M.B. (1982). Personal and group identity of Black children: An alternative synthesis. *Genetic Psycology Monographs, 106,* 59–84.

Spencer, M.B., & Horowitz, F.D. (1973). Effects of systematic social and token reinforcement on the modification of racial and color concept attitudes of black and white preschool children. *Developmental Psychology, 9,* 246–254.

Spencer, M.B., & Markstrom-Adams, C. (1990). Identity processes among racial and ethnic minority children in America. *Child Development, 61,* 290–310.

Spencer, M.S. (1998). Reducing racism in schools: Moving beyond rhetoric. *Social Work in Education, 20,* 25–37.

Stepick, A., Stepick, C.D., Eugene, E., Teed, D., & Labissiere, Y. (2001). Shifting identities and intergenerational conflict: Growing up Haitian in Miami. In R.C. Rumbaut & A. Portes (Eds.), *Ethnicities: Children of immigrants in America* (pp. 229–265). Berkeley: University of California Press.

Strickland, D.S., & Ascher, C. (1992). Low-income African-American children and public school. In P. Jackson, *Handbook of research on curriculum: A project of the American Educational Research Association* (pp. 609–625). New York: Macmillan/McGraw-Hill.

Sunia, J.H., & Smolken, L.B. (1994). From natal culture to school culture to dominant society culture: Supporting transitions for Pueblo Indian students. In P.M. Guenfield & R.R. Cocking (Eds.), *Cross-cultural roots of minority child development* (pp. 115–130). Mahwah, NJ: Lawrence Erlbaum Associates.

Takaki, R. (Ed.). (1994). *From different shores: Perspectives on race and ethnicity in America* (2nd ed.). New York: Oxford University Press.

Tharp, R.G. (1994). Intergroup differences among Native Americans in socialization and child cognition: An ethnogenetic analysis. In P.M. Greenfield & R.R. Cocking (Eds.), *Cross-cultural roots of minority child development* (pp. 87–106). Mahwah, NJ: Lawrence Erlbaum Assocaites.

Torres, R.D., Miron, L.F., & Inda, J.X. (1999). Introduction. In R.D. Torres, L.F. Miron, & J.X. Inda (Eds.), *Race, identity, and citizenship: A reader* (pp. 1–16). Malden, MA: Blackwell Publishers.

U.S. Bureau of the Census. (1999, March). *Table 3.1. Foreign-born population by world region of birth, age and sex: March 1999.* Ethnic and Hispanic Statistics Branch, Population Division, U.S. Bureau of Current Population Survey, 1999. Available on-line: http://www.census.gov/population/socdemo/foreign/cps1999/tab0301.txt

Vygotsky, L. (1978). *Mind in society.* Cambridge, MA: Harvard University Press.

Walker-Moffat, W. (1995). *The other side of the Asian American success story.* San Francisco: Jossey-Bass.

Wardle, F. (1996). An anti-bias and ecological model for multicultural education. *Childhood Education, 72*(3), 152–156.

Watson-Gegeo, K.A. (1992). Thick explanation in the ethnographic study of child socialization: A longitudinal study of the problem of schooling for Kwara'ae (Solomon Islands) children. In W.A. Corsaro & P.J. Miller (Eds.), *New directions for child development: No. 58. Interpretive approaches to children's socialization* (pp. 51–66). San Francisco: Jossey-Bass.

Webb-Johnson, G., Artiles, A.J., Trent, S.C., Jackson, C.W., & Velox, A. (1998). The status of research on multicultural education in teacher education and special education. *Remedial and Special Education, 19*(1), 7–16.

Whiting, B.B., & Edwards, C.P. (1988). *Children of different worlds: The formation of social behavior.* Cambridge, MA: Harvard University Press.

Winfield, L.F. (1986). Teacher beliefs toward academically at risk student in inner urban schools. *Urban Review, 18,* 253–267.

Young, V.H. (1974). A Black American socialization pattern. *American Ethnologist, 1,* 405–413.

Classroom Practices in Multicultural and Anti-bias Education

8

Peter Hoffman-Kipp

When I first began teaching, I thought that I needed to give an authoritative performance. Very quickly, I realized that this stance did not work. My class had a voice of its own, which included the many and different voices of each student. Our voices were often at odds. The moment I began to listen, I learned not only about the students themselves but also about their families, friends, and communities. Students are not isolated beings. They have histories, families, networks of friends, approaches to solving problems, and unique interests in different phenomena. These relationships and interests comprise the net that will catch—and, in turn, translate—whatever occurs in the classroom. Understanding and respecting students for their uniqueness and their connectedness is what multicultural and anti-bias education is all about.

Multicultural and anti-bias education seeks to assist students living in a diverse democracy where they can tolerate others but also work against their oppression and advocate for equality. Some have termed this goal *cultural democracy* (Romo & Salerno, 2000). In a cultural democracy, people work

> To find unity among diverse peoples, collaborate around mutual purposes, influence an exchange of knowledge and skills that results in shared meaning, take action for the purpose of significant change, and voluntarily engage in decision making, creative solutions, and implementations. (Banks & McGee Banks, 1997; Nava, 1995; Rost, 1991, cited in Romo & Salerno, 2000, p. 3)

These ideas resonate with teachers and researchers who speak of *social reconstruction* (Grant & Sleeter, 1999), *critical consciousness* (Freire, 1996), *transformative education* (Banks, 1996; Hooks, 1994), and *democracy in the classroom*.

Multicultural teacher education focuses on helping teachers learn to deal with student cultural diversity (Garcia, 1999); however, many teachers have no formal training in multicultural and anti-bias education. If you fall into this category, don't be intimidated! This chapter is meant to facilitate the progress teachers make toward implementation of a multicultural and anti-bias approach, which will encourage the "development of every child's fullest potential by actively addressing issues of diversity and equity in the classroom" (Hohensee & Derman-Sparks, 1992, p. 1).

TEACHER CONCERNS

Multicultural and anti-bias education requires change both in school environment and in teachers themselves, so it is natural for you to have concerns. These concerns will be eased if you receive the support and resources you need, including examples of how to implement a multicultural and anti-bias curriculum; open discussion about confusing feelings that arise; and help addressing issues of justice, fairness, diversity, and culture-specific parenting practices. It may benefit you to have a special person at your school to facilitate diversity.

Avoiding Miscommunication with Parents

Sometimes miscommunication can occur between parents and teachers. The difference between a valid home cultural practice and inadequate parenting of a child (e.g., discipline) can be confusing. Some cultures encourage their children to express their desires and choices more vocally than others. You may be overwhelmed by one student who has no problem stating what he or she feels while other children are silently waiting to be told what to do. In such a situation, knowing what parents are encouraging as well as understanding the dynamics of the child's home culture can assist you in working with the family instead of alienating them.

You also may run into problems if you want to celebrate a student's home culture, but the parents only want to Americanize their child. In addition, teaching students a democratic and social-justice approach to life may contradict lessons children are learning in the home (e.g., to unilaterally respect authority). In such situations, communication with parents is essential. Finding ways to involve parents in the classroom both physically and through telephone calls and letters sent home can help parents understand that their home cultural practices are an important bridge that their children will use to understand the culture of the United States.

   Teachers are often unaware of their own legal limitations when culture and religion intersect. Although you may fear the intersection between church and state, such an intersection is often supported on the grounds of the social studies standards of the district and state frameworks themselves. In fact, for many states, the question has changed from "Should we teach about religion" to "How should we include the study of religion in the curriculum?" (Risinger, 1993). You may need to research cultures and to develop plans of inclusion and strategies to approach parents.

Dealing with Colleagues Who Do Not Support Multicultural and Anti-Bias Education

In their efforts to realize a multicultural school climate, teachers are often surprised by their own colleagues' unwillingness to change. If this is the case, you must work to continue discussions with your colleagues in order to understand any personal experiences that have influenced the colleagues' philosophies about multicultural education. More information on this topic can be found in the section called "Four Phases of Adopting a New Approach."

Dealing with Personal Bias

Valuing human diversity and treating all people fairly is the basis of multicultural and anti-bias education. Regardless of the subject matter or age level, teachers who change curriculum and pedagogy to reflect multiculturalism and anti-bias must challenge prior beliefs and perspectives (e.g., how can I teach what I don't believe to be good for children?). Some teachers have prejudices or assumptions about certain ethnic, economic, or cultural groups that hinder their ability to embrace multicultural and anti-bias education. For instance, a teacher may be uneasy with gay and lesbian families. Or teachers may not be comfortable with families who do not speak English at home. They may feel that they must learn 30 different languages and cultures for each of the 30 students in their classrooms in order to do their job well. How teachers specifically deal with this task of handling their own bias is different, but a few practices seem to be present in all places where there is a real change of school culture and thinking:

- Open conversation among teachers, parents, students, administrators, and community members

- Experimentation with teaching styles
- Bridges between the home and school where both are construed as learning environments
- Recognition that the classroom community must make connections with the school and neighborhood for education to be meaningful

FOUR PHASES OF ADOPTING A NEW APPROACH

Once you address your concerns about multicultural and anti-bias education, it is important to spend time examining which approaches to multicultural education fit your style and your school culture. Then, begin to implement a strategy that you feel comfortable with. As you adopt this new approach to education, you can anticipate four phases: 1) creating the classroom climate, 2) nonsystematic implementation, 3) systematic implementation, and 4) ongoing integration. Let's explore the process with Julie, a first-grade teacher.

Phase 1: Creating the Classroom Climate

Julie became interested in multicultural and anti-bias education when she heard about it at a professional conference. She decided that it was something she wanted to try in her classroom and spoke with a few of her colleagues about the idea. Two colleagues were interested in the approach, so the three of them decided to form a support group. They planned to meet twice a month to give each other honest feedback about how they thought the new approach was working.

Julie knew that multicultural education would be a lot different from the school's current approach to education, so she decided it would be best to start by examining her own beliefs. She thought about her own identity and how her identity affected the way she viewed others. At the first group meeting, she brought index cards with introspective questions written on them. To help each other think about multiculturalism, the group members asked one another questions such as

- How did you become aware of the various aspects of your identity?
- What differences among people make you feel uncomfortable?
- When have you experienced or witnessed bias in your life, and how did you respond?

After examining her own beliefs, Julie decided to find out about her students' beliefs about diversity. During free time, she interviewed students with questions such as

- What do you know about Native Americans?

- What makes you a girl or a boy?

- What kind of work could a person in a wheelchair do?

She also observed the students' reactions during recess. Which students were excluded from games? How were girls encouraged to play? Were there any students who did not get along with other students? Inside the classroom, Julie read through the storybooks to see how groups of people were portrayed. She made a list of stereotypes that the students would encounter when they read the books. She also examined the books in the reading area. How diverse were they? She considered the languages spoken by students at home and realized that all of the books in her classroom were in English. She decided to ask the librarian for books in other languages, as well. She made a list of languages she would like to include.

Next, Julie looked at the displays in the room to see what messages they might be sending about diversity. She made a checklist to fill out for each display.

- Does the display show people of diverse abilities?

- Does the display show people from diverse ethnic backgrounds?

- Does the display show an equal number of men and women?

- Does the display represent people from diverse economic backgrounds?

- Do the display images include depictions of important individuals who participated in struggles for justice? (See the first chapter in Hohensee and Derman-Sparks, 1992, for more ideas for questions.)

This evaluation revealed that some of the displays were inappropriate and stereotypical. She made a list of the worst offenders to share with the support group. The group shared their thoughts on diversity in their classrooms. They decided that it might help if they each visited the others' classrooms and evaluated them, as well. This process provided such valuable feedback that they decided to invite parents into the classroom the following week to discuss their impressions of the displays and books.

Phase 2: Nonsystematic Implementation

After examining her beliefs and the classroom environment, Julie began to act on "teachable moments." These moments arose through unexpected statements or actions by students or other school personnel. For instance, while reading a book about a child with a visual impairment, one student asked how the child could recognize the people she met. Julie decided to start a discussion with her students by asking how they would react if they met a person who could not see. The discussion went so well that Julie invited a person with a visual impairment to speak to the class. The speaker taught the students about Braille. Julie's students were excited to experiment with glue on paper to create their own "Braille." Julie talked with them about how they could label the classroom to make it easier for a person with limited vision to walk around.

In continuation of the class's exploration of disabilities, Julie decided to plan a trip for the students to a cultural and educational center for people with visual impairments. At the center, students participated in activities that presumed certain ability levels the students did not have. Immediately, they became aware that they had crossed some sort of border between cultural worlds. They understood the ways in which participation in culturally organized activities presumes that people have certain interests, abilities, and identities. They realized how their activities outside of the center were organized differently. As an ongoing connection, Julie established a relationship between her class and the center so that students could, via computers, telephones, and their developing proficiency with Braille, communicate with the people they met at the center.

Julie also realized that continued parental involvement was vital. Through newsletters, meetings, and individual conferences, Julie explained to the parents the reasons behind the changes she had been making in the classroom. She acknowledged that the parents were not only learners, but teachers themselves, as well as an integral part of the learning and teaching community of the classroom. As Julie and her students' parents became partners in the project of multicultural education, they began to find ways to support each other and contribute to the multicultural and anti-bias approach. For instance, Julie set up a reading center and invited parents to bring in books they read with their children. She also asked parents to create a poster, which would remind her and her students that they bring family connections with them into new experiences.

Phase 3: Systematic Implementation

After 3–5 months, a multicultural and anti-bias climate had been present in Julie's classroom long enough for her to answer questions like

- What issues have surfaced?
- What has been accomplished?
- What areas need further work?

In answering these questions, Julie tried to use a systematic and comprehensive approach. Julie's main concern at this point was to reflect on her nonsystematic implementation through teachable moments to see what specific constants came up. She realized that her students had an interest in people, places, and cultures that they had not voiced before. In addition, she was happy to note that her classroom felt safer both to her and to her students. However, she realized that her responses to teachable moments did not satisfy her growing discomfort with her traditional curriculum. She had changed her methods and the climate of her classroom, but she continued to begin lessons the same and to end them with standard tests supplied by a teaching manual. She was interested in developing some units on her own.

Realizing this would take some time, she set her sights on the coming school year, even though it was only February. She began to record more diligently in a journal the experiences she had with teachable moments and to reflect on her lesson plans, their implementation, and the directions students' questions took. She presented these findings to her support group and asked them to reflect back to her what they heard and saw; she wanted to hear what an observer might notice were her main themes or objectives. The response she got prompted her to begin to develop a unit on justice, democracy, and accommodation that would reflect her growing interest in cultural democracy and participation of all members.

She continued to involve parents in the process by asking for their input early enough that she could wait a month for a response. She asked specific questions and created a worksheet for parents, asking them for guest speakers, supplies, and other specific needs she had for the unit. By late spring, she was ready to present the findings to her support group. During the support group meeting, the teachers advised her about planning and constructing the details. They also advised her how she might connect this unit to other elements of her existing curriculum.

Phase 4: Ongoing Integration

Julie began the new school year differently. She worked with students initially to feel at home in her classroom through a classroom-decoration project. She involved families immediately, and ended this first session of the class with a gathering for families and students in a ceremony to dedicate their classroom to respect, anti-bias, and listening. She then began her first unit, which she had been developing since early spring. She met with some success but some challenges because she had expected responses based on last year's students; she was surprised and frustrated, but her support group reminded her of her excitement over the unit and her successes in relationship to her previous year when dealing with these topics.

Eventually, Julie got the point where she automatically used the anti-bias perspective to design her lesson plans and to evaluate her interactions with her students, their parents, and her colleagues. She took time to reflect on the process and how far she had come since she first became interested in multicultural education. She realized the cycle through which an anti-bias and multicultural curriculum develops:

> As children engage in activities, they respond with comments and questions that become further "teachable moments." Teachers then plan more activities in response, which in turn lead to more teachable moments from the children, and the cycle continues as a part of daily classroom life. (Hohensee & Derman-Sparks, 1992, p. 4)

The goal is the process, Hohensee and Derman-Sparks argue, by which this work continues to occur and be renewed with each constituent that enters the equation whether he or she is a staff member, student, or parent.

Julie realized that, fundamentally, she wanted students, parents, colleagues, and other members of the school community to feel a part of the activities in her classroom. The process of creating curriculum was an organic process for her, and the school was a part of a larger community that deserved to be part of that process. Julie had become committed to participation as a foundation for her teaching.

PRACTICAL STRATEGIES

There are many ways teachers can implement a multicultural and anti-bias approach in diverse environments while addressing diverse topics. These examples suggest some concrete ideas as starting points for beginning work in your own classroom.

- *Teacher collaboration visuals:* When working with other teachers, give explicit instructions for how the activity will function, and talk about how roles will be divided. Break the project down into manageable parts.
- *Student collaboration visuals:* Allow students to work in groups to promote their creativity, teamwork, and reflection.
- *Teacher-created visuals:* Make your own visuals to explain and clarify lessons and to respond to student questions.
- *Student-created visuals:* Encourage students to make their own visuals for projects.
- *Connections to the home culture visuals:* Involve parents and the community in your classroom. Incorporate student's stories and language into your lesson plans. Use children's prior knowledge as a foundation for learning.
- *Project-oriented curriculum visuals:* Allow students to learn through projects that use different student strengths, skills, and abilities.

- *Group projects visuals:* Promote goal-directed collaboration and peer-to-peer communication.

Some other areas to consider are involving students in their learning; approaching gay, lesbian, bisexual, and transgender issues; and overcoming prejudice.

Involving Students in Their Learning

A multicultural approach to teaching involves creating a democratic classroom climate and teaching strategies that encourage students to take responsibility for their own learning (Steffey & Hood, 1994). Students who take responsibility for their learning are more engaged in the activity and use more creativity and collaboration. These children have greater intrinsic motivation because they care about what they are learning.

To find out what students are interested in, encourage them to ask questions. First, give children adequate time to think creatively about the material, to form opinions, and to think of questions to ask (Short, 1993). Encourage this by exploring several broad concepts throughout the year so that students have plenty of time to consider the relationships in the subject matter and to ask questions. Such concepts include change, democracy, community, and participation.

Encourage students to develop questions about material by letting them work in groups, helping them make connections to current events, and urging them to challenge their point of view (e.g., by asking how a certain person would feel about this issue). Ask them to bring in newspaper articles to discuss or to create a pictorial representation of what they are studying. Another activity is *hot seat,* in which one student role-plays as a character and the rest of the class asks the student questions. You can place a jar in the back of the room for students to place questions. At the end of the class, read two questions, and discuss possible answers.

These concepts are especially applicable to teaching social studies. Social studies teachers can challenge students to realize that all historical narrative has more than one perspective to it and help students see that history is not static but is made daily. History is changeable in the present, and students can learn to feel empowered by their story of history rather than weakened by its weight. Teachers can help students see the importance of recognizing others' perspectives as well as their own. They can communicate their love for the subject matter as well as present some of the engaging historical questions that prompt scholars to rethink perspective in historical analysis. This type of education challenges students with the problem-solving process that is at the heart of collaborative efforts to solve some of democracy's biggest challenges. Children of different ages will get different things out of a social studies class. Students in kindergarten will understand a sense of time, the cyclical quality of life, and where to look for answers to their questions (Crawford et al., 1994). First-grade students will develop a sense of being in charge of their own learning and will be able to evaluate what they have learned using portfolio self-assessment. Students in a multiage classroom of first, second, and third graders will develop independence and the ability to research historical events using interviews, classroom visitors they contacted, library resources, and letters they write themselves. All of these skills are part of multicultural and anti-bias education.

Approaching Gay, Lesbian, Bisexual, and Transgender Issues

Gay, lesbian, bisexual, and transgender issues present a personal, political, and cultural challenge, and you may be unsure of how to approach the subject with young children. Because two biological parents do not always live in the child's home, you need to be aware of the messages you send regarding family. Children raised in gay- and lesbian-headed households often undergo experiences based on the identification their parents have as a distinct group. During a discussion or study of family or during daily interactions, if these children's experiences are not being addressed and normalized, then the children are inevitably being hurt, excluded, and isolated. The visibility or invisibility of the experiences of children from gay- and lesbian-headed households is greatly linked to teachers' and the school's commitment, flexibility, and involvement with changing family structures, views on homosexuality and the sexual development of children, and ability to view children as individuals with varying experiences (Chapman, 1999).

One way to discuss these issues with children is to focus on the ideas of justice, fairness, diversity, and family. Scholars of early childhood education generally suggest the family and gender role definition as the best way to approach gay, lesbian, bisexual, and transgender issues with young children. Because young children have experience with parents and guardians and the kinds of work that men and women do in their home, they can often begin the conversation surrounding issues of difference.

However, in the event that gay, lesbian, bisexual, and transgender issues are foist on you due to an unforeseen event (e.g., name calling), you have the opportunity to respond in several ways. First, take the opportunity to instruct students about the true meaning of the term being used. Don't shy away from explaining the meaning of *gay* or *lesbian* if a student is using one of these words. Second, start a conversation about stereotyping and name-calling. In both cases, someone gets hurt. Explain how these behaviors are no different from another issue (e.g., race) being used. Finally, talk about family, as mentioned previously. Such a conversation is readily accessible by all students and can help students understand the ordinariness of gay, lesbian, bisexual, and transgender families (Gay, Lesbian and Straight Education Network, 1999).

Chapman (1999) mentions two anecdotes with 3-year-old children that illustrate the need for teachers to respond to the experiences of children from gay-, lesbian-, bisexual-, and transgender-headed families. In one instance, a boy stated that he wished to marry a male peer. A girl in the class stated that boys could not marry boys. The teacher clarified that this could be the case if a man loves another man, as in the case of Zoly, a student in their class whose parents were gay men. In the other instance, a student said he would complain to his mother about what was in his lunch. When the teacher suggested that he take up the issue with both his mother and his father, the student replied that only his mother makes his lunch, but then he said, "In Zoly's family, only his daddies can make his lunch because he has two daddies." The teacher agreed that yes, men can make lunches, too. In both of these situations, the teacher spoke to the students openly and honestly and took the opportunity to discuss stereotyping.

Overcoming Prejudice

Young children often have already developed prejudices like sexism and homophobia. In fact, research reveals that children notice (and construct) categories or stereotypes very early (Derman-Sparks & the ABC Task Force, 1989). Stereotyping and bias in the community (or immediate groups) influence children's attitudes and self-concept from a very early age. For example, by age 2, children use appropriate gender labels, and by age 3, children show signs of being influenced by societal biases and may show gender or racial prejudice. By 4 or 5 years old, children engage in active gender-appropriate behavior; they use racial reasons for refusing to interact with children who are different from themselves, and they reject people with disabilities (Derman-Sparks et al., 1989).

Teachers have an important role in helping students to become more accepting of diversity. Rather than ignoring prejudicial conversations between children, intercede and teach children that difference does not have a value judgement attached to it. (See http://www.atlasbooks.com/glsen/ordermid.htm for several books to read to primary students.)

Resistance from families of young children is one impediment of teachers implementing a multicultural and anti-bias curriculum. Chapman gives an example of how to make that bridge effective arguing that "[w]hen an open dialogue exists between teachers and parents it provides children with an opportunity to build compatible experiences between home and school" (1999, p. 12). One strategy for connecting with parents is to send home a parent letter and explain to children that the class will be focusing on families. Parents should be encouraged to bring in pictures or make a part of a collage that can be posted in the room. The result will demonstrate the diversity of members that make up a household and the variety of roles they play. Talking about gay, lesbian, bisexual, and transgender households and gender roles becomes a natural extension.

Homophobia may discourage female assertiveness and male sensitivity and may prevent children of gay and lesbian parents from talking about their families in school (Chapman, 1999). Therefore, teachers have the responsibility to expand children's awareness of these differences. Some activities to try include

- Reading books on different ways families are organized (see http://www.atlasbooks.com/glsen/ordermid.htm for ideas)
- Inviting family members who do nontraditional, sex-stereotyped jobs to speak to the class (e.g., a female construction worker, male child care provider)
- Supporting children's dramatic play in nontraditional roles and in different family structures (Derman-Sparks et al., 1989)

Literature, role models, and role play can make dynamic the lived truths of different family structures and cultures. Chapman wrote, "Stories influence children. They also empower children because they give validity to their actions . . . .They provide children with alternatives and also empower them to make and observe choices regardless of one's gender identity" (1999, p. 13).

TEACHERS AS SOCIAL JUSTICE EDUCATORS

Most students in American teacher education programs are Caucasian, speak one language, come from rural or suburban communities, and have very little direct intercultural experience (American Association of Colleges for Teacher Education [AACTE], 1987, 1989; Gomez, 1994; Irvine, 1989; LaFontaine, 1988). This fact alone often is utilized to recommend multicultural education for teachers. Consider the comparative demographic of Los Angeles' teacher-to-student racial profile. Approximately 90% of the students in the Los Angeles Unified School District are students of color, and approximately 60% of its teaching force is Caucasian (Genzuk & Baca, 2001).

Experiments in teacher education search for ways to meet the need for more culturally sensitive teachers. Several theorists and teacher education programs have labored to produce a definition of *social justice education* and sought to design a system that assists teachers in coming to know what this term means. Integral to this definition is the sense that teachers must be facilitators and not just all-knowing sources of knowledge. This definition seeks to deal with the power teachers wield and the changes teachers have to undergo in order to share that power with students, parents, and community members who constitute the school community and are often the most knowledgeable resources for new teachers.

Jeannie Oakes and Martin Lipton offered a definition of social justice education as one that does three things:

1. It considers the values and politics that pervade education, as well as the more technical issues of teaching and organizing schools;

2. It asks critical questions about how conventional thinking and practice came to be, and who in society benefit from them; and

3. It pays particular attention to inequalities associated with race, social class, language, gender, and other social categories, and looks for alternatives to the inequalities. (1999, p. xviii)

A possible fourth perspective is, "It treats cultural and linguistic diversity as an asset to teaching and learning" (TEP Research Group, 1999–2000).

The notions of sharing power and treating diversity as an asset to teaching and learning have important repercussions. Students are not seen as empty containers waiting for knowledge to be thrown at them. Learning occurs when teachers and students interact and share ideas. In an atmosphere where students come from diverse backgrounds that do not match the teacher's or the dominant group, open discussion between students and teachers is particularly important.

If you are a student in a teacher education program, you can find out about community assets and cultural routines by participating in community activities prior to and during your time in the program. Similar to the California state preliminary field experience requirement that compels teachers to observe an urban, multicultural classroom prior to acceptance into an internship program, community observations seek to assist you in bridging the gap between your own cultural background and the diversity of backgrounds you will face in your classroom. Regardless of the location of your school, observations in the community help you understand the background your students will bring to the classroom. You probably do not have an implicit understanding of the community unless you are returning to a school you attended. Even in such cases, the school demographics may have changed, and certainly, your perspectives change as you return as an adult. Carrying this process on while teaching should be a priority for teachers interested in an anti-bias, multicultural approach.

BECOMING A MEMBER OF A SOCIAL MOVEMENT

Many teacher education programs that face these goals struggle to address and connect teachers to social movements. Seeing teaching as embedded in an ongoing movement that involves other aspects of the community makes teachers feel a part of something, prevents burnout, and assists in remedying the isolation that new and continuing teachers often feel, especially when trying to bring about organizational and community change. In so doing, these teacher education programs work within a larger progressive community that prioritizes social issues (e.g., affordable housing, health care, educational opportunity, citizenship, union organizing) in impoverished communities because these issues shape the needs of students in schools. School is seen as interconnected and teaching as part of a force for progressive change. Simultaneously, teachers demonstrate for their students that learning in school is connected to learning in the community.

You should ask the following questions:

- What problems or issues are facing the community?

- What main improvements would community members like to see?

- What kinds of additional resources could the community best use, and for what?

- What resources does the community have for addressing these issues, and what is the community trying to do about them?

- What are the community's greatest strengths?

- What should future citizens learn in order to contribute best to the local community's growth, development, and improvement? (Grant & Sleeter, 1999)

As the community's needs emerge, so also will discussions with early elementary school students as to what interests them as a class or small group project. Often, these discussions alone provide rich fodder for teaching topics, but action is important. As students realize that their actions have repercussions for their community, they see history as dynamic and their lives as important in the process of change that they can affect.

CONCLUSION

Children come to understand their world through the lens of their identity. Teachers must think about how early childhood classroom environments, curricula, and pedagogy help students to develop a proactive vision of themselves as important participants in the community. How are students developing their voice? As students learn to trust the classroom atmosphere established by the teachers in conjunction with parents and students, a microcosm of cultural democracy is established. In this milieu, students and teachers realize that knowledge is constructed through collaboration, a key lesson for full participation in society.

REFERENCES

American Association of Colleges for Teacher Education. (AACTE). (1987). *Teaching teachers: Facts and figures. Research about teacher education project.* Washington, DC: Author.

American Association of Colleges for Teacher Education. (AACTE). (1989). *Rate III—teaching teachers: Facts and figures.* Washington, DC: Author.

Banks, J.A., & McGee Banks, C.A., (Eds.). (1997). *Multicultural education: Issues and perspectives* (4th ed.). San Francisco: Jossey-Bass.

Chapman, S.K. (1999, January 1). *The power of children's literature: Gay and lesbian themes in a diverse childhood curriculum.* Retrieved from http://www.glsen.org/binary-data/GLSEN_ARTICLES/pdf_file/391.pdf

Crawford, K., Ferguson, M., Kauffman, G., Laird, J., Schroeder, J., & Short, K. (1994). In S. Steffey & W.J. Hood (Eds.), *If this is social studies, why isn't it boring.* Portland, ME: Stenhouse Publishers.

Derman-Sparks, L., & the ABC Task Force. (1989). *The anti-bias curriculum: Tools for empowering young children.* Washington, DC: National Association for the Education of Young Children.

Freire, P. (1996) *Pedagogy of the oppressed.* New York: The Continuum International Publishing Group.

Garcia, E. (1999). *Student cultural diversity: Understanding and meeting the challenge* (2nd ed.). Boston: Houghton Mifflin.

Gay, Lesbian and Straight Education Network. (1999, January 1). *Advice to teachers: Tinky wicky in the classroom.* Retrieved from http://www.glsen.org/binary-data/GLSEN_ARTICLES/pdf_file/36.pdf

Genzuk, M., & Baca, R. (2001). The paraeducator-to-teacher pipeline. *Education and Urban Society, 31*(1), 73–98.

Gomez, M.L. (1994). Teacher education reform and prospective teachers: Perspectives on teaching other people's children. *Teaching and Teacher Education, 10*(3), 319–224.

Grant, C.A., & Sleeter, C.E. (1999). *Turning on learning: Five approaches for multicultural teaching plans for race, class, gender, and disability* (2nd ed.). New York: John Wiley & Sons.

Hohensee, J.B., & Derman-Sparks, L. (1992). Implementing an anti-bias curriculum in early childhood classrooms. *ERIC Digest.* Urbana, IL: ERIC Clearinghouse on Elementary and Early Childhood Education. (ERIC Reproduction Services No. ED351146)

Hooks, B. (1994). *Teaching to transgress: Education as the practice of freedom.* New York: Routledge.

Irvine, J.J. (1989, December). *Cultural responsiveness in teacher education: Strategies to prepare majority teachers for successful instruction of minority students.* Paper presented at the annual meeting of Project 30, Monterey, CA.

LaFontaine, H. (1988). Educational challenges and opportunities in serving limited-English-proficient students. In Council of Chief State School Officers (Ed.), *School success for students at risk* (pp. 120–153). Orlando, FL: Harcourt.

Nava, A. (1995). (Ed.). *Educating Americans in a multiethnic society* (3rd ed.). New York: McGraw-Hill.

Oakes, J., & Lipton, M. (1999). *Teaching to change the world.* New York: McGraw-Hill Higher Education.

Risinger, C.F. (1993, August). Religion in the social studies curriculum. *ERIC Digest.* Bloomington, IN: ERIC Clearinghouse for Social Studies/Social Science Education. (ERIC Document Reproduction Service No. ED363553)

Romo, J.J., & Salerno, C. (2000). *Toward cultural democracy: The journey from knowledge to action in diverse classrooms.* Boston: Houghton Mifflin.

Rost, J.C. (1991). *Leadership for the twenty-first century.* Westport, CT: Praeger Publishers.

Short, K. (1993, April). *Integrating curriculum through inquiry cycles.* Paper presented at the Annual Convention of the International Reading Association, San Antonio.

Steffey, S., & Hood, W.J. (1994). *If this is social studies, why isn't it boring.* Portland, ME: Stenhouse Publishers.

TEP Research Group. (1999–2000). *A social justice perspective: Working definition.* Unpublished manuscript, University of California-Los Angeles.

Afterword

Carollee Howes

Thinking about practices in early childhood education, reading these chapters, and participating in the conference that inspired this volume have made it clear to me that having every child in an early childhood education program that enacts practices that are both culturally competent *and* associated with succeeding in elementary school is a monumental task. A few themes seem important to highlight: changing or enhancing our theoretical framework, the early childhood workforce, and clarity about practices.

CHANGING OR ENHANCING OUR THEORETICAL FRAMEWORK

When teachers at the National Center for Early Development & Learning (NCEDL) conference, Teaching and Learning in the Classroom: Practices for Four- to Eight-Year-Old Children, met in small groups to discuss how to apply the research paper topics to classroom activity, they often began with the phrase, "But we already do that." Sharon Ritchie, who had worked for years with many of these teachers and with others in University of California–Los Angeles's teacher training program, suggested that the discussion would be enhanced if the group began with the phrase, "How can we do this better?" She argued that more complex and nuanced teaching practices would emerge from this kind of discussion. I suspect that these two phrases, one leading to a dead end and the other to innovative thinking, are as applicable to researchers in early childhood as they are to teachers.

We researchers have spent our research careers examining associations between experiences of young children and their contemporary and long-term development as well as the associations between young children and their teachers and caregivers. We "grew up" with Bronfenbrenner's (1986)

173

theory of ecological contexts of human development and already know about examining the meaning of behavior in context. But as recent work by Rogoff (Rogoff, Matusov, & White, 1996), the chapters in this volume by Jean Baker and Aisha Ray, and challenges from the reconceptualizing early childhood group (Lubeck, 1996, 1998) illustrate, there is much that we can do better in understanding and explaining how and with whom practices in early childhood education are enacted so that practices enhance development. For example, thanks to a massive public education program, it would be hard to not know that the practice of reading to children is good for their future development.

But this is insufficient information. We need theories that help us examine, for example, if reading a culturally relevant book in the context of a secure teacher–child relationship is sufficient to predict early literacy or whether we also need theories of practice about how to read (e.g., collaborative sounding out words, engaging the child in exploring the meaning of the story, making a puppet show to act out the story) or whether one-to-one adult–child reading is different from reading to the entire group of children or using collaborative peer reading.

It will not be easy to hold in the same theory the importance of relationships between adults and children, of culture and home language, of teacher behaviors that respectfully enhance collaborative adult–child and child–child learning, *and* content knowledge (e.g., counting). Yet, the chapters in this volume present compelling evidence that theories to explain associations between experiences of young children in early childhood programs and their contemporary and long-term development must include all of these elements—relationships, culture and home language, collaborative adult–child interaction, and content knowledge—if they are to succeed. To do this task, I suspect that researchers who identify as developmental psychologists and researchers who identify as early childhood educators must collaborate.

THE EARLY CHILDHOOD WORKFORCE

As this volume has illustrated, teachers of 4- to 8-years-old children bring commitment and enthusiasm to enhancing the lives of children. Teachers are working hard to develop and implement practices around classroom community, literacy, mathematics, and multiculturalism as they strive to meet the needs of the diverse children in their programs. At the conference, it was difficult to end the small groups because discussions were intense, complicated, and lengthy. Yet, I cannot help but reflect that perhaps we are expecting far too much of a workforce that is underpaid and increasingly not trained for what is expected of it.

In the late 1980s, the National Child Care Staffing Study pointed out that the early childhood workforce was both significantly better educated than the average worker in the United States but significantly less well paid (Whitebook, Howes, & Phillips, 1990). A decade later, the workforce was even less well paid relative to other workers but not quite as well educated (Whitebook, Howes, & Phillips, 1998). As might be expected, teachers who were well educated tended to move into higher paying jobs outside the classroom, and programs were unable to replace those teachers with similarly well-educated teachers.

In order to use the practices that help children learn, teachers need to be as enthusiastic about reading and literature, science and mathematics, and geography and history as they are about loving children. In order to prepare children for further school success, early childhood teachers need to be highly successful in their own schooling. Accessing postsecondary education is difficult for early childhood education teachers, especially if they are women from lower socioeconomic groups. Beyond the financial barriers, there are gender, class, and race barriers to college degree programs. For many of the preschool teachers who attended the NCEDL conference, this was the first time they had been on the campus of a university.

The field struggles with these issues—reducing the barriers to higher education, making the content of classes accessible, and changing the science of early childhood education to include children who are not white, who live in poverty, who are immigrants, who do not speak English, and who are living under difficult life circumstances. However, children need teachers right now who can work with them in a content-sophisticated manner. We have much to do to resolve these dilemmas.

CLARITY ABOUT PRACTICES

It is clear that there are no shortcuts. We cannot enhance children's learning by simply providing a set of materials, nor can we put all teachers through a small number of focused workshops that provide the "right way" to do things. The authors have presented a large numbers of successful practices—none of them simple. Even Megan Loef Franke's suggestion of counting everything in sight may sound deceptively simple until you realize that it is paired with a complex analysis of understandings and misunderstandings of numbers. We can't possibly "already do" all of that. But to move to "How can we do this better?" will require a deep understanding not only of content as we have discussed but also of theories about when to use what practice and with whom. My hope is that this volume will have moved us further along this path.

REFERENCES

Bronfenbrenner, U. (1986). Ecology of the family as a context for human development research perspectives. *Developmental Psychology, 22,* 723–742.

Lubeck, S. (1996). Deconstructing "child development knowledge" and "teacher preparation." *Early Childhood Research Quarterly, 11,* 147–167.

Lubeck, S. (1998). Is DAP for everyone?: A response. *Childhood Education, 74,* 299–301.

Rogoff, B., Matusov, E., & White, C. (1996). Models of teaching and learning. In D.R. Olson et al. (Eds.), *The handbook of education and human development* (pp. 388–414). Malden, MA: Blackwell Publishers.

Whitebook, M., Howes, C., & Phillips, D. (1990). *Who cares? Child care teachers and the quality of care in American: National Child Care Staffing Study.* Oakland, CA: Center for the Child Care Workforce.

Whitebook, M.H., Howes, C., & Phillips, D.A. (1998). *A decade following the National Child Care Staffing Study.* Washington, DC: Center for the Child Care Workforce.

Index

Page references followed by *f* or *t* indicate figures or tables, respectively.

Active teachers, 146
   constructive, 147
   nonconstructive, 146
Activism, social, 169–170
Activities
   community-building, 15–16
   to expand children's awareness of differences, 168
   letter of the week, 82
   linking to children's lives, 87
   name card and sign-in, 80–81
   phonemic awareness, 57
   that support literacy, 77–83
   Treasure Box, 82
Addition and subtraction, 97, 99–102
   problems, 100, 101*t*
   strategies for solving problems, 100
Additive Approach, 144–145
African-American families, 59, 135, 136
   culture of, 137, 138
   ethnic and racial identity of, 141
   living in poverty, 136
Alphabetic principles, 50
   mastering, 56–57
America, diversity in, 135–136
Anecdotal records, 125–126
Anger, coping with, 36–37
Anti-bias education, 135–155
   classroom practices in, 157–172
   colleagues who do not support, 159
   curricular development cycle, 164
   nonsystematic implementation in, 161–162
   ongoing integration of, 163–164

   parent and community involvement in, 150
   phases of adopting, 160–164
   practical strategies for, 164–168
   research in, 148–149
   suggestions for future areas of work, 148–150
   support for, 149
   systematic implementation in, 162–163
   teacher concerns for, 158–160
   teacher preparation for, 148–149
   value of, 149
Audiotape books, 79
Autonomous moral reasoning, 141

Behavior, linking to activities and rewards, 33
Beliefs, examination of, 72–75
"Belonging" to school culture, 11
Bias
   anti-bias education, 135–155, 157–172
   personal, 159–160
Bilingual education, 61
Bisexual issues, 166–167
Books, 74
   nonfiction, 84
   placing throughout the classroom, 89
   problem-solving and feeling, 80
   rhyming, 82–83
   on tape, 79
"Buddy" programs, 19

CDP, *see* Child Development Project

Charts
  data displays, 118
  song charts, 78
Child associates, 20
Child care, 51–52
Child care workforce, 174–175
Child development, 139–142
Child Development Project (CDP), 18–20
Child poverty, 136
Child-initiated learning, 73
Children
  culturally and linguistically diverse, 58–62
  older, as role models, 87–88
  positive teacher–child relationships, 25–46
  praising them in genuine and specific ways, 33
  reading to, 76
  sick and injured, 32–33
  teacher–child relationships, 90–91
  topics for conversations with, 84
  who need extra attention, 40–41
Children's literature
  integrating into mathematics lessons, 132
  problems from, 119–120
  see also Books
Civic activism, 145
Civic development, 8–9
Class meetings, 17
Classroom(s)
  community-oriented, 1–24, 42–45
  democracy in, 158
  diversity in, 146–147
  early childhood, 71–92
  events that regularly occur in, 76–77
  learning diversity in, 142–148
  placing books throughout, 89
  preschool and primary, 142–148
  stocking and creating, 114–116
Classroom climate, 160–161
Classroom practices
  community-oriented, 25–46
  emergent literacy, 71–92
  linking to children's lives, 87
  in multicultural and anti-bias education, 157–172
  that build community, 10–12
  that enhance instruction while establishing and fostering care, 13
  that support mathematical ideas, 113–133
Climate, classroom, 160–161
Cognitive skills, development of, 7
Collaboration
  with colleagues, 129–130
  student, 164
  teacher, 164
Colleagues
  collaboration with, 129–130

who do not support multicultural and anti-bias education, 159
Collections, counting, 116
Communication
  about mathematics, 106–108
  miscommunication with parents, 158–159
  student to teacher, 107
  teacher to student, 107
Community
  caring classroom, 13
  classroom-based practices that build, 10–12
  connection to school learning, 170
  involvement in multicultural and anti-bias education, 150
Community-building activities, 15–16
Community-oriented approaches
  classroom practices, 25–46
  classrooms, 1–24, 42–45
  recommended readings, 46
  to schooling, 2–5
Community-oriented skills, teaching, 34–35
Comparison problems, 100, 101t
Comprehension, reading, 57–58
Conceptual knowledge, 49–50
Conflict resolution, 26–29
Consciousness, critical, 158
Constructive teachers, 145–146
  active, 147
  passive, 146–147
Constructivist theory, 139, 140
Contributions Approach, 144
Conversations
  with children, 84
  genuine, 121
  topics for, 84
Coping with anger and frustration, 36–37
Counting, 97–99
  extending, 98–99
  rote, 97
Counting collections, for mathematical instruction, 116
Critical consciousness, 158
Cultural democracy, 157
Cultural differences, 137–139
Cultural diversity, 136
Culturally and linguistically diverse children, 58–62
Culturally relevant instruction, 142
Culturally responsive curriculum, 63–64
Culture
  definition of, 137
  home, 164
  and learning, 58–59
  school, 11
Curriculum, 142
  anti-bias and multicultural, 164

approaches that promote diversity and justice, 144–145
culturally responsive, 63–64
project-oriented, 164–165

Daily schedules, 73–74
Data displays, 118–119
Development
  environmental aspects that promote, 9–12
  first and second grade, 7–8
  kindergarten, 6–7
  nurturing, 1–24
  preschool, 6–7
Developmental tasks, 6–9
Discipline, 17–21
Displays
  data, 118–119
  messages about diversity, 161
Diversity, 135–136
  child development and, 140
  cultural, 136
  curricular approaches that promote, 144–145
  display messages about, 161
  early literacy for diverse children, 58–62
  ethnic, 136
  instructional responses to, 145–146
  learning, 142–148
  nonsystematic implementation of, 161–162
  patterns of teacher responses to, 146–147
  in preschool and primary classrooms, 142–148
  racial, 136
  student beliefs about, 160–161
  tolerance for, 137
Diversity education, theories on, 137–142
Division, 97

Early childhood classrooms, 71–92
Early childhood workforce, 174–175
Early literacy
  areas for new knowledge, 64
  for culturally and linguistically diverse children, 58–62
  for young children and English-language learners, 47–69
Education
  anti-bias, 135–155
  bilingual, 61
  community-oriented approaches to, 2–5
  connection to community, 170
  diversity, 137–142
  multicultural, 135–155
  social justice, 169
  traditional, 3–4

transformative, 158
  see also Instruction
Emergent literacy
  examination of practices, 72–75
  practices in early childhood classrooms, 71–92
  skills and knowledge base of, 75–77
Emotion, reading with, 83–84
English as a Second Language (ESL) programs, 61
English language
  fluency in, 63
  immersion in, 60–61
English-language learners, 47–69
  ideas about good practice for, 73
  literacy programs for, 60–62
  needs of, 87
  suggestions for, 63
Environment
  aspects that promote development, 9–12
  mathematically rich, 115
  print-rich, 52–53, 76–77
  supportive, 83–90
ESL programs, see English as a Second Language programs

Family participation and support, 73, 77
  see also Parents
Feeling books, 80
First- and second-grade development, 7–8
First-grade classrooms, 122
Flannel board stories, 78–79
Fractions, 97
Friendship building, 29–31
Frustration, coping with, 36–37

Gay issues, 166–167
Gestures, 85–86
Greeting children warmly, 31
Group writing, 79

Heroes and Holidays Approach, 144
Home culture, 164
Home support, 77
Homophobia, 168

Identity, ethnic and racial, 140–141
Immersion, English, 60–61
Individualizing responses, 35–36
Injured children, soothing and caring for, 32–33
Instruction
  culturally relevant, 142
  intensified, 50

Instruction *(continued)*
  nonsystematic implementation, 161–162
  ongoing integration, 163–164
  responses to diversity, 145–146
  systematic implementation, 162–163
  teacher practices that enhance, 13
  teaching community-oriented skills,
      34–35
  teaching conflict resolution, 26–29
  teaching practices, 16–17
Interpretive Approach, 139, 140
Interviews, 126–127

Joining action problems, 100, 101*t*
Justice
  curricular approaches that promote,
      144–145
  knowledge of, 141–142
  positive, 140, 142
  social justice education, 169
  social justice educators, 168–169

Kindergarten development, 6–7
Knowledge, conceptual, 49–50

Language
  mathematical talk, 121–124
  natural, 105
  oral, 53–55
  shared with teachers, 14–15
  use of, 13–15
Language development, 49–50
  primary language support, 62–63
Language programs
  bilingual education, 61
  English as a Second Language (ESL) pro-
      grams, 61
  primary, 61
Late preschool development, 6–7
Learning
  child-initiated versus teacher-initiated, 73
  community, 170
  culture and, 58–59
  literacy, 73
  nurturing, 1–24
  from others, 108
  poverty and, 60
  school, 170
  student involvement in, 165–166
Lesbian issues, 166–167
Letter of the week activities, 82
Linguistically diverse children, 58–62
Literacy
  activities, 84–85
  early

  areas for new knowledge, 64
  for culturally and linguistically diverse
      children, 58–62
  for young children and English-
      language learners, 47–69
  emergent
    practices in early childhood class-
        rooms, 71–92
    skills and knowledge base of, 75–77
  opportunities for young children, 49–50
  practices that support, 77–83
  programs, 61–62
  utility of, 50
Literature, children's
  see also Book suggestions
  problems from, 119–120

Manipulatives, 114–115
Mathematical assessment, 125
Mathematical reading, 120–121
Mathematical talk, 121–124
Mathematical tasks, 116–121
Mathematical thinking
  detailing, 97–103
  eliciting and building, 121–123
  listening to, 103–104
  representing, 105–106
  sharing, 122
Mathematical understanding
  development of, 94–96
  fostering, 93–111
  guiding principles for, 103–109
  theoretical perspectives on, 94–96
Mathematically rich environments, 115
Mathematics
  assessment of ideas, 124–128
  classroom practices that support, 113–133
  communication about, 106–108
  drawing on everyday experiences,
      117–118
  problems from children's literature,
      119–120
  resources for integrating children's litera-
      ture into, 132
  talking about, 115
  working with parents in, 130–131
Meetings, class, 17
Miscommunication with parents,
      158–159
Mistakes, responding to, 124
Morality, 140
  autonomous moral reasoning, 141
  knowledge of, 141–142
Mother Read program, 90
Multicultural education, 135–155
  classroom practices in, 157–172
  colleagues who do not support, 159

curricular development cycle, 164
essential characteristics for transformed
    schools, 143
nonsystematic implementation in,
    161–162
ongoing integration of, 163–164
parent and community involvement, 150
phases of adopting, 160–164
practical strategies for, 164–168
research, 148–149
suggestions for future areas of work,
    148–150
support for, 149
systematic implementation in, 162–163
teacher concerns for, 158–160
teacher preparation for, 148–149
value of, 149
Multiculturalism, 160
Multiplication and division, 97

Name card and sign-in activities, 80–81
Nonconstructive teachers, 146
    active, 146
    passive, 146
Noncontingent responses, 33–34
Nonfiction books, 84
Number sense, 116
Numbers
    operating on, 99
    webs of connections associated with, 95t,
        95–96
Nursery rhyme rebus, 77–78

Observations, 126
Operating on numbers, 99
Oral language development, 53–55

Parents
    inclusion of, 89–90
    involvement in multicultural and anti-bias
        education, 150
    miscommunication with, 158–159
    Mother Read program, 90
    working with, 38–40, 130–131
Participation
    encouraging, 37–38
    family, 73
    parent, 38–40
    student involvement in learning,
        165–166
Part–part–whole problems, 100, 101t
Passive constructive teachers, 146–147
Passive nonconstructive teachers, 146
Passive teachers, 146
Peer interactions, positive, 8

Personal bias, 159–160
Personal-, Social-, and Civic-Action
        Approach, 145
Phonemic awareness activities, 57
Phonological training, 57
Play, 52
PMHP, see Primary Mental Health Project
Portfolios, 127–128
Positive teacher–child relationships, 25–46
Poverty, 49
    child, 136
    and learning, 60
Praise, genuine and specific, 33
Prejudice, 167–168
Preschool classrooms, 142–148
Preschool development, 6–7
Primary classrooms, 142–148
Primary language
    development, 62
    programs, 61
    support, 62–63
Primary Mental Health Project (PMHP),
        18, 19–20
Print
    functions of, 50
    understanding, 55–56
Print-rich environment, 52–53, 76–77
Proactive teachers, 147
Problem solving
    addition and subtraction, 100
    drawing on everyday experiences,
        117–118
    mathematical tasks, 116–121
    offering help with the next step, 86
    problems from children's literature,
        119–120
    rehearsing strategies for, 108–109
    talking about mathematical situations,
        115
Problem-solving and feeling books, 80
Project-oriented curriculum, 164–165

Questions to help expand number sense, 116

Racial differences, 137–139
Racial identity, 140–141
Reading
    with emotion, 83–84
    enthusiasm for, 50–53
    mathematical, 120–121
    pretending to read, 76
    storybook, 50–51
    talking about how reading is used, 84
Reading ability, 47
Reading comprehension, 57–58
Reading nonfiction books, 84

Reading to children, 76
  Mother Read program, 90
Reasoning, autonomous moral, 141
Rebus, nursery rhyme, 77–78
Reconstruction, social, 158
Records, anecdotal, 125–126
Rehearsing strategies, 108–109
Representations, 115–116
Representing mathematical thinking,
    105–106
Responses
  to diversity, 145–146
  individualizing, 35–36
  instructional, 145–146
  noncontingent, 33–34
  to student mistakes, 124
Rewards, linking behavior to, 33
Rhyming books, 82–83
Rhyming songs, 83
Role models, 87–88
Room labels, 81
Rote counting, 97
Rules
  for conflict resolution, 28–29
  implementation of, 29

Schedules, daily, 73–74
Schooling, see Education; Instruction
Schools
  discipline in, 17–18
  relationally oriented, 17–18
  transformed multicultural, 143
Second grade development, 7–8
Self-knowledge, 140
Separating action problems, 100,
    101t
Sign-in activities, 80–81
Social activism, 145
Social justice educators, 168–169
Social movements, joining, 169–170
Social reconstruction, 158
Solution paths, 96, 96f
Song charts, 78
Stocking classrooms, 114–116
Storybook reading, 50–51
Storytelling, 76
Student collaboration, 164
Student thinking
  eliciting and building, 121–123
  sharing, 122
Student to teacher communication,
    107
Student work portfolios, 127–128
Student-created visuals, 164
Students
  beliefs about diversity, 160–161
  involvement in learning, 165–166

who may need extra help, 48–50
Subtraction, 97, 99–102
Success, contexts that promote, 49
Support for multicultural and anti-bias
    education, 149

Teachable moments, 74–75, 161, 164
Teacher to student communication, 107
Teacher–child relationships, 25–46,
    90–91
Teacher-created visuals, 164
Teacher-initiated learning, 73
Teachers
  active, 146
  active constructive, 147
  active nonconstructive, 146
  collaboration with colleagues, 129–130,
    164
  concerns of, 158–160
  constructive, 145–146
  early childhood workforce, 174–175
  joining social movements, 169–170
  nonconstructive, 146
  passive, 146
  passive constructive, 146–147
  passive nonconstructive, 146
  personal bias of, 159–160
  preparation for multicultural and anti-
    bias education, 148–149
  proactive, 147
  as social justice educators, 168–169
  working with parents, 130–131
Teaching community-oriented skills,
    34–35
Teaching conflict resolution, 26–29
Teaching practices, 16–17
Theories
  changing or enhancing, 173–174
  of diversity education, 137–142
  of mathematical understanding,
    94–96
Tolerance for diversity, 137
Tracing words visually, 77
Traditional education, 3–4
Transformation Approach, 144
Transformative education, 158
Transformed multicultural schools, 143
Transgender issues, 166–167
Transitions, smooth, 34–35
Treasure Box activity, 82
Trust, 90–91

Visuals
  student-created, 164
  teacher-created, 164
Vocabulary, 49–50

Webs of connections, 95*f*, 95–96
Writing, 74
   group, 79

Young children
   early literacy for, 47–69
   literacy opportunities for, 49–50
   mathematical understanding of, 93–111